'This previously untold story of economic history in Australia exposes the centrality of economic thought and scholarship to Australian intellectual and political life. Deftly positioning economic history in an innovative institutional, place-based and person-focused narrative, Claire Wright entangles economics with the history of education to produce a tale of university interdisciplinarity, influence and impact. Written with vitality and bursting with both data and anecdote, this book makes an exceptional contribution to the intersecting fields of history, economics and higher education studies.'

– Hannah Forsyth, author of *A History of the Modern Australian University*

'Few readers would expect to find a classical tragedy in the story of an academic field. Yet that is what Claire Wright shows us in this study of Economic History, as it has been practiced in Australia. She traces the field from legendary beginnings to triumphant growth to organizational collapse – and renaissance on other terms. Carefully researched and vigorously written, this book raises questions about disciplines and interdisciplinary fields, universities and markets, and social bases of intellectual work, that are relevant to all fields today.'

– Raewyn Connell, author of *The Good University*

'Australia proved a pioneer in the study of economic history, nurturing a discipline with innovative data and understanding of material trends. Yet by the 1990s economic history departments closed as senior scholars retired and the field was subsumed by conventional economics. In this absorbing study, Dr Claire Wright challenges the conventional account. She is tough-minded about financial and institutional pressures on the field, but cautiously optimistic about the future. It is a mistake, she argues, to see institutional representation as the benchmark of influence. Instead, the interdisciplinary nature of economic history has encouraged new research and teaching across the humanities and social sciences. With close attention to individual scholars and their university departments, and a deep sense of the trajectory of the field, *Australian Economic History: Transformations of an Interdisciplinary Field* is an original and important contribution to Australian intellectual history.'

– Glyn Davis, Distinguished Professor of Political Science in the Crawford School of Public Policy, The Australian National University

AUSTRALIAN ECONOMIC HISTORY

TRANSFORMATIONS OF AN
INTERDISCIPLINARY FIELD

AUSTRALIAN ECONOMIC HISTORY

TRANSFORMATIONS OF AN
INTERDISCIPLINARY FIELD

CLAIRE E. F. WRIGHT

ANU PRESS

ANU PRESS

Published by ANU Press
The Australian National University
Canberra ACT 2600, Australia
Email: anupress@anu.edu.au

Available to download for free at press.anu.edu.au

ISBN (print): 9781760465124
ISBN (online): 9781760465131

WorldCat (print): 1316690658
WorldCat (online): 1316689072

DOI: 10.22459/AEH.2022

This title is published under a Creative Commons Attribution-NonCommercial-NoDerivatives 4.0 International (CC BY-NC-ND 4.0) licence.

The full licence terms are available at
creativecommons.org/licenses/by-nc-nd/4.0/legalcode

Cover design and layout by ANU Press

This book is published under the aegis of the Social Sciences Editorial Committee of ANU Press.

This edition © 2022 ANU Press

Contents

List of figures	ix
List of tables	xi
List of abbreviations	xiii
Acknowledgements	xv
1. The interdisciplinary space	1
Universities and interdisciplinary research	7
Structure	20
2. Early economic history in Australia	21
Colonial writings	22
Interwar	25
Wartime transition	42
3. The big bang	45
The words and the numbers	46
Orthodox recruitment	52
The revolution	62
Conclusions	66
4. A moment in the sun	69
Growth	70
Enclaves	79
A fragmented community	111
5. The resistance	113
The crisis in Australian economic history	115
Adaptation and survival	138
Conclusions	161
6. Renaissance	163
The revival	164
Persistent challenges	173
Conclusions	185
7. Epilogue	187
Appendix and data	191
Departments of economic history in Australia	191
Oral history interviews	199
Index	201

List of figures

Figure 1: Timothy Augustine Coghlan, early twentieth century	24
Figure 2: Professor Noel G. Butlin, ANU, 10 October 1989	47
Figure 3: Professor Syd Butlin, University of Sydney, 1960	89
Figure 4: Professors Gus Sinclair (left) and Allan Fels from the Monash Faculty of Economics and Politics	96
Figure 5: Participants at the second workshop for the *Cambridge Economic History of Australia*, Trinity College, University of Melbourne, February 2013	171

List of tables

Table 1: Economic history staff of ANU　　　　　　　　　　192
Table 2: Economic history staff of Flinders University　　　194
Table 3: Economic history staff of La Trobe University　　　194
Table 4: Economic history staff of University of Melbourne　195
Table 5: Economic history staff of Monash University　　　　196
Table 6: Economic history staff of University of Sydney　　　197
Table 7: Economic history staff of UNE　　　　　　　　　　197
Table 8: Economic history staff of UNSW　　　　　　　　　198
Table 9: Interviews conducted for this text's research　　　　199

List of abbreviations

AAHANZBS	Academic Association of Historians in Australian and New Zealand Business Schools
ABDC	Australian Business Dean's Council
ANU	The Australian National University
APEBH	Asia-Pacific Economic and Business History
ARC	Australian Research Council
CSIR	Council for Scientific and Industrial Research
CSIRO	Commonwealth Scientific and Industrial Research Organisation
CUC	Canberra University College
ECHOSEA	Economic History of Southeast Asia Project
EHSANZ	Economic History Society of Australia and New Zealand
ERA	Excellence in Research for Australia
FoR	Field of Research code
HECS	Higher Education Contribution Scheme
IDRF	interdisciplinary research field
IEHA	International Economic History Association
MBA	Masters of Business Administration
RSPacS	Research School of Pacific Studies (ANU)
RSSS	Research School of Social Sciences (ANU)
the Faculties	The School of General Studies (ANU)
the Institute	The Institute of Advanced Studies (ANU)
UNE	University of New England

AUSTRALIAN ECONOMIC HISTORY

UNSW	University of New South Wales
UWA	University of Western Australia
WEA	Workers' Educational Association
WEHC	World Economic History Congress

Acknowledgements

My story starts towards the end of this book. In 2013, I needed a job. Working in hospitality as an introvert is a genuine nightmare, and I was looking for something, anything, so I didn't have to pull beers and talk to people. A meeting with Simon Ville at the University of Wollongong changed my professional trajectory. I was brought on board to ease some of the administrative burden associated with the final stages of the *Cambridge Economic History of Australia*, providing feedback, compiling the index and liaising between the authors, editors, copyeditors and publishers. In the process, I read every word.

When it came time to choose a topic for my PhD, my interest in professional communities and knowledge was combined with Simon's work in Australian economic history. I set out to map (quite literally) the various networks among members of the field in the postwar decades, and the impact of these connections on knowledge. As I wrote this book, I was increasingly interested in the labour of academic work and professional networks: the structural matters that determine who is employed, what groups they work in, and what sort of work they do. There are no networks if no one has a job. It meant taking a step back to examine the production of interdisciplinary knowledge not simply in terms of the scholars involved, but also university policy and government and public priorities. Although this is a substantial departure from the initial work, I hope it is now a more practical account of the field's development and possible futures.

This book is about places and ways of work, and I would be remiss not to mention mine. My laptop and I have been on quite the journey through the course of writing, presenting and refining this book, from accidentally being held at gunpoint in Poland (a misunderstanding) to the coastal vistas on the train from Wollongong to Sydney. Those I interviewed were kind enough to invite me into their homes, and I have fond memories of eating apple crumble with Jonathan Pincus and his wife Priscilla, tea with Gus Sinclair, being stopped for autographs with Geoffrey Blainey, watching the waves off Maroubra beach with Alan Hall, Ian McLean's architectural tour of Adelaide, inspecting post-bushfire Blue Mountains with Barrie Dyster, and a look inside the very secretive O'Connell St Associates offices with Peter Shergold, to name a few. Each conversation, whether in person or virtually, has enriched my understanding of this craft, and I am grateful to each for their kindness and generosity.

This project has encompassed nine years of my life, and I have many people to thank. The economics and history departments at the University of Wollongong, at different points, trained me, and I am grateful for their support and encouragement. More recently, the Department of Management at Macquarie University provided the space, time and resources needed to finalise this book. I was very fortunate in this job, and am particularly grateful to Nikki Balnave, Murray Taylor and Lucy Taksa for their support.

I would like to thank members of the Economic History Society of Australia and New Zealand for welcoming me into the profession, making time for interviews and providing feedback through conferences and conversations. Lionel Frost, Martin Shanahan, Jim McAloon and Andy Seltzer have been particularly helpful with their insights and the provision of data. I am extraordinarily grateful to Simon Ville for his supervision and mentorship. Matthew and Judy Butlin have generously allowed me stewardship over part of Noel and Syd's stories. Archivists from the Noel Butlin Archives Centre (The Australian National University), National Library of Australia, La Trobe and the universities of Sydney, New South Wales, Western Australia, Melbourne and New England have assisted with records. Members of the History of Economic Thought Society of Australia, The Academic Association of Historians in Australian and New Zealand Business Schools, and the New Histories of Capitalism have also been kind and helpful. Thanks to Beth Battrick for the care taken with copyediting and indexing this work, and to Emma Wright for creating the concept for the cover design. I would also like to extend my sincere thanks to two anonymous reviewers, as well as Frank Bongiorno and the team at ANU Press, for suggestions and assistance that have been of enormous benefit to this book.

ACKNOWLEDGEMENTS

I have had the distinct pleasure of being surrounded by intelligent and insightful women throughout my career – including Claire Seaman, Leonie Noble, Claire Lowrie, Lauren Samuelsson, Liz Carnuccio, Susannah Clement and Zoe Richards – each of whom has shaped this work through their discussions and insights. Hannah Forsyth has been an inspiration, as a supportive colleague, and as the model for how to make those not in universities care about what goes on in universities. Emma Mabin would modestly tell you she had nothing to do with this, but her ongoing guidance in flourishing in uncertainty not only allowed this book to be written, but informed its conclusions.

Finally, I dedicate this book to my family: Kathy, Paul, Emma, Ben and David. Thank goodness they do not take me very seriously – I'm sure they will refer to me as Claire Bear or C-Biscuit well into my dotage – but I am always assured of their support.

1

The interdisciplinary space

Interdisciplinary research is the key to addressing the challenges of our current moment. Climate change, global development, pandemics and so on are infuriatingly complex, and rarely respect disciplinary boundaries. As we have all learnt recently, responding to the COVID-19 pandemic has required not only understanding epidemiology, but also political science, economics, sociology, psychology and geography. Interdisciplinary fields communicate between disciplines and integrate this knowledge to produce something new.[1] Interdisciplinary research is advocated as a source of innovation and scientific breakthroughs,[2] and in Australia, discourse in favour of interdisciplinarity has voiced the need for 'job-ready' graduates and 'useful' real-world research.[3] Universities have responded, redesigning curricula in some areas to incorporate cross-disciplinary instruction, and invoking its benefits in public statements about learning and graduate outcomes.[4] However, despite this rhetoric, university policy and practice

---

1   Claire EF Wright and Simon Ville, 'Visualising the Interdisciplinary Research Field: The Life Cycle of Economic History in Australia', *Minerva* 55, no. 3 (2017): 321–40, doi.org/10.1007/s11024-017-9319-z.
2   National Academies, *Facilitating Interdisciplinary Research* (Washington DC: The National Academies Press, 2005); Her Majesty's Treasury, *Science and Innovation Investment Framework 2004–2014: Next Steps* (London: Her Majesty's Treasury, 2006); Dian Rhoten, 'Interdisciplinary Research: Trend or Transition', *Items and Issues* 5, no. 1–2 (2004): 6–11; Peter Woelert and Victoria Millar, 'The "Paradox of Interdisciplinarity" in Australian Research Governance', *Higher Education* 66, no. 6 (2013): 755–67, doi.org/10.1007/s10734-013-9634-8; Wright and Ville, 'The Interdisciplinary Research Field'.
3   Woelert and Millar, 'Paradox of Interdisciplinarity'; Victoria Millar, 'Interdisciplinary Curriculum Reform in the Changing University', *Teaching in Higher Education* 21, no. 4 (2016): 471–83, doi.org/10.1080/13562517.2016.1155549.
4   Millar, 'Interdisciplinary Curriculum Reform'.

continues to reinforce the dominance of disciplines. Everyone *wants* interdisciplinary research, but very few understand how it is produced, and even fewer actively implement policies to encourage it.

Economic history is one of the world's oldest interdisciplinary fields. It emerged alongside the large social science and humanities fields of the modern period, with the formalisation of economics and history disciplines in nineteenth-century universities providing the stability for scholars to begin conducting economic history research.[5] The expansion of universities in the twentieth century, particularly post–World War II, provided new students and additional space for economic history – and other interdisciplinary fields – to flourish.[6] As with the university sector more generally, the field expanded first in metropole nations such as the US and Britain, though it has had a strong presence in most nations and regions across the world. In 2011 there were approximately 10,000 economic historians and 44 economic history societies representing at least 59 countries.[7] The World Economic History Congress has run triennially since 1960, and there are a dozen or more international journals focused on publishing work in the field.[8]

Australian economic history has been a part of these global trends. The common narrative of the field's progress is that it has experienced a 'rise and fall' in three acts: dedicated research began in late nineteenth and early twentieth centuries, with the intellectual foundations laid by Sir Timothy

---

5   Francesco Boldizzoni, *The Poverty of Clio: Resurrecting Economic History* (Princeton: Princeton University Press, 2011), doi.org/10.23943/princeton/9780691144009.001.0001; Herman Van Der Wee, 'Economic History: Its Past, Present and Future', *European Review* 15, no. 1 (2007): 33–45, doi.org/10.1017/S106279870700004X; NB Harte, ed., *The Study of Economic History* (London: Frank Cass, 1971); Pat Hudson, 'Economic History in Britain: The "First Industrial Nation"', in *Routledge Handbook of Global Economic History*, ed. Francesco Boldizzoni and Pat Hudson (London: Routledge, 2015), 17–34, doi.org/10.4324/9781315734736-2; John S Lyons, Louis P Cain and Samuel H Williamson, eds, *Reflections on the Cliometrics Revolution: Conversations with Economic Historians* (New York: Routledge, 2008), doi.org/10.4324/9780203799635; Alfred William Coats, 'Disciplinary Self-Examination, Departments, and Research Traditions in Economic History: The Anglo-American Story', *Scandinavian Economic History Review* 38, no. 1 (1990): 3–18, doi.org/10.1080/03585522.1990.10408164; Jon S Cohen, 'The Achievements of Economic History: The Marxist School', *Journal of Economic History* 38, no. 1 (1978): 29–57, doi.org/10.1017/S002205070008815X; Naomi Lamoreaux, 'Beyond the Old and the New: Economic History in the United States', in Boldizzoni and Hudson, *Global Economic History*, 35–54, doi.org/10.4324/9781315734736.
6   Boldizzoni and Hudson, *Global Economic History*.
7   Joerg Baten and Julia Muschallik, 'The Global Status of Economic History', *Economic History of Developing Regions* 27, no. 1 (2012): 93–113, doi.org/10.1080/20780389.2012.682390.
8   Gianfranco Di Vaio and Jacob Louis Weisdorf, 'Ranking Economic History Journals: A Citation-Based Impact-Adjusted Analysis', *Cliometrica* 4, no. 1 (2010): 1–17, doi.org/10.1007/s11698-009-0039-y.

Coghlan, E. O. G. Shann and Brian Fitzpatrick. The publication of Noel G. Butlin's two volumes in the early 1960s was a significant event, and his work inspired a wealth of other research in a similar vein. Butlin's contribution gave the field focus and identity, and although economists generally approved, historians kept their distance. Following from this intellectual success and the postwar emphasis on higher education, the 1960s and 1970s were characterised by expansion of scholars, students and research, and closer relationships with the economics discipline. In the 1990s, higher education reform was responsible for the closure of departments and 'institutional reversal in the fortunes of economic history in Australasia'. To the present day, Australian economic history is considered a bit of 'corpse', albeit one that 'still twitches'.[9]

Vicissitudes in economic history's fortunes mean it has been subject to regular reflection. The field's progress has been covered most comprehensively in the US and Britain,[10] though Francesco Boldizzoni and Pat Hudson's recent *Routledge Handbook of Global Economic History* has incorporated a variety of voices to understand the study of economic history across the world.[11] Research generally examines the field's ideas

---

9   Stephen Morgan and Martin Shanahan, 'The Supply of Economic History in Australasia: The *Australian Economic History Review* at 50', *Australian Economic History Review* 50, no. 3 (2010): 217–39, doi.org/10.1111/j.1467-8446.2010.00303.x, 220; David Meredith and Deborah Oxley, 'The Rise and Fall of Australian Economic History', in Boldizzoni and Hudson, *Global Economic History*, 73–94, 84.
10 Coats, 'Disciplinary Self-Examination'; Hudson, 'Economic History in Britain'; Lamoreaux, 'Beyond the Old and the New'; Harte, *Study of Economic History*; Alfred William Coats, 'The Historical Context of the "New" Economic History', *Journal of European Economic History* 9, no. 1 (1980): 185–207; Arthur H Cole, 'Economic History in the United States: Formative Years of a Discipline', *Journal of Economic History* 28, no. 4 (1968): 556–89, doi.org/10.1017/S002205070010097X; Cristel de Rouvray, '"Old" Economic History in the United States: 1939–1954', *Journal of the History of Economic Thought* 26, no. 4 (2004): 221–39, doi.org/10.1080/1042771042000219046; David Mitch, 'Economic History in Departments of Economics: The Case of the University of Chicago, 1892 to the Present', *Social Science History* 35, no. 2 (2011): 237–71; DC Coleman, *History and the Economic Past: An Account of the Rise and Decline of Economic History in Britain* (Oxford: Clarendon Press, 1987); Gerard M Koot, 'English Historical Economics and the Emergence of Economic History in England', *History of Political Economy* 12, no. 2 (1980): 174, doi.org/10.1215/00182702-12-2-174; Gerard M Koot, *English Historical Economics, 1870–1926: The Rise of Economic History and Neomercantilism* (Cambridge, MA: Cambridge University Press, 1987), doi.org/10.1017/CBO9780511983832; Gerard M Koot, 'Historians and Economists: The Study of Economic History in Britain ca. 1920–1950', *History of Political Economy* 25, no. 4 (1993): 641–75, doi.org/10.1215/00182702-25-4-641. Also briefly in Lyons et al., *Reflections*; Ángela Milena Rojas, 'Cliometrics: A Market Account of a Scientific Community (1957–2006)', *Lecturas de Economia Universidad de Antioquia-Lecturas de Economia* 66, no. 1 (2007): 47–82; Robert Whaples, 'Where Is the Consensus among American Economic Historians? The Results of a Survey on Forty Propositions', *Journal of Economic History* 55, no. 1 (1995): 139–54, doi.org/10.1017/S0022050700040602.
11 Boldizzoni and Hudson, *Global Economic History*.

and traditions, in relation to individual scholars, or as motivated by the national economic and political context.[12] The relationship between knowledge and universities has been discussed briefly for the US, UK, Italy, Netherlands, Africa and Japan.[13] For example, the innovativeness and success of the cliometrics revolution in the US has been argued to be due to the expansion of the higher education system, and the nature of Purdue University in the postwar period.[14] For the UK, A. W. 'Bob' Coats and D. C. Coleman examined departments of economic history, linking the departmental form to the field's insularity and lethargy in the postwar period.[15] Despite the fact that economic history has experienced vastly different outcomes in different places, there has been very little systematic analysis of the impact of universities on knowledge in this field.

---

12   Tirthankar Roy, 'The Rise and Fall of Indian Economic History 1920–2013', *Economic History of Developing Regions* 29, no. 1 (2014): 15–41, doi.org/10.1080/20780389.2014.9228 43; Gareth Austin and Stephen Broadberry, 'Introduction: The Renaissance of African Economic History', *Economic History Review* 67, no. 4 (2014): 893–906, doi.org/10.1111/1468-0289.12081; AG Hopkins, 'The New Economic History of Africa', *Journal of African History* 50, no. 2 (2009): 155–77, doi.org/10.1017/S0021853709990041; Morten Jerven, 'A Clash of Disciplines? Economists and Historians Approaching the African Past', *Economic History of Developing Regions* 26, no. 2 (2011): 111–24, doi.org/10.1080/20780389.2011.625244; John H Coatsworth, 'Structures, Endowments, and Institutions in the Economic History of Latin America', *Latin American Research Review* 40, no. 3 (2005): 126–44, doi.org/10.1353/lar.2005.0040.
13   Lamoreaux, 'Beyond the Old and the New'; Francesco Boldizzoni, 'The Flight of Icarus: Economic History in the Italian Mirror', in Boldizzoni and Hudson, *Global Economic History*, 130–45, doi.org/10.4324/9781315734736; Erik Aerts and Ulbe Bosma, 'The Low Countries, Intellectual Borderlands of Economic History' in Boldizzoni and Hudson, *Global Economic History*, 175–92, doi.org/10.4324/9781315734736; Meredith and Oxley, 'Australian Economic History', 73–94; Ayodeji Olokoju, 'Beyond a Footnote: Indigenous Scholars and the Writing of West African Economic History', in Boldizzoni and Hudson, *Global Economic History*, 377–93, doi.org/10.4324/9781315734736; Bill Freund, 'Reflections on the Economic History of South Africa', in Boldizzoni and Hudson, *Global Economic History*, 394–408, doi.org/10.4324/9781315734736; Per Boje, 'Danish Economic History – Towards a New Millenium', *Scandinavian Economic History Review* 50, no. 3 (2002): 13–34, doi.org/10.1080/03585522.2002.10410815; H Borton, 'Modern Japanese Economic Historians', in *Historians of China and Japan*, ed. William G Beasley and Edwin G Pulleyblank (London: Oxford University Press, 1961), 288–306; M Mehl, *Historiography and the State in Nineteenth-Century Japan* (London: Macmillan, 1998); Osamu Saito, 'A Very Brief History of Japan's Economic and Social History Research' (paper presented at the XVIIth World Economic History Congress, Kyoto, Japan, 2015); K Sugihara, 'The Socio-Economic History Society of Japan', *Information Bulletin of the Union of National Economic Associations in Japan* 21, no. 1 (2011): 99.
14   Coats, 'The Historical Context'; Coats, 'Disciplinary Self-Examination'; Lyons et al., *Reflections*.
15   Coats, 'Disciplinary Self-Examination'; Coleman, *History and the Economic Past*.

Economic history in Australia has been subject to similar interest.[16] Individual ideas and texts have been examined,[17] with William Coleman emphasising biographical elements for Noel and Syd Butlin, who were economic historians, and brothers, who both grew up in the Maitland region of New South Wales.[18] David Meredith and Deborah Oxley have incorporated some contextual and institutional elements, examining the role of Australia's background as an affluent British colony, and the place of postwar economic historians within economics departments.[19] Contemporary commentary during the field's crisis in the 1990s has also highlighted the role of higher education policy on economic history.[20] The field's experience has been aggregated at the national level, with Butlin's approach seen as the guiding framework in the post–World War II decades. Some have attempted to define an 'Australian approach', though

---

16   William Coleman, 'The Historiography of Australian Economic History', in *Cambridge Economic History of Australia*, ed. Simon Ville and Glenn Withers (Melbourne: Cambridge University Press, 2015), 11–28, doi.org/10.1017/CHO9781107445222.004; Brian Fitzpatrick, 'Counter Revolution in Australian Historiography?', *Meanjin Quarterly* 22, no. 2 (1963): 197–213; Timothy Jetson, 'Economic History–the Neglected Relative of Australian Historiography?', *Tasmanian Historical Studies* 15, no. 1 (2010): 7–37; Martin Shanahan, 'Discipline Identity in Economic History: Reflecting on an Interdisciplinary Community', *Arts and Humanities in Higher Education* 14, no. 2 (2015): 181–93; Christopher Lloyd, 'Economic History and Policy: Historiography of Australian Traditions', *Australian Journal of Politics and History* 41, no. 3 (1995): 61–79, doi.org/10.1111/j.1467-8497.1995.tb01082.x; Christopher Lloyd, 'Can Economic History Be the Core of Social Science? Why the Discipline Must Open and Integrate to Ensure the Survival of Long-Run Economic Analysis', *Australian Economic History Review* 37, no. 3 (1997): 256–66, doi.org/10.1111/aehr.373005; Christopher Lloyd, 'Analytical Frameworks of Australia's Economic History', in Ville and Withers, *Cambridge Economic History of Australia*, 52–69, doi.org/10.1017/CHO9781107445222.006; C Boris Schedvin, 'Economic History in Australian Universities, 1961–1966', *Australian Economic History Review* 7, no. 1 (1967): 1–18, doi.org/10.1111/aehr.71001; C Boris Schedvin, 'Midas and the Merino: A Perspective on Australian Economic Historiography', *Economic History Review* 32, no. 3 (1979): 542–56, doi.org/10.1111/j.1468-0289.1979.tb02058.x; William Angus Sinclair, 'Economic History', in *Australians: A Guide to Sources*, ed, DH Borchardt (Sydney: Fairfax, Syme & Weldon, 1987), 245–51; Jonathan Pincus and Graeme Snooks, 'The Past and Future Role of the *Australian Economic History Review*: Editorial Reflections and Aspirations', *Australian Economic History Review* 28, no. 2 (1988): 3–7, doi.org/10.1111/aehr.282001; Morgan and Shanahan, 'Supply of Economic History'; Meredith and Oxley, 'Australian Economic History'.
17   Jetson, 'Economic History'; Lloyd, 'Economic History and Policy'; Schedvin, 'Midas and the Merino'; Sinclair, 'Economic History'; Lloyd, 'Analytical Frameworks'.
18   Coleman, 'Historiography'.
19   Meredith and Oxley, 'Australian Economic History'.
20   Stephen Nicholas, 'The Future of Economic History in Australia', *Australian Economic History Review* 37, no. 3 (1997): 267–74, doi.org/10.1111/aehr.373006; Greg Whitwell, 'Future Directions for the *Australian Economic History Review*', *Australian Economic History Review* 37, no. 3 (1997): 275–81, doi.org/10.1111/aehr.373007; HM Boot, 'Some Developments in Teaching Practice in the Department of Economic History at the Australian National University', *Australian Economic History Review* 37, no. 3 (1997): 282–97, doi.org/10.1111/aehr.373008; Lloyd, 'Core of Social Science'.

only very loose unifying characteristics have been identified.[21] Chris Lloyd and C. B. 'Boris' Schedvin have argued that the approach had unique origins through the national income accounting tradition.[22] Schedvin has argued that a major characteristic of Australian economic history has been to 'under-interpret', letting the numbers speak for themselves.[23] Coleman, on the other hand, has argued that there is no uniform style in the field, though has conceded that the practice was distinctive to both Britain and the US.[24]

Higher education policy has not featured heavily in understanding the progress of Australian economic history. The institutional situation is used as a barometer – the presence of separate departments accepted as evidence of the field's success, and their closure more recently demonstrating its decline.[25] Meredith and Oxley have identified one of the primary issues associated with departments: that the structure isolated scholars from the history discipline – though they also argue that the closure of departments 'inevitably narrows the disciplinary backgrounds of practitioners and thus the intellectual influence on the discipline, reduces research output and decimates teaching capacity, constraining future prospects'.[26] This book contributes to these existing conversations by systematically demonstrating the impact of higher education policy on Australian economic history. Incorporating work on intellectual communities and the history of education (see below), I differ from the mainstream 'rise and fall' narrative in my assessment of economic history's progress. University departments were designed with disciplines in mind, by a higher education system that fundamentally misunderstood interdisciplinary knowledge. For Australian economic history, this structure has been, at once, both protagonist and antagonist, contributing to the perceived success of the field as well as restricting its ability to perform core functions. Under this framework, there is neither a 'rise' nor a 'fall', simply different ways of organising scholarship that then had an influence on the sort of knowledge produced.

---

21   Coleman, 'Historiography'; Lloyd, 'Analytical Frameworks'; C Boris Schedvin, 'Australian Economic History', *Economic Record* 65, no. 190 (1989): 287–90, doi.org/10.1111/j.1475-4932.1989.tb00938.x.
22   Lloyd, 'Analytical Frameworks'; Schedvin, 'Australian Economic History'.
23   Schedvin, 'Australian Economic History', 288.
24   Coleman, 'Historiography'.
25   Nicholas, 'Future of Economic History'; Lloyd, 'Core of Social Science'; Whitwell, 'Future Directions'; Meredith and Oxley, 'Australian Economic History'; Morgan and Shanahan, 'Supply of Economic History'.
26   Meredith and Oxley, 'Australian Economic History', 86.

By offering a theoretically grounded assessment of economic history's progress, I hope to encourage broader conversations about what it means to be a 'successful' interdisciplinary field.

Universities and interdisciplinary research

A key innovation of this book is embedding the progress of Australian economic history within its knowledge community, particularly the nature of interdisciplinary research and the policy and practice of the higher education sector. Intellectual historians have been concerned not only with knowledge itself, but examining the development of ideas within scholars' personal, professional and institutional contexts. Some see knowledge as a form of internal expression, and thus largely independent of the context in which it is produced.[27] Others embed knowledge within the scholar's context, including their childhood, education, workplace, political orientation, class and social relationships.[28] Intellectual communities have received attention, with formal research schools and informal collaborative circles demonstrating the way groups of scholars develop research agendas and exchange support, ideas and criticism.[29] Activities

---

27 Arthur Lovejoy's examination of molecule-like 'unit-ideas' over the course of history is an early example of this. See Arthur O Lovejoy, *The Great Chain of Being: A Study of the History of an Idea* (New York: Harper and Row, 1936).
28 Quentin Skinner, 'Meaning and Understanding in the History of Ideas', *History and Theory* 8, no. 1 (1969): 3–53, doi.org/10.2307/2504188; Margaret Schabas, 'Breaking Away: History of Economics as History of Science', *History of Political Economy* 24, no. 1 (1992): 187–203, doi.org/10.1215/00182702-24-1-187; JGA Pocock, 'The Reconstruction of Discourse: Towards the Historiography of Political Thought', *MLN* 96, no. 5 (1981): 959–80, doi.org/10.2307/2906228; Malachi Haim Hacohen, *Karl Popper – The Formative Years, 1902–1945* (Cambridge: Cambridge University Press, 2000); Louis Menand, *The Metaphysical Club: A Story of Ideas in America* (New York: Farrar, Straus and Giroux, 2001); Alfred William Coats, 'The Sociology of Economics and Scientific Knowledge, and the History of Economic Thought', in *A Companion to the History of Economic Thought*, ed. Warren J Samuels, Jeff E Biddle and John B Davis (Malden: Blackwell, 2003), 507–22; D Wade Hands, 'Conjectures and Reputations: The Sociology of Scientific Knowledge and the History of Economic Thought', *History of Political Economy* 29, no. 4 (1997): 695–739, doi.org/10.1215/00182702-29-4-695.
29 JB Morrell, 'The Chemist Breeders: The Research Schools of Liebig and Thomas Thomson', *Ambix* 19, no. 1 (1972): 1–46, doi.org/10.1179/amb.1972.19.1.1; Gerald L Geison, 'Scientific Change, Emerging Specialties, and Research Schools', *History of Science* 19, no. 43 (1981): 20–40, doi.org/10.1177/007327538101900103; Alan J Rocke, 'Group Research in German Chemistry: Kolbe's Marburg and Leipzig Institutes', *Osiris* 8, no. 1 (1993): 52–79, doi.org/10.1086/368718; Randall Collins, *The Sociology of Philosophies* (Harvard: Harvard University Press, 1998); Harriet Zuckerman, 'Nobel Laureates in Science: Patterns of Productivity, Collaboration, and Authorship', *American Sociological Review* 32, no. 3 (1967): 391–403, doi.org/10.2307/2091086; MP Farrell, *Collaborative Circles: Friendship Dynamics and Creative Work* (Chicago: University of Chicago Press, 2001); Claire

associated with groups – seminars, conferences, collaboration, graduate supervision, social activities, meetings and so on – bring scholars together. These interactions contribute to communication, debate, challenge, compromise and learning. Communication then reinforces, alters or expands the way individuals think, the research questions they ask and the answers they find.[30] This body of work reminds us that no scholar is an island, and sometimes even casual conversations may, gradually, change how they see the world.

Research institutions have been seen as powerful organising structures for ideas. Some intellectual communities have been independent of universities, for example the Bloomsbury group of British intellectuals, or the marginalised *Anschluß*-era Viennese scholars.[31] However, universities have been important for enabling hierarchies, focused research programs, graduate research and publication outlets.[32] Universities often structure the physical space where scholars interact, including things as basic as the placement of offices along a hallway.[33] Universities have been found to determine groupings – faculties, departments and so on – that match scholars with like-minded colleagues. Institutions have also controlled the cash: they have decided who to hire, the incentives for funding and promotion, and the degrees they will offer.[34] These policy decisions have been found to direct scholars' time and attention in certain ways. Institutions can thus be responsible for the overt barriers and covert inconveniences that influence the way that knowledge is produced.

EF Wright, 'The 1920s Viennese Intellectual Community as a Centre for Ideas Exchange: A Network Analysis', *History of Political Economy* 48, no. 4 (2016): 593–634, doi.org/10.1215/00182702-3687271.
30   Scott L Feld, 'The Focused Organisation of Social Ties', *American Journal of Sociology* 86, no. 5 (1981): 1015–35, doi.org/10.1086/227352.
31   Craufurd D Goodwin, 'The Bloomsbury Group as Creative Community', *History of Political Economy* 43, no. 1 (2011): 59–82, doi.org/10.1215/00182702-2010-044; Wright, 'The 1920s Viennese Intellectual Community'.
32   Morrell, 'The Chemist Breeders'; Geison, 'Scientific Change'; Rocke, 'Group Research in German Chemistry'; Zuckerman, 'Nobel Laureates in Science'.
33   Claire EF Wright and Simon Ville, 'The University Tea Room: Informal Public Spaces as Ideas Incubators', *History Australia* 15, no. 2 (2018): 236–54, doi.org/10.1080/14490854.2018.1443701.
34   Woelert and Millar, 'Paradox of Interdisciplinarity'; Andrew Abbott, *Chaos of Disciplines* (Chicago: University of Chicago Press, 2001); Hermann Röhrs, 'The Classical Idea of the University', in *Tradition and Reform of the University Under an International Perspective*, ed. Hermann Röhrs and Gerhard Hess (Verlag: Peter Lang, 1987), 13–27.

Despite growing attention to intellectual communities overseas, Australian historians rarely examine ideas in this context. For the most part, work has examined a particular discipline, tracing the main research themes and attributing the development of ideas to individual capabilities or sociopolitical context. The transformation of prominent international ideas has been of key concern, with work uncovering the extent to which Australian intellectual traditions are 'unique'.[35] Connections between various knowledge domains and the policy sphere have also been prominent.[36] This research is often framed individualistically: while authors discuss prominent collective research themes, current work lacks a systematic analysis of the way interpersonal networks and university structures have influenced ideas.[37]

Historians of education, on the other hand, have focused on university policies and the production of knowledge. Scholars internationally have traced the underlying logic of universities around three distinct systems of learning. Medieval universities in the UK and Europe were elite enclaves tied to the clergy. This 'English' or 'Oxbridge' model of higher education aimed to provide a common moral, intellectual and social experience for the ruling elite, with academic disciplines relatively unimportant and students instead grounded in general intellectual skills. The 'Scottish' model was more secular and egalitarian, emphasising practical subjects and applied knowledge. Universities served the professions, and educators were responsible for imparting practical knowledge to students. Scottish-led universities placed emphasis on academic disciplines as a way to organise knowledge into discrete categories. Finally, the 'German' or 'Humboldtian'

---

35 Alex Millmow, *A History of Australasian Economic Thought* (London: Taylor & Francis, 2017), doi.org/10.4324/9781315716152; Alison Bashford and Joyce E Chaplin, *The New Worlds of Thomas Robert Malthus: Rereading the Principle of Population* (Princeton: Princeton University Press, 2016); Deborah Gare, Geoffrey Bolton, Stuart Macintyre and Tom Stannage, eds, *The Fuss That Never Ended* (Melbourne: Melbourne University Press, 2003); Geoffrey Bolton, 'Rediscovering Australia: Hancock and the Wool Seminar', *Journal of Australian Studies* 23, no. 62 (1999): 159–70, doi.org/10.1080/14443059909387515; Peter Groenewegen and Bruce McFarlane, *A History of Australian Economic Thought* (London: Routledge, 1990); Craufurd D Goodwin, *Economic Inquiry in Australia* (Durham: Duke University Press, 1966).

36 Millmow, *Australasian Economic Thought*; William Coleman, Selwyn Cornish and Alf Hagger, *Giblin's Platoon: The Trials and Triumphs of the Economist in Australian Public Life* (Canberra: ANU E Press, 2006), doi.org/10.22459/GP.04.2006; Neville Cain, 'The Economists and Australian Population Strategy in the Twenties', *The Australian Journal of Politics and History* 20, no. 3 (1974): 346–59, doi.org/10.1111/j.1467-8497.1974.tb01123.x; Stuart Macintyre, *The Poor Relation* (Melbourne: Melbourne University Press, 2010).

37 Stuart Macintyre's history of the social sciences – particularly the way their constitution within universities has impacted their practice and progress – is a key exception. See Macintyre, *The Poor Relation*.

model of higher education emerged in the early nineteenth century through an emphasis on scientific training and research. The university professor, in this system, develops new knowledge and supervises postgraduate research students, with instruction in undergraduate knowledge a secondary activity. The Humboldtian university model strongly emphasises research at the frontier of siloed academic disciplines.[38]

Closer to home, Australian historians of education have examined the way universities combined these systems of learning, and the impact of policy design on education and research.[39] The older sandstone universities, one in each Australian state capital city, were established in the nineteenth century on principles similar to the Oxbridge elite Liberal Arts education.[40] However, they quickly incorporated professional instruction, expanding to include law and medicine. The 'Scottish model' has been prevalent, with nineteenth- and early twentieth-century tertiary education designed to prepare students for professional work.[41] The Workers' Educational Association (WEA) was also established in the interwar period to complement university professional education by providing extension tutorials in discrete subjects for blue-collar workers.[42] Postwar mass expansion of higher education was designed along similar lines: to multiply the supply of skilled labour, particularly in professions such as engineering, accountancy, law, teaching, business, medicine and science.[43] Universities came to command greater space in professional work, and simultaneously a much greater proportion of Australia's workforce trained as professionals through tertiary education.[44] Postwar universities also incorporated the German model of higher education.

---

38 John C Smart, Kenneth A Feldman and Corinna A Ethington, *Academic Disciplines: Holland's Theory and the Study of College Students and Faculty* (Nashville: Vanderbilt University Press, 2000); John Gascoigne, 'The Cultural Origins of Australian Universities', *Journal of Australian Studies* 20, no. 50–51 (1996): 18–27, doi.org/10.1080/14443059609387275; Röhrs, 'The Classical Idea'.
39 Hannah Forsyth, *A History of the Modern Australian University* (Sydney: University of New South Wales Press, 2014).
40 Gascoigne, 'Cultural Origins'; Tamson Pietsch, *Empire of Scholars: Universities, Networks and the British Academic World, 1850–1939* (Manchester: Manchester University Press, 2013).
41 Gascoigne, 'Cultural Origins'; Hannah Forsyth, 'Census Data on Universities, Professions and War', in *The First World War, the Universities and the Professions in Australia 1914–1939*, ed. Kate Darian-Smith and James Waghorne, 1–25 (Melbourne: Melbourne University Press, 2019).
42 Gerald Friesen and Lucy Taksa, 'Workers' Education in Australia and Canada: A Comparative Approach to Labour's Cultural History', *Labour History*, no. 71 (1996): 170–97, doi.org/10.2307/27516453.
43 Forsyth, *Modern Australian University*; Stuart Macintyre, Andre Brett and Gwilym Croucher, *No End of a Lesson: Australia's Unified National System of Higher Education* (Melbourne: Melbourne University Press, 2017).
44 Forsyth, *Modern Australian University*.

Primary research became part of the compact of the establishment of new universities and the expansion of old ones, with governments funding a greater proportion of research through universities, and the role of university workers expanding to include both professional instruction and research.[45] The Australian National University (ANU) was the only true 'Humboldtian' university, with work at the institution consisting of frontier discovery and supervision of graduate students. Since the late 1980s, neoliberal reform corporatised Australia's higher education system. While the underlying logic of universities – focusing on professional education and frontier research – remained the same, principles of 'New Public Management' were introduced to encourage performance through competition in new and expanded markets for students and research.[46]

Others have incorporated the discussion of Australia's higher education policy into an understanding of the global hierarchy of knowledge. Our nation has profited from the dispossession of Indigenous people, and our education systems are based on, and constantly look to, the British and US metropoles. Raewyn Connell's *Southern Theory* argues that ideas in the humanities and social sciences are based on imperial education structures. 'Southern tier' countries such as Australia provide much of the raw information on which mainstream knowledge is based, and to which it is then later applied. The North, the 'metropole', on the other hand, is the main site of theoretical processing of global knowledge. Data and information from the periphery flow to the metropole, are legitimised and then flow back to be applied in the periphery again. Modern universities are a European invention, and the knowledge they produce is seen as universal and objective. While there has been remarkable growth of higher education beyond the metropole, particularly since the decolonisation movement from the mid-twentieth century, a Eurocentric curriculum

---

45   Gascoigne, 'Cultural Origins'; Forsyth, *Modern Australian University*; Macintyre, *The Poor Relation*; DS Anderson and E Eaton, 'Part 1: Post-War Reconstruction and Expansion 1940–1965', *Higher Education Research and Development* 1, no. 1 (1982): 8–93, doi.org/10.1080/0729436820010102.
46   Forsyth, *Modern Australian University*; Macintyre et al., *No End of a Lesson*; Peter Woelert and Lyn Yates, 'Too Little and Too Much Trust: Performance Measurement in Australian Higher Education', *Critical Studies in Education* 56, no. 2 (2015): 175–89, doi.org/10.1080/17508487.2014.943776 ; Jill Blackmore, Marie Brennan and Lew Zipin, *Re-Positioning University Governance and Academic Work* (Rotterdam: Sense Publishers, 2010), doi.org/10.1163/9789460911743; Simon Marginson and Mark Considine, *The Enterprise University: Power, Governance and Reinvention in Australia* (Cambridge: Cambridge University Press, 2000); Hugh Lauder et al., *Educating for the Knowledge Economy? Critical Perspectives* (London: Routledge, 2012); Raewyn Connell, 'The Neoliberal Cascade and Education: An Essay on the Market Agenda and Its Consequences', *Critical Studies in Education* 54, no. 2 (2013): 99–112, doi.org/10.1080/17508487.2013.776990.

prevails, and instruction is increasingly conducted in English. University policies around hiring, funding and promotion encourage research palatable to the global North, under the assumption that this process of legitimacy implies research 'quality'.[47]

These insights from Australian historians of education – the credentialisation of universities, increased bureaucracy and competition from the 1980s, and the global hierarchy of knowledge – have been applied to the sector in general,[48] a particular university[49] or a large discipline such as economics.[50] Interdisciplinary fields have been left out of these conversations, as they are often small, unstable or amorphous, thus presenting challenges for historical inquiry. Contemporary educationists, on the other hand, have emphasised the importance of interdisciplinary research, adopting a case study approach to understanding the progress of this form of knowledge within university structures.[51] Margaret Boden's work on the cognitive science field is a rare exception of a historical approach to understanding

---

47 Raewyn Connell, *Southern Theory: The Global Dynamics of Knowledge in Social Science* (Crows Nest: Allen & Unwin, 2007); Raewyn Connell, *The Good University: What Universities Actually Do and Why It's Time for Radical Change* (London: Zed Books Ltd., 2019); Fran Collyer et al., *Knowledge and Global Power: Making New Sciences in the South* (Johannesburg: Wits University Press, 2019).
48 Forsyth, *Modern Australian University*; Pietsch, *Empire of Scholars*; Connell, *Southern Theory*.
49 William James Breen and John A Salmond, *Building La Trobe University: Reflections on the First 25 Years 1964–1989* (Melbourne: La Trobe University Press, 1989); Peter Groenewegen, *Educating for Business, Public Service and the Social Sciences: A History of the Faculty of Economics at the University of Sydney 1920–1999* (Sydney: Sydney University Press, 2009), doi.org/10.2307/j.ctv1wmz4h4; Ross Williams, *Balanced Growth: A History of the Department of Economics, University of Melbourne* (Melbourne: Australian Scholarly Publishing, 2009); Fay Anderson and Stuart Macintyre, eds, *The Life of the Past: The Discipline of History at the University of Melbourne* (Melbourne: RMIT Publishing, 2006); WGK Duncan and RA Leonard, *The University of Adelaide, 1874–1974* (Adelaide: Rigby Ltd, 1973); Stephen G Foster and Miriam M Varghese, *The Making of the Australian National University* (Sydney: Allen & Unwin, 1996); Wilfrid Prest, ed., *Pasts Present: History at Australia's Third University* (Kent Town: Wakefield Press, 2014).
50 Alex Millmow, 'The State We're In: University Economics 1989/1999', *Economic Papers* 19, no. 4 (2000): 43–51, doi.org/10.1111/j.1759-3441.2000.tb00974.x; Tim Thornton, 'The Economics Curriculum in Australian Universities 1980 to 2011', *Economic Papers* 31, no. 1 (2012): 103–13, doi.org/10.1111/j.1759-3441.2011.00163.x; John Kees Lodewijks, 'The History of Economic Thought in Australia and New Zealand', *History of Political Economy* 34, no. 5 (2002): 154–64, doi.org/10.1215/00182702-34-Suppl_1-154.
51 Guy G Gable et al., *The Information Systems Academic Discipline in Australia* (Canberra: ANU E Press, 2008), doi.org/10.22459/ISADA.09.2008; Chris Gibson, 'Geography in Higher Education in Australia', *Journal of Geography in Higher Education* 31, no. 1 (2007): 97–119, doi.org/10.1080/03098260601033050; Christina Raasch et al., 'The Rise and Fall of Interdisciplinary Research: The Case of Open Source Innovation', *Research Policy* 42, no. 5 (2013): 1138–51, doi.org/10.1016/j.respol.2013.01.010; Thomas Pfister, 'Coproducing European Integration Studies: Infrastructures and Epistemic Movements in an Interdisciplinary Field', *Minerva* 53, no. 3 (2015): 235–55, doi.org/10.1007/s11024-015-9275-4 .

interdisciplinarity, with others calling for similar efforts offering the benefit of hindsight.[52] This book is the first systematic study of an interdisciplinary field in the Australian history of education.

Education scholars have argued that contemporary universities promote disciplinary knowledge through the emphasis on professional instruction in Scottish-style universities, and the Humboldtian focusing on frontier research. Universities have an incentive to encourage disciplinary research and teaching, as professional accreditation requires standardisation, collaboration between those with similar knowledge occurs more efficiently, and research within disciplines is more likely to receive funding and citations.[53] As a result, universities are designed to encourage work around disciplines: appointment and promotion is based on assessment within the 'tribe', which means being published in the 'right' places, cited by the right people and accredited by the appropriate professional bodies.[54] Inward communication is encouraged by clustering offices together, with each group conducting their own meetings, seminars and joint projects.[55] Degrees and majors are designed to match students and instructors based on their intellectual alignment, with students progressing through a standardised program from first year to the end of their PhD.

---

52 Margaret Ann Boden, *Mind as Machine: A History of Cognitive Science* (Oxford: Clarendon Press, 2006); Jerry A Jacobs and Scott Frickel, 'Interdisciplinarity: A Critical Assessment', *Annual Review of Sociology* 35, no. 1 (2009): 43–65, doi.org/10.1146/annurev-soc-070308-115954.
53 Clark Hu and Pradeep Racherla, 'Visual Representation of Knowledge Networks: A Social Network Analysis of Hospitality Research Domain', *International Journal of Hospitality Management* 27, no. 1 (2008): 302–12, doi.org/10.1016/j.ijhm.2007.01.002; JS Coleman, 'Social Capital in the Creation of Human Capital', *American Journal of Sociology* 94, Supplement (1988): S95–S120, doi.org/10.1086/228943; Julia Nieves and Javier Osorio, 'The Role of Social Networks in Knowledge Creation', *Knowledge Management Research and Practice* 11, no. 1 (2013): 62–77, doi.org/10.1057/kmrp.2012.28; Ray Reagans and Bill McEvily, 'Network Structure and Knowledge Transfer: The Effects of Cohesion and Range', *Administrative Science Quarterly* 48 no. 2 (2003): 240–67, doi.org/10.2307/3556658; Katja Rost, 'The Strength of Strong Ties in the Creation of Innovation', *Research Policy* 40, no. 4 (2011): 588–604, doi.org/10.1016/j.respol.2010.12.001; Andrea Bonaccorsi, 'New Forms of Complementarity in Science', *Minerva* 48, no. 4 (2010): 355–87, doi.org/10.1007/s11024-010-9159-6; R Whitley, *The Intellectual and Social Organisation of the Sciences* (Oxford: Clarendon, 1984); Ronald S Burt, 'The Network Structure of Social Capital', *Research in Organisational Behaviour* 22, no. 1 (2000): 345–423, doi.org/10.1016/S0191-3085(00)22009-1; Ismael Rafols et al., 'How Journal Rankings Can Suppress Interdisciplinary Research: A Comparison between Innovation Studies and Business and Management', *Research Policy* 41, no. 7 (2012): 1262–82, doi.org/10.1016/j.respol.2012.03.015; Ehud Shapiro, 'Point of View: Correcting the Bias against Interdisciplinary Research', *eLife* 3, no. 1 (2014): 1–3, doi.org/10.7554/eLife.02576; Jochen Gläser and Grit Laudel, 'Evaluation without Evaluators: The Impact of Funding Formulae on Australian University Research', in *The Changing Governance of the Sciences*, ed. Richard Whitley and Jochen Gläser (Dordrecht: Springer, 2007), 127–51, doi.org/10.1007/978-1-4020-6746-4_6; Woelert and Millar, 'Paradox of Interdisciplinarity'.
54 Woelert and Millar, 'Paradox of Interdisciplinarity'; Rafols et al., 'Journal Rankings'.
55 Wright and Ville, 'University Tea Room'.

This establishes hierarchies, frequent interactions and adherence to group norms, meaning that scholars and students are identifiable among themselves and to outsiders.[56] Instruction within the discipline shapes the pool of those in the labour market, which then determines those appointed to train the next generation, beginning the cycle again.[57]

While these policies are entirely appropriate for disciplines, they are not cognisant of the nature and value of interdisciplinary knowledge, which integrates concepts, methodologies and perspectives from two or more disciplines.[58] As disciplines grow over time, they develop more inward-looking structures and thus greater gaps in understanding between them. Interdisciplinary practitioners take pieces of knowledge from 'parent' disciplines, combine them into something new, and then communicate this knowledge back to parent disciplines. The process of communication and integration essentially bridges the two otherwise separate knowledge domains, and develops new, innovative insights.[59] Much of the theoretical work sees interdisciplinary knowledge as either the residue of disciplines evolving over time, or as separate and mutually exclusive groups.[60] More recently, however, these different forms of knowledge production have been seen as complementary.[61] Some have advocated for division of labour and cooperation between disciplines and interdisciplinary fields, with the

---

56   Alan Collins, John Seely Brown and Susan E Newman, 'Cognitive Apprenticeship: Teaching the Crafts of Reading, Writing, and Mathematics', in *Knowing, Learning and Instruction*, ed. Lauren B Resnik (Hillsdale: Erlbaum, 1989), 453–94, doi.org/10.4324/9781315044408-14; Alston Lee, 'How Are Doctoral Students Supervised? Concepts of Doctoral Research Supervision', *Studies in Higher Education* 33, no. 3 (2008): 267–81, doi.org/10.1080/03075070802049202; Margot Pearson and Angela Brew, 'Research Training and Supervision Development', *Studies in Higher Education* 27, no. 2 (2002): 135–50, doi.org/10.1080/03075070220119986c.
57   Abbott refers to this as 'dual institutionalisation'. See Abbott, *Chaos of Disciplines*.
58   Thomas S Kuhn, *The Structure of Scientific Revolutions* (Chicago: University of Chicago Press, 1962); C Lyall and LR Meagher, 'A Masterclass in Interdisciplinarity: Research into Practice in Training the Next Generation of Interdisciplinary Researchers', *Futures* 44, no. 6 (2012): 608–17, doi.org/10.1016/j.futures.2012.03.011; Scott E Page, *The Difference: How the Power of Diversity Creates Better Groups, Firms, Schools, and Societies* (Princeton: Princeton University Press, 2007), doi.org/10.1515/9781400830282; Frank J van Rijnsoever and Laurens K Hessels, 'Factors Associated with Disciplinary and Interdisciplinary Research Collaboration', *Research Policy* 40, no. 3 (2011): 463–72, doi.org/10.1016/j.respol.2010.11.001; Rafols et al., 'Journal Rankings'.
59   Wright and Ville, 'The Interdisciplinary Research Field'.
60   Abbott, *Chaos of Disciplines*; Stephen Turner, 'What Are Disciplines? And How Is Interdisciplinarity Different?', in *Practising Interdisciplinarity*, ed. Peter Weingart and Nico Stehr (Toronto: University of Toronto Press, 2000), 46–65, doi.org/10.3138/9781442678729-005.
61   John D Aram, 'Concepts of Interdisciplinarity: Configuration of Knowledge and Action', *Human Relations* 57, no. 4 (2004): 379–412, doi.org/10.1177/0018726704043893; Bonaccorsi, 'Complementarity in Science'; Robert Frodeman and Carl Mitcham, 'New Directions in Interdisciplinarity: Broad, Deep, and Critical', *Bulletin of Science, Technology and Society* 27, no. 6 (2007): 506–14, doi.org/10.1177/0270467607308284; Pfister, 'European Integration Studies'.

former providing coherent intellectual foundations and systematic research techniques, as well as credibility strategies that underpin interdisciplinary integration.[62] They argue that broad interdisciplinary groups are able to produce innovative synergies, whereas the interrogation and application of these new ideas is efficiently done within the disciplinary tribe.

Empirical research has found that interdisciplinarity can take a number of different forms. Specific projects or funded research centres can serve as 'boundary organisations' that bring relevant scholars together to solve a particular problem.[63] Liberal arts 'colleges', with the broad ideals of Oxbridge universities, integrate knowledge and personnel from a range of backgrounds. Simon Ville and I have used the case study of Australian economic history to specify the interdisciplinary research field (IDRF) as a more enduring organising framework.[64] The IDRF is an organisational structure that brings scholars into the space between disciplines, and helps mediate the relationships between them. Professionally, *communicating infrastructures* such as publications, events, collaborations and teaching activities facilitate interactions between scholars from different groups. Intellectually, a body of knowledge with a spectrum of approaches also acts as a communicating infrastructure, bridging the interdisciplinary space by providing overlapping frameworks for members of the IDRF and parent disciplines to interact. As with any intellectual community, there is interdependence between the places where scholars interact and the knowledge they produce. The field's progress over time depends on the success of its communicating infrastructures, as well as the interests of parent disciplines and the nature of the higher education environment.

Disciplinary forms of organisation can restrict the IDRF's ability to perform core functions. As discussed above, universities often adopt a 'one size fits all', specifically disciplinary, policy with regard to its research groups. Even within the field, there is strong temptation to colonise, with scholars understandably building capacity through training, research projects and administrative structures. However, they are faced with opportunity costs – a vibrant seminar program within the group

---

62 Ken Fuchsman, 'Rethinking Integration in Interdisciplinary Studies', *Issues in Integrative Studies* 1, no. 27 (2009): 72–73; Bonaccorsi, 'Complementarity in Science'; Abbott, *Chaos of Disciplines*; Rost, 'Strong Ties'; Burt, 'Network Structure'.
63 David H Gunston, *Between Politics and Science: Assuring the Integrity and Productivity of Research* (New York: Cambridge University Press, 2000); Jacobs and Frickel, 'Interdisciplinarity'; Rhoten, 'Interdisciplinary Research'.
64 Wright and Ville, 'The Interdisciplinary Research Field'.

means scholars are not able to host or attend as many events in other groups. Collaborations that deepen connections within the field reduce the time and energy available for developing interdisciplinary bridges. If scholars and students all emerge from a particular major, then they have a comprehensive understanding of that knowledge domain, at the expense of broad knowledge and networks.[65] On the other hand, the complete absence of institutional resources, collaboration and shared ideas can lead to the dispersal of the field's members. Communicating infrastructures that are too strong or too weak both represent, without being too dramatic, the 'death' of the IDRF. In either scenario the knowledge domain no longer exists in an integrative position. A long-lasting 'hybrid' is the aim, with the IDRF maintaining a degree of autonomy as well as links to larger disciplines.[66] As the following chapters will examine in detail, this is a very complicated balance to maintain.

The place of interdisciplinary research, over time and within university structures, is the key issue this book will address. Economic history has flourished in the empty spaces created by two disciplinary silos, and scholars have existed along a spectrum from the humanist on the one end to the social scientist on the other. The nature of interdisciplinary integration has depended on the quality of professional interactions, the nature of the higher education system and the field's pertinent research questions within local and temporal contexts. As such, traditions in economic history are part of global conversations, but can also be specific to the particular place and historical moment.[67] Analysing the development of Australian economic history as part of its knowledge community thus reveals the way scholars worked together to develop new ideas, the opportunities and challenges associated with moving between intellectual paradigms, and the ways universities have encouraged (and discouraged) interdisciplinary research.

---

65   JS Coleman, *Foundations of Social Theory* (Cambridge: Harvard University Press, 1990); Julie T Klein, *Interdisciplinarity: History Theory, and Practice* (Detroit: Wayne State University, 1990); Julie T Klein, *Crossing Boundaries: Knowledge, Disciplinarities, and Interdisciplinarities* (Charlottesville: The University of Virginia Press, 1996); Whitley, *Organisation of the Sciences*; Frodeman and Mitcham, 'New Directions'; Jacobs and Frickel, 'Interdisciplinarity'.
66   Wright and Ville, 'The Interdisciplinary Research Field'; Raasch et al., 'Rise and Fall of Interdisciplinary Research'.
67   This is the subject of Boldizzoni and Hudson, *Global Economic History*.

As with any interdisciplinary field, economic historians have had some autonomy regarding how they spend their time. These choices reflect deeper questions of identity, about how the scholar sees economic history and their place in it. Some see the field as interdisciplinary, others see it as a subdiscipline of economics or history. Some identify as economic historians, and others see themselves as, say, an economist who sometimes works on historical matters. These questions of identity are not new, with Pat Hudson's edited *Living Economic and Social History* collating responses of over 100 prominent economic historians who reflected on 'what economic and social history means to me'.[68] The diversity of scholars' self-identification, and views on what economic history should be, is quite astounding. Joel Mokyr has similarly argued that:

> It has never been easy to be an economic historian. Much like Jews in their diaspora, they belong simultaneously in many places and nowhere at all. They are perennial minorities, often persecuted, exiled, accustomed to niche existences, surviving by their wits and by (usually) showing solidarity to one another.[69]

In Australia, William Coleman has asked 'what is economic history for?', with Ben Huf commenting that successive generations of scholars have 'contested what economic history ought to encompass'.[70] Some, like Chris Lloyd, see it as the 'core of social science', while others argue that it is a key component of Australian historiography.[71] The interviews that follow in this book express the diversity of perspectives in Australian economic history. As Huf comments, it is inherently political to draw lines around what *is* economic history, and what is *not*.[72] Such lines often betray what the practitioners themselves want the field to be, and where they would like it to go in the future.

Those who examine intellectual communities – interdisciplinary fields or otherwise – make these identity judgements. I do myself in this book. Describing a profession and a body of knowledge has meant that I have

---

68 Pat Hudson, ed., *Living Economic and Social History* (Glasgow: Economic History Society, 2001).
69 Joel Mokyr, 'On the Supposed Decline and Fall of Economic History', *Historically Speaking* 11, no. 2 (2010): 23–25, doi.org/10.1353/hsp.0.0101.
70 Ben Huf, 'Making Things Economic: Theory and Government in New South Wales, 1788–1863' (PhD thesis, The Australian National University, 2018), 52; Coleman, 'Historiography', 27.
71 Lloyd, 'Core of Social Science'; Jetson, 'Economic History'; Hannah Forsyth and Sophie Loy-Wilson, 'Seeking a New Materialism in Australian History', *Australian Historical Studies* 48, no. 1 (2017): 169–88, doi.org/10.1080/1031461X.2017.1298635.
72 Huf, 'Making Things Economic'.

drawn boundaries around what I consider to be the main scholars, projects and ideas. As uncomfortable as it is to admit, the nature of interdisciplinary research means that my identification (and anyone's) is inherently flawed. Interdisciplinary fields have cascading spheres of centrality: overlap with parent disciplines means that members can be more, or less, central to economic history, but there are no hard lines to determine who is in and who is out. Members can also change scholarly identity over the course of their career. My group of scholars and texts will not please everyone. I have been guided by major works of economic historical writing and scholars involved in the field's primary professional structures. In the colonial and interwar period, the lack of formal structures means I have discussed those who made a major contribution to understanding Australian economic history, regardless of their institutional base. For the postwar period, a very strong professional community means I primarily discuss members of departments, and those involved in the field's key journal and society, the *Australian Economic History Review* and the Economic History Society of Australia and New Zealand (EHSANZ). In the period of resistance since the 1990s, I have been more inclusive institutionally, in recognition that work in the field has come from those in economics, history, business and other groups.

To understand Australian economic history, I have drawn on a range of complementary sources. Qualitative or content analysis has been applied to texts written on an aspect of the Australian economy or economic matters (including business and policy) in a historical time period or over the long run. This follows others who have reflected on the field's progress, examining the main themes, frameworks, methods and interpretations.[73] I discuss the major monographs, as well as edited collections where members of the field worked together. The field's main journal, the *Australian Economic History Review*, has also been very influential, and I have paid particular attention to work published in its pages. Work in the field has, of course, also been published in adjacent forums, such as journals overseas, parent discipline outlets and other interdisciplinary publications such as *Labour History*. The analysis of organisational structure and its influence on knowledge draws on university records regarding personnel and department activities. The chronology of EHSANZ activities were often mentioned in the *Review*, and discussion of informal collaborations through acknowledgments uncover the various ways that scholars have interacted.

---

73   Similar to a combination of Lloyd, 'Analytical Frameworks'; Coleman, 'Historiography'.

Oral history interviews provide one of the main empirical contributions of this book. Oral history provides details of undocumented experiences, recreates the 'multiplicity of standpoints' from a historical moment, and can be used to reaffirm or challenge received wisdom.[74] It's widely used in intellectual history to illuminate the more nuanced aspects of what it means to 'do research' – aspects often missing from written records.[75] Between 2015 and 2020, I interviewed 35 economic historians prominent in the field's key professional structures and intellectual debates. Earlier interviews for the most part focused on the postwar period.[76] Latterly, through the process of writing this book, interviews have focused more on the period from the 1980s onwards. Some interviews were in person, and some were conducted virtually. Occasionally, interviewees brought along someone else – as was the case with Tony Dingle and Graeme Davison, and Deborah Oxley and David Meredith. Interviews ranged in length from about 45 minutes to 2 hours, though I also had follow-up conversations with several scholars as the research progressed. The list of interviewees is incomplete, with some no longer with us, and some declining to be interviewed. I also had to draw my own lines around the interview material. Aligning with best practice in oral history, when I reached a 'saturation point' of hearing similar things about a particular theme or event, I generally moved on.[77] I also tried to balance between different types of scholars, with the aim of representing a range, rather than the totality, of possible voices. Lines of questioning were broad, focusing on scholars' professional communities, their approach to research, and the links between economic history and other fields. While all were undoubtedly based on subjective experiences, that is the point.[78] These conversations describe, in detail, the lived experiences of negotiating the interdisciplinary space.

---

74 Robert Perks and Alistair Thomson, *The Oral History Reader* (New York: Routledge, [1998] 2006); Alistair Thomson, 'Fifty Years On: An International Perspective on Oral History', *Journal of American History* 85, no. 2 (1998): 581–95, doi.org/10.2307/2567753; Paul Thompson, *The Voice of the Past: Oral History*, 3rd ed. (Oxford: Oxford University Press, [1978] 2000).
75 Ronald E Doel, 'Oral History of American Science', *History of Science* 41 (2003): 349–78, doi.org/10.1177/007327530304100401; Charles Weiner, 'Oral History of Science: A Mushrooming Cloud?', *Journal of American History* 75, no. 2 (1988): 548–59, doi.org/10.2307/1887871.
76 For a preliminary discussion of these early interviews, see Claire EF Wright and Simon Ville, 'The Evolution of an Intellectual Community through the Words of Its Founders: Recollections of Australia's Economic History Field', *Australian Economic History Review* 57, no. 3 (2017): 345–67, doi.org/10.1111/aehr.12110.
77 Charles T Morrissey, 'On Oral History Interviewing', in *Elite and Specialised Interviewing*, ed. Lewis Anthony Dexter (Evanston: Northwestern University Press, 1970), 109–18; Perks and Thomson, *The Oral History Reader*.
78 See Wright and Ville, 'Evolution of an Intellectual Community', for a detailed discussion of the oral history method.

Structure

This book progresses through five thematic–chronological chapters that examine major episodes in the relationship between Australian economic history and universities. Chapter 2 discusses the early period of colonial writing through to Coghlan's work on historical national income. It then examines the field's tripartite institutional structure in the interwar period, with cooperation between scholars in government agencies, universities and the WEA. This institutional flexibility resulted in knowledge that connected Australian economic history with a range of other groups. Chapter 3 focuses on the production and reception of Noel Butlin's major contribution to understanding Australian economic development in the latter half of the nineteenth century. The nature of ANU, and the resulting professional community of economic historians had an important role in the production of Butlin's work, and its transmission as an intellectual movement. Chapter 4 analyses the 'departmental era'; the period during the 'golden age' of Australian higher education, where economic historians were largely placed within separate departments and the field experienced 'disciplinary'-style growth. While this structure was important for developing resources and recognition, it isolated scholars from parent disciplines, and encouraged tribalism within each group.

Chapter 5 follows the field's progress from higher education reforms in the late 1980s, particularly scholars' resistance and adaptation in the face of a very hostile university sector. The closure of departments provided opportunities for renewed interdisciplinary engagement, particularly with economics and business schools. Chapter 6 discusses the shape of the recent revival in interest in economic historical matters, as well as the field's enduring uncertainties: uneven connections with parent disciplines, fragmentation between different clusters and the escalation of neoliberal policies that disadvantage the production of interdisciplinary research. Finally, Chapter 7 summarises the lessons from understanding this field's history, including the ways that scholars, universities and policymakers can develop robust interdisciplinary conversations now and in the future.

2

Early economic history in Australia

> In Australia, it's sort of a path dependency [...] This materialistic, statistical kind of understanding of the world. Coghlan developed it, and he was, you know, the great founder of the statistical business.
>
> Christopher Lloyd, June 2019[1]

Sir Timothy Coghlan is a rare example of a celebrity economic historian. Born in Sydney to Irish working-class parents, he attended Sydney Grammar School on a scholarship. He tried his hand at wool-broking and teaching before joining the New South Wales Department of Public Works as a cadet in 1873. Although very successful as an engineer, Coghlan was more passionate about mathematics and statistics, and in 1886 was appointed government statistician.[2] His work sought to understand the colony through quantitative material, elucidating influential theories on the link between economic growth and population in the Australian context. By expanding the work of his office, acting as a consultant on a range of government issues and developing his professional networks, Coghlan earned an enviable national and international reputation as an expert in national income accounting; the first in the world to record and examine the economy's production, distribution and disposition.[3] A member of the Royal Statistical Society from the 1890s, in 1914 he was

---

1   Lloyd interview with author. Unless otherwise specified, interviews cited are those conducted by the author: see Appendix for details.
2   Neville Hicks, 'Coghlan, Sir Timothy Augustine (1855–1926)', *Australian Dictionary of Biography* (hereafter *ADB*), Volume 8 (Canberra: National Centre of Biography, The Australian National University, 1981).
3   Heinz W Arndt, 'A Pioneer of National Income Estimates', *Economic Journal* 59, no. 236 (1949): 616–25, doi.org/10.2307/2226600.

knighted. From his vantage in London, Coghlan's earlier statistical efforts culminated in *Labour and Industry in Australia*, which, in 2,449 pages, provides a 'pullulating Victorian panorama in words and numbers that seemingly capture every person, law, and landmark'.[4] With regards to the accuracy of the material, he argued 'I am my own authority'.[5]

Australian economic history prior to World War II is usually a footnote. Coghlan looms large, as do E. O. G. Shann and Brian Fitzpatrick.[6] The lack of formal professional structures has led most to discount this era as simply the origin story before the 'real' work began in the post–World War II decades. However, this time in the field's history has an important story to tell, with this chapter focusing on interdisciplinary research conducted in the absence of formal professional structures. The field's main contributions at this time were produced through formal and informal partnership between governments, universities and the Workers' Educational Association (WEA), allowing scholars to move between different modes of knowledge production and between disciplines. Although the field lacked strong communicating infrastructures and collective action, the result was a diverse corpus of scholarship with economic history engaged in the interdisciplinary space.

Colonial writings

Some have argued that 'the Australian Commonwealth came into existence in 1901 without an economic history'.[7] Reflecting Walter Scott's famous assertion of the same, the general understanding has been that an 'Australian' economic history tradition waited on the development of a national consciousness.[8] Colonial writers may beg to differ. As Ben Huf

---

4 William Coleman, 'The Historiography of Australian Economic History', in *Cambridge Economic History of Australia*, ed. Simon Ville and Glenn Withers (Melbourne: Cambridge University Press, 2015), 11–28, 12, doi.org/10.1017/CHO9781107445222.004.
5 Timothy A Coghlan, *Labour and Industry in Australia*, vol. 1 (London: Oxford University Press, 1918), v.
6 Coleman, 'Historiography'; Christopher Lloyd, 'Analytical Frameworks of Australia's Economic History', in Ville and Withers, *Economic History of Australia*, 52–69, doi.org/10.1017/CHO9781107 445222.006; David Meredith and Deborah Oxley, 'The Rise and Fall of Australian Economic History', in *Routledge Handbook of Global Economic History*, ed. Francesco Boldizzoni and Pat Hudson, 73–94, doi.org/10.4324/9781315734736; Timothy Jetson, 'Economic History – the Neglected Relative of Australian Historiography?', *Tasmanian Historical Studies* 15, no. 1 (2010): 7–37.
7 Coleman, 'Historiography'.
8 Coleman, 'Historiography'; Walter Scott, 'The Cash Nexus', *Australian Economist: Journal of the Australian Economic Association* 1 (1888): 2–6.

has examined, a literary tradition developed throughout the nineteenth century in which the nature, history and future of Australian economic matters were broadcast to the public. Adopting eighteenth- and early nineteenth-century political economy, administrators and policymakers in the colonies began to write about Australian life through distinctly economic categories such as 'capitalist' and 'labourer'.[9] Colonial writing reflected this transition, with authors gradually defining the 'economic' as a sphere of interest throughout the first half of the nineteenth century, and deploying comprehensive evidence to demonstrate the progress of economic matters in the colonies. While there was very little aggregated quantitative material, historical arguments regarding agriculture, exports, import of capital and immigration were developed through smaller samples of data, as well as anecdotes and observation. Authors wrote with political agendas, using historical events to convince colonial masters to boost immigration, invest in agriculture and encourage free trade. These writers began to conceive of economic matters, and their history, as important to policymakers and the public.[10]

Quantitative, data-driven economic history began primarily through government work rather than universities. After writers defined and understood economic matters as separate categories in the colonial project, statistics were then used to provide evidence to govern these categories. Colonial Blue Books were used to report on each colony from 1822, and the first census was conducted shortly after in 1828. The British Government used number-gathering as a way to ensure fiscal responsibility, and as a technique of surveillance and control throughout many of their colonies. Statistics in Britain and other settler colonies had risen to prominence as – depending on who you asked – a political tool or a scientific form of 'fact'.[11] By the mid to late nineteenth century – at a time when sandstone universities were established as small, Scottish-style teaching institutions – government statisticians had the capacity to conduct extensive primary research into the nature and progress of the economy. Government statisticians, including Coghlan, William Archer, Henry Hayter, George Knibbs, Robert Johnston, James Sutcliffe and Stanley Carver were experts in the management of the colonies, and cultivated an

---

9   Ben Huf, 'Making Things Economic: Theory and Government in New South Wales, 1788-1863' (PhD thesis, The Australian National University, 2018), 7.
10 Huf, 'Making Things Economic'.
11 Huf, 'Making Things Economic'; Eli Cook, *The Pricing of Progress: Economic Indicators and the Capitalization of American Life* (Cambridge, MA: Harvard University Press, 2017), doi.org/10.4159/ 9780674982529.

international reputation for quality and objective statistics.[12] Others then used these statistics to develop political arguments regarding their view of Australia's destiny.[13] Although not historians themselves (they were too engrossed in 'progress' to turn their lens backwards), this generation of 'statistician-participant-observers' developed the quantitative foundation on which historical analysis was built.[14]

Figure 1: Timothy Augustine Coghlan, early twentieth century
Source: National Library of Australia, PIC Box PIC/7639.

---

12 Meredith and Oxley, 'Australian Economic History'.
13 William Westgarth, *Australia: Its Rise, Progress, and Present Condition* (Edinburgh: Adam and Charles Black, 1861).
14 Coleman, 'Historiography'.

Upon his retirement, Coghlan published *Labour and Industry*, a historical chronicle based on his work as the New South Wales government statistician.[15] Coghlan was a social scientist, free of university structures and moving between disciplines such as political economy, sociology, economics and demography with ease.[16] *Labour and Industry* is encyclopaedic in nature, narrating seemingly endless data on different aspects of the continent.[17] His aim was to be a 'just reasoner',[18] enumerating a broad range of 'progress' indicators and aiming to let the 'facts' speak for themselves. However, even under the guise of objectivity, the collection and description of certain material was an ontological choice that betrayed his perception of what economic history should be: numbers were good; theoretical frameworks to explain the numbers were not. Despite his diverse career, Coghlan is primarily remembered as a statistician and economist, contributing to an understanding of Australia's industrial structure, capital–output ratio and per capita income. Historians have acknowledged Coghlan's role in Left and Labor intellectual movements,[19] while a more critical strain has targeted his construction of statistics.[20] For economic historians, Coghlan pioneered a sustained, long-run statistical account of Australia's material development, providing the quantitative infrastructure for future research. *Labour and Industry* maintained its status as one of the 'standard' Australian economic history texts throughout the rest of the twentieth century.

Interwar

In the interwar period, a diverse set of institutional structures provided the basis for a small community of economic history scholars. Government agencies, particularly statisticians, continued as a hub for the collection and analysis of quantitative material. Universities expanded in size and

---

15   Hicks, 'Coghlan'.
16   Sandra S Holton, 'T.A. Coghlan's *Labour and Industry in Australia*: An Enigma in Australian Historiography', *Historical Studies* 22, no. 88 (1987): 336–51, doi.org/10.1080/10314618708595755; Christopher Lloyd, 'Economic History and Policy: Historiography of Australian Traditions', *Australian Journal of Politics and History* 41, no. 3 (1995): 61–79, doi.org/10.1111/j.1467-8497.1995.tb01082.x; Lloyd, 'Analytical Frameworks'.
17   Coghlan, *Labour and Industry*.
18   Lloyd, 'Analytical Frameworks'.
19   For example, Ben Maddison, '"The Day of the Just Reasoner": TA Coghlan and the Labour Public Sphere in Late Nineteenth Century Australia', *Labour History* 77 (1999): 11–26, doi.org/10.2307/27516667.
20   See the discussion of feminist scholarship in Chapter 4.

function from the end of World War I, with newly admitted women and returned servicemen expanding the student base and providing employment for many of those working on economic history.[21] The WEA then worked alongside universities to provide practical undergraduate education in a range of subjects, including economic history. These relatively good employment prospects provided stability for some scholars, with cooperation between these three institutions developing the field's diverse identity.

Shann and Fitzpatrick were both prominent university-based economic historians. Shann was born into a middle-class family in Hobart, who later moved to Melbourne. In 1904 he completed a Bachelor of Arts at Queen's College, University of Melbourne, graduating with first-class honours in both history and political economy. A 'smallish, neatly dressed man, who wore round, gold-rimmed spectacles', Shann held positions in philosophy, politics, history and economics throughout the first few of decades of the twentieth century.[22] He settled in Perth in 1912 as the foundation professor of history and economics at the University of Western Australia. During his time in Perth, Shann penned *An Economic History of Australia*, adopting Coghlan's broad periodisation of Australia's material progress in the first thorough history of economic events, actions and processes.[23] His central theme was the struggle of good, enterprising men against the controlling forces of government, seen through analysis of the 'failure' of land settlement schemes, the inefficiencies of tariffs, the importance of squatters and the wool industry, and the triumph of the exchange economy over the communism of government food production in the early days of Botany Bay. He has been remembered as 'quick in movement and temperamental in reaction', characteristics that were reflected in his written work through dramatic generalisations, 'vivid', 'lively' prose and analyses that included many 'tasty morsel[s]' alongside

---

21 The first course in the subject was established at the University of Sydney in 1911, with others following at the universities of Adelaide and Melbourne in 1920 and 1927, respectively. See Peter Groenewegen, *Educating for Business, Public Service and the Social Sciences: A History of the Faculty of Economics at the University of Sydney 1920–1999* (Sydney: Sydney University Press, 2009), doi.org/10.2307/j.ctv1wmz4h4; Kym Anderson and Bernard O'Neil, *The Building of Economics at Adelaide, 1901–2001* (Adelaide: University of Adelaide Press, 2002); Ross Williams, *Balanced Growth: A History of the Department of Economics, University of Melbourne* (Melbourne: Australian Scholarly Publishing, 2009).

22 Graeme Snooks, 'Shann, Edward Owen Giblin (1884–1935)', *ADB*, adb.anu.edu.au/biography/shann-edward-owen-giblin-8395/text14741 (published first in hardcopy 1988).

23 Edward OG Shann, *An Economic History of Australia* (Melbourne: Cambridge University Press, 1930).

'more solid fare'.[24] Shann's work improved the reach of economic history, and remained on undergraduate reading lists well into the 1960s. On the back of this success, Shann accepted the Chair of Economics at the University of Adelaide in 1933. The appointment was cut short with his tragic death on campus on the evening of 23 May 1935. He fell from an office window – an event that the coroner decided was suicide, but which remains unresolved.[25]

Fitzpatrick, the younger by 20 years, was the other side of Shann's coin. He was born in Warrnambool, Victoria, before his family moved to suburban Melbourne. Like Shann, he won a scholarship to attend the University of Melbourne, earning his Bachelor of Arts in 1925. Fitzpatrick was an active Labor member from his time at the University of Melbourne, founding both the student newspaper *Farrago* and the Melbourne University Labor Club. He committed to left-leaning writing and politics for the rest of his life, working for a variety of newspapers until he chose to focus on historical research from the late 1930s.[26] Although Fitzpatrick worked outside the tertiary education sector (as a journalist) for much of his career, from 1936 to 1945 his major historical work was funded by a series of research scholarships from the University of Melbourne.[27] Fitzpatrick's primary contributions to Australian history during this time – *British Imperialism and Australia* and *The British Empire in Australia* – were Marxist responses to Shann's liberalism.[28] He analysed economic change from the perspective of the division of labour, class struggle, and conflict between imperial policy and the interests of the Australian State, accounting for changes in the structures of social

---

24   Roland Wilson, 'Review: Shann, *An Economic History of Australia*', *Journal of Political Economy* 41, no. 2 (1933): 248–50, doi.org/10.1086/254460; Frederic Benham, 'Review: Shann, *An Economic History of Australia*', *Economic Journal* 41, no. 163 (1931): 480–83, doi.org/10.2307/2223916.
25   Alex Millmow, 'The Mystery of Edward Shann', *History of Economics Review* 42, no. 1 (2005): 67–76, doi.org/10.1080/18386318.2005.11681215.
26   Geoffrey Serle, 'Fitzpatrick, Brian Charles (1905–1965)', *ADB*, adb.anu.edu.au/biography/fitzpatrick-brian-charles-10195/text18015 (published first in hardcopy 1996).
27   He was awarded the Harbison-Higinbotham prize in 1937 and 1939, a major university research scholarship (£200 per year) from 1940 to 1942, and an annual grant (£500 per year) from 1944 to 1945. See Serle, 'Fitzpatrick'.
28   Brian Fitzpatrick, *British Imperialism and Australia* (Sydney: Sydney University Press, 1939); Brian Fitzpatrick, *The British Empire in Australia* (Melbourne: Melbourne University Press, 1941).

and economic development, and the distribution of wealth and power.[29] He was dismissive of analysing Australia as an independent economic entity, arguing that 'New South Wales expanded as Britain expanded', and that the colony was primarily the 'scenes of British private capital investment'.[30] Once this capital entered Australia, it was then controlled by a dominant class who were closely associated with the imperial project and established bourgeois governments to serve their own interests. Capital investment, in Fitzpatrick's view, was thus not neutral (as it appears in Shann's work), but determined the character of Australia's economic, social and political structure.

Contemporaries actively compared Shann and Fitzpatrick, praising the latter for his detail and abstinence from generalisations.[31] Sydney James 'Syd' Butlin, at that point lecturer in economics at the University of Sydney, reviewed *British Imperialism* as having 'the advantage over Coghlan that it is not a chronicle but a connected story, and it is more detailed, more accurate, and better balanced than Shann's episodic, romanticized *History*'.[32] However, Syd later commented that Fitzpatrick's reliability was uneven, and that the more recent past was treated particularly poorly.[33] Shann and Fitzpatrick's scholarship, though of very different analytical and political persuasions, had commonalities. They had a strong underlying theme, a skilled command of the written word and each added spice to Coghlan's more sober treatment of Australian economic history.

Economic history within universities at this time was a concert between the humanities and social sciences. Both economics and history had relatively porous disciplinary identities and institutional structures,

---

29 Graeme Snooks, 'Orthodox and Radical Interpretations of the Development of Australian Capitalism', *Labour History*, no. 28 (1975): 1–11, doi.org/10.2307/27508159; Lloyd, 'Economic History and Policy'; Lloyd, 'Analytical Frameworks'; C Boris Schedvin, 'Midas and the Merino: A Perspective on Australian Economic Historiography', *Economic History Review* 32, no. 3 (1979): 542–56, doi.org/10.1111/j.1468-0289.1979.tb02058.x; William Angus Sinclair, 'Economic History', in *Australians: A Guide to Sources*, ed. DH Borchardt (Sydney: Fairfax, Syme & Weldon, 1987), 245–51.
30 Fitzpatrick, *British Imperialism*, 299; Fitzpatrick, *The British Empire*, xiii.
31 WB Reddaway, 'Review: Fitzpatrick, *British Imperialism and Australia*', *Economic Journal* 49, no. 195 (1939): 528–29, doi.org/10.2307/2224828.
32 Syd J Butlin, 'Review: Fitzpatrick, *British Imperialism and Australia*', *Australian Quarterly* 11, no. 2 (1939): 108–12, doi.org/10.2307/20630753.
33 Syd J Butlin, *Foundations of the Australian Monetary System 1788–1851* (Melbourne: Melbourne University Press, 1953), preface; Schedvin, 'Midas and the Merino', 544.

enabling scholars to move between paradigms with ease.[34] Interwar economics was characterised by pragmatism and the public–academic nexus, with scholars drawn from different areas to provide advice on a range of economic issues.[35] In the history discipline, scholars were also preoccupied with tracking Australian colonial 'progress', with Mark McKenna arguing that 'politics, archaeology, classics and literature [were] commonly subsumed in the study of history'.[36] These conditions allowed economic historians to work across paradigms, with Shann appointed to positions, variously, in economics and history. He mentored John Andrew La Nauze at the University of Western Australia, who went on to hold positions in economics, economic history and history in Sydney, Melbourne and Canberra.[37] Herbert 'Joe' Burton trained as a historian, but often wrote on contemporary economic matters and was appointed senior lecturer of economic history at the University of Melbourne as early as 1930.[38] Sir Robert Madgwick, similarly, trained in both economics and history. After a DPhil at Balliol College, Oxford, Madgwick returned to the University of Sydney in 1935 as an 'economist who saw the light' and turned to history, taking up a lectureship in economic history.[39] A. G. L. Shaw graduated in history and political science at the University of Melbourne in 1935, and in philosophy, politics and economics at Oxford in 1940. Returning to Melbourne, Shaw lectured in economic history before a deepening career in the history discipline.[40] Garnet Vere 'Jerry' Portus was, similarly, depending on who you asked, a historian and an economist (and an industrial relations scholar and a theologian). Portus studied history and economics at Oxford between 1908 and

---

34   Mark McKenna, 'The History Anxiety', in *The Cambridge History of Australia*, ed. Alison Bashford and Stuart Macintyre vol. 2 (Melbourne: Cambridge University Press 2013), 561–80, doi.org/10.1017/CHO9781107445758.055; William Coleman, 'A Young Tree Dead? The Story of Economics in Australia and New Zealand', in *Routledge Handbook of the History of Global Economic Thought*, ed. Vincent Barnett (London: Routledge, 2015), 291–303.
35   Alex Millmow, *A History of Australasian Economic Thought* (London: Taylor & Francis, 2017), doi.org/10.4324/9781315716152; Coleman, 'A Young Tree Dead?'; Peter Groenewegen and Bruce McFarlane, *A History of Australian Economic Thought* (London: Routledge, 1990).
36   McKenna, 'The History Anxiety', 568.
37   Stuart Macintyre, 'La Nauze, Andrew John (1911–1990)', *ADB*, adb.anu.edu.au/biography/la-nauze-andrew-john-575/text25044 (published first in hardcopy 2012).
38   Selwyn Cornish, 'Burton, Herbert (Joe) (1900–1983)', *ADB*, adb.anu.edu.au/biography/burton-herbert-joe-180/text22025 (published first in hardcopy 2007).
39   Andrew Spaull, 'Madgwick, Sir Robert Bowden (1905–1979)', *ADB*, adb.anu.edu.au/biography/madgwick-sir-robert-bowden-11032/text19627 (published first in hardcopy 2000).
40   Graeme Davison, 'Alan George Lewers Shaw, 1916–2012', *2012 Annual Report* (Canberra: Australian Academy of the Humanities, 2012), www.humanities.org.au/wp-content/uploads/2017/04/AAH-Obit-Shaw-2012.pdf.

1917, acted for George C. Henderson as professor of history and English at the University of Adelaide in 1914, and from 1918 was director of WEA tutorial classes and part-time lecturer in economic history at the University of Sydney. Portus also contributed to early Australian labour studies and was a founding member of the Australian Institute of Political Science, eventually moving to a Chair in History and Political Science at the University of Adelaide from 1934. According to his biographer, Portus 'opposed the increasing specialization within universities', and expanded the scope of his lectures on economic history so much so that they 'became virtually a cultural history of mankind'.[41]

Social scientists embraced the field, with economic history taught widely in faculties of economics or commerce. Economist Douglas Copland started his professional life through a joint appointment in history and economics at the University of Tasmania, and later held chairs in both commerce and economics at the University of Melbourne.[42] Copland emphasised the interdisciplinarity of economic history, arguing it was the 'halfway house' between the abstract and the concrete.[43] Copland's successor as professor of commerce, Gordon Leslie Wood, also contributed to Australian economic history with a social sciences perspective. In Sydney, R. C. Mills completed his DPhil at the London School of Economics in 1915, and eventually settled in Sydney as the university's professor of economics from 1922. The following year Mills recruited economist Frederic Benham from London. Both contributed frequently to economics and economic history.[44] Benham left Sydney for the London School of Economics in 1929, but Mills continued as an economist and university administrator, serving as dean of faculty of economics until Syd Butlin relieved him in the mid-1940s.

---

41 WGK Duncan, 'Portus, Garnet Vere (Jerry) (1883–1954)', *ADB*, adb.anu.edu.au/biography/portus-garnet-vere-jerry-8082/text14103 (published first in hardcopy 1988).
42 Marjorie Harper, 'Copland, Sir Douglas Berry (1894–1971)', *ADB*, adb.anu.edu.au/biography/copland-sir-douglas-berry-247 (published first in hardcopy 1993).
43 Williams, *Balanced Growth*, 37.
44 Peter Groenewegen, 'Mills, Richard Charles (1886–1952)', *ADB*, adb.anu.edu.au/biography/mills-richard-charles-7593 (published first in hardcopy 1986); Neville Cain, 'Benham, Frederic Charles Courtenay (1900–1962)', *ADB*, adb.anu.edu.au/biography/benham-frederic-charles-courtenay-5201/text8751 (published first in hardcopy 1979).

The field also had institutional ties with the history discipline. For instance, at the University of Adelaide, economic history was housed in a large Department of Economics and History.[45] Sir W. Keith Hancock was one of Australia's most distinguished historians, and while he mostly held appointments in the history discipline, he worked with Shann in Perth in the early 1920s and maintained interest and research on economic history for the rest of his career.[46] Stephen Henry Roberts similarly wrote his *History of Australian Land Settlement*, published in 1924, from his Masters thesis in history, and then his vantage as a 'young lecturer in British History in the University of Melbourne'.[47] He went on to accept the Challis Professorship of History at the University of Sydney in 1929, before writing *The Squatting Age* in 1935.[48] Also at Melbourne, Fitzpatrick had trained in history, and his contributions to Australian economic history were facilitated by support from Melbourne's history Chair R. M. 'Max' Crawford.[49] La Nauze's transition from economic history to Melbourne's Ernest Scott Chair of History was also facilitated by his friendship with Max Crawford.[50]

Coghlan's work had set a precedent for the field's integration between government and academic knowledge. In the interwar period, Roland Wilson was a member of 'Giblin's Platoon' of public economists.[51] His *Capital Imports* was written from his Oxford DPhil thesis, and from 1932 Wilson held positions as an economist in the Commonwealth Statistician's branch in Hobart, as an economic adviser to the Treasury in Canberra, and as the Commonwealth statistician.[52] In the early 1940s, Shaw lectured in economic history part-time while working for the Commonwealth Departments of Information, Army and Postwar Reconstruction.[53] Mills, similarly, was an active member of government advisory bodies, consulting on wages, monetary and banking systems,

---

45 Anderson and O'Neil, *Economics at Adelaide*; W Prest, ed., *Pasts Present: History at Australia's Third University* (Kent Town: Wakefield Press, 2014).
46 Jim Davidson, 'Hancock, Sir William Keith (1898–1988)', *ADB*, adb.anu.edu.au/biography/hancock-sir-william-keith-460/text22673 (published first in hardcopy 2007).
47 Stephen H Roberts, *History of Australian Land Settlement 1788–1920* (Melbourne: Macmillan of Australia, [1924] 1968), xii.
48 DM Schreuder, 'Roberts, Sir Stephen Henry (1901–1971)', *ADB*, adb.anu.edu.au/biography/roberts-sir-stephen-henry-11539/text20589 (published first in hardcopy 2002).
49 Serle, 'Fitzpatrick'; Fitzpatrick, *The British Empire*, xii.
50 Macintyre, 'La Nauze'.
51 William Coleman, Selwyn Cornish and Alf Hagger, *Giblin's Platoon: The Trials and Triumphs of the Economist in Australian Public Life* (Canberra: ANU E Press, 2006), doi.org/10.22459/GP.04.2006.
52 John Farquharson, 'Wilson, Sir Roland (1904–1996)', *Sydney Morning Herald*, 29 October 1996.
53 Davison, 'Shaw'.

taxation, and education policy throughout his career. Sir Frederic Eggleston alternated between elected politician and appointed public official throughout his career, while also participating in WEA activities and writing for local and British press on Australian politics.[54] *State Socialism in Victoria*, published in 1932, was written out of Eggleston's 'intense political experience involved in [...] occupying several Ministerial posts in Victorian Governments from 1924 to 1927'.[55] Colin Clark and John G. Crawford were both well-known public economists. Clark was a British-Australian statistician who, after work as a lecturer in statistics at Cambridge, was appointed the Queensland government statistician (among other portfolios) from 1938 to 1952. Crawford worked as an economic adviser for the Rural Bank of New South Wales from 1935 to 1944, and then as the post–World War II director for the Bureau of Agricultural Economics and Department of Commerce and Agriculture.[56] Although Shann was primarily employed within universities, he also engaged in various government advisory committees, and acted as the Bank of New South Wales's economic consultant (the first economist to ever hold such a position in Australia) in the early years of the Great Depression. Shann used these platforms to argue for liberal factor markets, flexible exchange rates, free trade and conservative fiscal policies. He was 'one of the pioneers promoting the status of the economist as an adviser and consultant in a developing country'.[57]

Complementing universities and public servants, the third branch of interwar economic history knowledge work was the Workers' Educational Association. The organisation began in Britain, and the Australian offshoot expanded from 1919. It partnered with universities and the trade union movement to provide university extension tutorial studies for part-time students, who were usually full-time blue-collar workers.[58] Meredith Atkinson was the organisation's main disciple, arriving in Australia in 1914 to organise tutorial classes for the WEA and, soon after, to lecture in

---

54 Warren Osmond, 'Eggleston, Sir Frederic William (1875–1954)', *ADB*, adb.anu.edu.au/biography/eggleston-sir-frederic-william-344/text10409 (published first in hardcopy 1981).
55 Frederic William Eggleston, *State Socialism in Victoria* (London: PS King & Son, 1932), vii.
56 Alex Millmow, *The Gypsy Economist: The Life and Times of Colin Clark* (Singapore: Springer, 2021), doi.org/10.1007/978-981-33-6946-7; JDB Miller, 'Crawford, Sir John Grenfell (Jack) (1910–1984)', *ADB*, adb.anu.edu.au/biography/crawford-sir-john-grenfell-jack-1391/text22223 (published first in hardcopy 2007).
57 Snooks, 'Shann'.
58 Gerald Friesen and Lucy Taksa, 'Workers' Education in Australia and Canada: A Comparative Approach to Labour's Cultural History', *Labour History*, no. 71 (1996): 170–97, doi.org/10.2307/27516453.

economic history at the universities of Sydney and Melbourne.[59] A number of other scholars who contributed to the field – including Eggleston, Portus, Herbert Heaton and Clarence Northcott – were members of the tutorial class movement across the country. Research in Australian economic history was explicitly motivated by the WEA, with Portus commenting that his edited series of monographs on Australia's 'economic, social and political problems' was prompted by the assembly of material by WEA instructors.[60] Herbert Heaton, the organiser of WEA tutorials and lecturer in history and economics at the University of Tasmania, wrote that his *Economic History*, published in 1921, 'had its origins in a series of pamphlets published [...] by the Workers' Educational Association of South Australia'. Atkinson's *New Social Order*, published two years prior, was similarly based on 'numerous lectures' and was written 'to provide the students of the Workers' Educational Association throughout the Commonwealth with a text book which they can conveniently use in their tutorial classes'.[61] Northcott contributed to economic history from outside the primary parent disciplines. He was a sociologist by trade, and gave the organisation's first sociology classes in 1915–16.[62]

There was substantial professional crossover between these three institutions. Scholars were often employed by a combination of universities, the WEA and the public service throughout their career, and brought these contacts into their published research. While some – such as Roberts and Heaton – were professionally embedded in a single sector, they were the exceptions.[63] For example, Sydney's WEA leader Portus informally collaborated with university colleagues Mills, Shann and

---

59   Warren Osmond, 'Atkinson, Meredith (1883–1929)', *ADB*, adb.anu.edu.au/biography/atkinson-meredith-5081/text8477 (published first in hardcopy 1979).
60   Garnet Vere Portus, *Australia: An Economic Interpretation* (Sydney: Angus and Robertson, 1933).
61   Herbert Heaton, *Modern Economic History with Special Reference to Australia* (Adelaide: WEA South Australia, 1921), preface; Meredith Atkinson, *The New Social Order: A Study of Post-War Reconstruction* (Melbourne: Workers' Educational Association of Australia, 1919), xiii–xiv; Jack King, 'Herbert Heaton: A Scholar "Exiled" from Australia', *History of Economics Review* 43, no. 1 (2006): 56–70, doi.org/10.1080/18386318.2006.11681221.
62   Northcott's PhD thesis, published as *Australian Social Development* (New York: Longmans, 1918), was produced as a Columbia University PhD under the supervision of American sociologist Franklin H Giddins. Following this, Northcott worked for private industry and became a pioneer of industrial relations overseas. Helen Bourke, 'Northcott, Clarence Hunter (1880–1968)', *ADB*, adb.anu.edu.au/biography/northcott-clarence-hunter-11256 (published first in hardcopy 2000).
63   Roberts attributed his 'inspiration' for *Land Settlement* to his mentor Professor Ernest Scott. See Roberts, *Land Settlement*, xv. Heaton exclusively acknowledged WEA colleagues W Ham, VE Cromer, and FA Bland for their assistance. See, Heaton, *Economic History*, preface.

Hancock.[64] Melbourne's WEA leader Atkinson edited a volume on the economic and political life of Australia, with chapters by his WEA contacts as well as those at several different universities.[65] Northcott, another WEA advocate, acknowledged Atkinson for encouraging him to publish *Australian Social Development*, in addition to Commonwealth Statistician G. H. Knibbs, and scholars at Sydney and Columbia universities.[66] Clark and Crawford moved between universities, the government and, in Crawford's case, private industry. They acknowledged university workers – including Syd Butlin, economist Trevor Swan and cartographer Joyce Wood – those with connections to the public service such as Professor Jim Brigden, as well as Crawford's colleagues at the Rural Bank of New South Wales.[67] Eggleston, similarly, acknowledged assistance from colleagues in the public service alongside university scholars.[68] Fitzpatrick noted diverse contacts, including those from universities, the WEA, the public service, and leaders of the trade union movement.[69]

The field's relatively weak professional structures, and movement of scholars between disciplines and organisations enabled a broad intellectual tradition in the interwar period. International trade of goods and money became an important explainer of Australia's progress. In *The Prosperity of Australia*, published in 1928, Benham examined protectionism and trade, evaluating the efficiency with which European Australians had exploited resources.[70] He found Australia's record wanting, particularly regarding tariff protection, arguing that only an unobstructed price mechanism could allocate resources 'ideally'.[71] Wilson and Wood both explored the role of international capital imports in the Australian economy.[72] Wilson examined Australia's capital borrowings and the terms of trade, finding that – although economic theory would suggest otherwise – the Australian evidence exhibited no robust relationship between the

---

64 Shann, *An Economic History*, xi.
65 Portus on the Australian Labour movement, and Herbert Heaton on land settlement. See Meredith Atkinson, *Australia: Economic and Political Studies* (Melbourne: Macmillan, 1920).
66 Northcott, *Australian Social Development*, 10.
67 Colin Clark and JG Crawford, *The National Income of Australia* (Sydney and London: Angus and Robertson, 1938), viii.
68 Eggleston, *State Socialism*, vii–xi.
69 Fitzpatrick, *British Imperialism*, preface; Fitzpatrick, *The British Empire*, xiii.
70 Frederic Benham, *The Prosperity of Australia: An Economic Analysis* (London: PS King & Son, 1928).
71 Cain, 'Benham'.
72 Roland Wilson, *Capital Imports and the Terms of Trade* (Melbourne: Melbourne University Press, 1931); Gordon L Wood, *Borrowing and Business in Australia* (Oxford: Oxford University Press, 1930).

two. Wood also interrogated the link between borrowing and inflation relative to Australia's business cycle from the 1840s to 1929. He argued cheap loan money had contributed to speculation, disadvantage in trade, reduced private sector efficiency and, ultimately, reduced prosperity for Australia. Excessive capital imports were touted as the chief reason for the instance and relative magnitude of Australia's economic downturns. Fitzpatrick examined international flows – particularly trade and capital – from the perspective of colonial dependence and imperial exploitation.[73] Similarly, during his time in economics at the University of Sydney, La Nauze examined imperial dependence and the Australian tariff.[74] Wool was seen as a major vehicle of Australia's international trade, with Shann, for example, arguing the 'big sheep men' were the 'most characteristic and economically important Australians'.[75] Portus's and Shaw's generalist textbooks both featured the wool trade, and Hancock commented that wool 'made Australia a solvent nation, and in the end, a free one'.[76]

Land settlement was another key theme, drawing together a focus on the wool trade, migration and interest in Australia as a net capital importer. Squatters formed a substantial portion of Shann's work, and he examined their bonds of legislature, and political dramas with the imperial government. As an individualist, Shann was on the side of the squatters, bemoaning their lack of representation in government and inefficiencies of the land legislation system.[77] Mills evaluated colonist Edward Gibbon Wakefield's theory of 'systematic colonisation' in Australia for his DPhil at the London School of Economics in 1915. He argued that although the system was sensible at the time, it was only so at a certain stage of colonial development.[78] Roberts, a wide-ranging historian, also contributed to Australian economic history on the issue of land settlement and pioneers. His *History of Australian Land Settlement* did what it said on the tin, synthesising the development of land settlement from European invasion to 1920, as written by Coghlan, Mills and so on. It was necessarily a survey

---

73 Fitzpatrick, *British Imperialism*; Fitzpatrick, *The British Empire*.
74 John Andrew La Nauze, 'Australian Tariffs and Imperial Control', *Economic Record* 24, no. 1 (1948): 1–17, doi.org/10.1111/j.1475-4932.1948.tb01203.x; John Andre La Nauze, 'Merchants in Action: The Australian Tariffs of 1852', *Economic Record* 31, no. 1–2 (1955): 77–89, doi.org/10.1111/j.1475-4932.1955.tb02918.x.
75 Coleman, 'Historiography', 14.
76 Coleman, 'Historiography'; Portus, *Australia*; Alan GL Shaw, *The Economic Development of Australia* (New York: Longmans, Green and Company, 1944).
77 Shann, *An Economic History*.
78 Richard C Mills, *The Colonisation of Australia, 1829–1842* (London: Sidgwick and Jackson, 1915).

of parts of the story woven elsewhere, but in true interwar style was written with the panache that was missing from Coghlan. In *The Squatting Age* a decade later, Roberts focused on the squatting period, describing with vibrant detail the lives of early pastoralists, and their impressions of political, economic and social events in New South Wales.[79] Land settlement also provided a link between migration and material progress, with Madgwick's *Immigration into Eastern Australia* examining, as Mills did, Wakefield's systematic colonisation.[80] Madgwick emphasised the human capital dimensions of immigrants, characterising them as deceitful, fraudulent and disreputable, and arguing that Australia's development was hampered by its use for the disposal of British poorhouses and prisons. Migration and land settlement was also crucial for Fitzpatrick's account of dependence between Australia and Britain, arguing that free immigration supplied cheap labour for pastoralism, which in turn provided cheap wool for English textiles.[81]

The role of government was woven throughout these themes. The *laissez faire* scholars held the balance of power, with most critical of past interventions by the State in the economy.[82] Shann, trained in the individualism of the classical school of economics, reported on the triumph of market-based activities over State monopolies.[83] Benham's *Prosperity* adopted a similar classical economic model to Shann, advocating for an unobstructed, market-based price mechanism.[84] Although not as explicitly 'classical' as Shann and Benham, the WEA group were generally critical of State intervention. Portus disapproved of the 'autocratic communism' of the early years of European invasion.[85] Northcott's *Australian Social Development* examined the different functions of the State, arguing that public enterprises were 'invading' capitalism, that Labor's social ideals were short-sighted and that they ignored that 'private enterprise […] can perform its function more efficiently than the state'.[86] Atkinson's *New Social*

---

79 Roberts, *Land Settlement*; Stephen H Roberts, *The Squatting Age in Australia, 1835–1847* (Melbourne: Melbourne University Press, 1935).
80 RB Madgwick, *Immigration into Eastern Australia, 1788–1851* (London: Longmans, 1937).
81 Fitzpatrick, *The British Empire*.
82 Schedvin, 'Midas and the Merino'; Brian Galligan, 'The State in Australian Political Thought', *Politics* 19, no. 2 (1984): 82–92, doi.org/10.1080/00323268408401923; Tod Moore and James Walter, 'State Socialism in Australian Political Thought: A Reconsideration', *Australian Journal of Politics & History* 52, no. 1 (2006): 13–29, doi.org/10.1111/j.1467-8497.2006.00405a.x.
83 Snooks, 'Orthodox and Radical Interpretations'.
84 Cain, 'Benham'.
85 Portus, *Australia*.
86 Clarence Hunter Northcott, *Australian Social Development* (New York: Longmans, 1918), 71.

Order supported Northcott's argument that State socialism had 'failed' and advocated a corporatist approach to solving problems in each industry.[87] Eggleston also critiqued government intervention in the economy, with his *State Socialism in Victoria* examining the colony that had 'possibly the largest and most comprehensive use of State power outside Russia'.[88] He traced the history of Victoria's use of public enterprises in social and economic infrastructure, the development of local manufacturing and the alleviation of depressions. Although he acknowledged that sometimes the dominance of State enterprise was for practical reasons, he ultimately concluded that publicly owned essential services, taken from the Victorian case, were not economically or politically sound.[89] Hancock's *Australia* included a chapter on 'State Socialism', and although it narrowly preceded Eggleston's work, Hancock acknowledged his debt to Eggleston 'who ha[d] for several years been collecting, with great industry and skill, a vast mass of facts' on the issue.[90] While Hancock saw state socialism as holding the nation back throughout its history, he was more sympathetic, arguing that the State's role was to provide public utility and 'collective power at the service of individualistic rights'.[91]

Others wrote from the Left. Fitzpatrick linked, pejoratively, market economics and political exploitation, using a Marxist lens to argue that the economic utilisation of the colonies was entirely to meet the needs of the imperial country.[92] Heaton's discussion of the development of Australian capitalism came from his position as a socialist. Although he did not necessarily want to overthrow capitalism – instead he argued for an ethical capitalism in which capital worked alongside unions and government – Heaton certainly advocated for greater tempering of the market economy by collective action.[93]

The field's porous professional boundaries manifested in a body of work that demonstrated a range of approaches. Most were comfortable using the vast statistical material that had been built by Coghlan and the colonial statisticians. They were also, on balance, engaged with the humanities, fashioning published work with a narrative style that added 'spice' to

---

87 Atkinson, *The New Social Order*, 216.
88 Eggleston, *State Socialism*, 1.
89 Moore and Walter, 'State Socialism'.
90 W. Keith Hancock, *Australia* (London: Ernest Benn, 1930), 107–8.
91 Hancock, *Australia*, 55.
92 Fitzpatrick, *The British Empire*.
93 Heaton, *Economic History*.

Coghlan's quite sober and impersonal treatment of the economy.[94] The use of a range of sources, and the engagement of economic history alongside social, political and geographic history, were key features of the interwar approach. Shann's training in both history and classical economics created a story based on Coghlan's quantitative material, but with the flair of a master storyteller.[95] Similarly, Fitzpatrick's approach to understanding economic matters combined statistical material with the literary edge of a journalist trained in history and sensitive to social and political context. Heaton's *Modern Economic History*, released and updated a number of times throughout the 1920s, integrated social and political themes with a disposition towards quantitative chronicle. Heaton argued that the 'best approach to the study of Economics lies in a *historical and descriptive survey* of modern economic life and organisation'.[96] Roberts's work on land settlement described historical economic and geographic matters, incorporating a range of quantitative, government, personal and family historical sources to paint a vibrant picture of life on the land. Roberts walked the line between 'history and the arts as civilising morally uplifting agents', and an empirical historian who 'aimed to train professionals for work'.[97] Madgwick's *Immigration* similarly bridged social science and humanities paradigms, incorporating analysis of economic theory and the labour market, with discussion of the personalities and political machinery of the British Colonial Office. Hancock's *Australia* blended economics, history and politics in his study of Australian population, soil, political institutions, foreign policy, tariffs, literature and art. His work was praised for its integration of economic matters with the skills of a humanities scholar:

> Life had fashioned him as a scholar, but happily, experience or chance or the fates, or the gods had lavished on him the gifts and burden of the artist.[98]

Social science approaches were also present, with Clark and Crawford continuing Coghlan's legacy of national income accounting by compiling longitudinal national data from the 1890s to the 1930s. Their work was an

---

94 Sinclair, 'Economic History', 245.
95 Coleman, 'Historiography'.
96 Herbert Heaton, *Modern Economic History with Special Reference to Australia*, 3rd ed. (Adelaide: Vardon and Sons, [1922] 1925), 'Author's Preface' (emphasis mine).
97 Schreuder, 'Roberts'.
98 CMH Clark, 'Hancock's *Australia* and Australian Historiography: A Note', *Historical Studies* 13, no. 51 (1968): 329–32, 329, doi.org/10.1080/10314616808595381.

exercise in Keynesian business cycle specification, on par with the trend in economics elsewhere towards national income accounting.[99] Wilson also used an economist's lens to discuss capital imports and the terms of trade. *Capital Imports* progressed in three parts: Wilson estimated Australian borrowing between 1871 and 1930, developed a theory of international capital movements, and then tested the theoretical conclusions against the Australian evidence.[100] His approach was deductive, and his use of economic theory was world class. The book was reviewed primarily for economics outlets (for example, *Economic Record, Journal of Political Economy, The Economic Journal*) and was praised for its contribution to international trade theory rather than its historical material. Benham's approach was also deductive. His *Prosperity* was based on national income measurement, and used formal economic ideas to 'test' Australia's economic success.[101] Wood's work was less deductive, but still used the tools of economics to integrate economic history and economic theory. Wood assembled substantial quantitative material on borrowing, inflation and the business cycle, and used economic theory to interpret this evidence.[102] While scholars such as Benham were sceptical about Wood's conclusions, his work was praised for the same reason as most of the field's heroes – for assembling valuable estimates of key economic indicators. Mills, although sympathetic to both history and economics, favoured the latter. His work on systematic colonisation was an exercise in the history of economic policy, examining the genesis and implementation of Wakefield's views within his context of contemporary political economy.[103]

Encouraged, perhaps, by the relative infancy of the field within universities, the balance between these three 'arms' of interwar economic history was distinctive for the field globally. The interwar period was a time of consolidation for many other communities of economic historians, such as in Britain where the period culminated in the foundation of the Economic History Society in 1926, the first issue of the *Economic History Review* in 1927, and the first chair in the subject established at Cambridge in 1928.[104] In the US, although independent specialist departments of economic history never materialised, the interwar period saw the foundation of the

---

99 Clark and Crawford, *National Income*.
100 Wilson, *Capital Imports*.
101 Benham, *Prosperity*.
102 Wood, *Borrowing*.
103 Mills, *Colonisation*.
104 Pat Hudson, 'Economic History in Britain: The "First Industrial Nation"', in Boldizzoni and Hudson, *Global Economic History*, 17–34, doi.org/10.4324/9781315734736.

National Bureau of Economic Research to integrate economics, statistics and historical research, and the establishment of both the Economic History Association and its flagship journal the *Journal of Economic History*.[105] The professionalisation of the field occurred at a similar time elsewhere, with chairs established in Germany, Italy, Poland and Hungary in the 1920s. The French journal *Annales d'histoire économique et sociale* – the model for research in the *Annales* school – was established in 1929; the Italian specialist journal *Rivista di Storia Economica* first appeared in 1936; professional journals on Chinese economic history were established in the 1930s; and in Japan, seminars, journals, institutes and a nationwide association were established between 1929 and 1931.[106] Compared to the development of economic history elsewhere, Australia was a late starter.

The relative infancy of Australian economic history was a boon for the field's interdisciplinary connections, allowing communication across the disciplinary divide. However, it also reinforced a dependence on the metropole. Australian society was, of course, established on a British model, and work in economic history began as part the colonial project. The description of the economy and the collection of statistics was used as a way for London to rationalise, understand and govern the colonies. Colonial economic historical writers spent some time visiting Australia, but then wrote, published and distributed their research in Britain.[107] Even Sydney-born Coghlan facilitated this intellectual imperialism. While his research was based on his time on the ground as the New South Wales government statistician, *Labour and Industry* was written and distributed from London during Coghlan's time there in various diplomatic roles from 1904.[108] Coghlan had been back and forth to London since the 1890s, and was well received into London society, including a fellowship

---

105 Naomi Lamoreaux, 'Beyond the Old and the New: Economic History in the United States', in Boldizzoni and Hudson, *Global Economic History*, 35–54, doi.org/10.4324/9781315734736; Alfred William Coats, 'Disciplinary Self-Examination, Departments, and Research Traditions in Economic History: The Anglo-American Story', *Scandinavian Economic History Review* 38, no. 1 (1990): 3–18, doi.org/10.1080/03585522.1990.10408164.
106 Jean-Yves Grenier, 'Economic History in France: A *Sonderweg*?', in Boldizzoni and Hudson, *Global Economic History*, 113–29, doi.org/10.4324/9781315734736; Francesco Boldizzoni, 'The Flight of Icarus: Economic History in the Italian Mirror', in Boldizzoni and Hudson, *Global Economic History*, 130–45, doi.org/10.4324/9781315734736-8; Li Bozhong, 'Economic History in China: Tradition, Divergence and Potential', in Boldizzoni and Hudson, *Global Economic History*, 293–309, doi.org/10.4324/9781315734736; K Sugihara, 'The Socio-Economic History Society of Japan', *Information Bulletin of the Union of National Economic Associations in Japan* 21, no. 1 (2011): 99.
107 Huf, 'Making Things Economic'.
108 Hicks, 'Coghlan'.

of the Royal Statistical Society from 1893. Knowledge about Australia was thus produced at home but its legitimacy, distribution and use was controlled by the metropole.[109]

The expansion of economic history within universities reinforced the degree to which scholars looked to Britain. Sandstone universities were established with Eurocentric systems of learning in mind, primarily Scottish logics of training in discrete areas of inquiry.[110] The WEA was similarly imported, with Atkinson emigrating to Australia from Durham in 1914 specifically for the purpose of promoting working-class education. In addition to the use of the metropole's curriculum, the Australian academy prioritised recruitment and training from Britain.[111] This was the form in which both imperialism and cultural cringe manifested, with overseas training seen as increasingly important to establish the scholar's pedigree. The model was simple, and very common at this time: the bright young man (yes, mostly men) would complete an undergraduate degree at an Australian university, would then be selected for either a Rhodes or Rockefeller scholarship to attend Oxford, Cambridge or the London School of Economics, where he would complete another Bachelors degree, and then either a Masters or DPhil. With small variation, the majority of interwar economic historians took this path. Roberts, for example, earned no less than three degrees at the University of Melbourne in the 1920s, though British legitimacy was still required. He won a scholarship to study for his DSc at the University of London.[112] Heaton, Benham and Atkinson were born in the UK, and trained there before recruitment to Australia.[113] Crawford and Wilson both studied in the US, at Harvard and Chicago, respectively.[114] The only true exceptions to this pattern were Fitzpatrick and Eggleston. Fitzpatrick studied at the University of Melbourne, and although he went to England intending further study, he spent a year in London as a journalist before working his passage home

---

109 This is consistent with Raewyn Connell, *Southern Theory: The Global Dynamics of Knowledge in Social Science* (Crows Nest: Allen & Unwin, 2007).
110 John C Smart, Kenneth A Feldman and Corinna A Ethington, *Academic Disciplines: Holland's Theory and the Study of College Students and Faculty* (Nashville: Vanderbilt University Press, 2000); Hannah Forsyth, *A History of the Modern Australian University* (Sydney: University of New South Wales Press, 2014).
111 Tamson Pietsch, *Empire of Scholars: Universities, Networks and the British Academic World, 1850–1939* (Manchester: Manchester University Press, 2013).
112 Schreuder, 'Roberts'.
113 Helen Bourke, 'Heaton, Herbert (1890–1973)', *ADB*, adb.anu.edu.au/biography/heaton-herbert-6626/text11413 (published first in hardcopy 1983); Cain, 'Benham'; Osmond, 'Atkinson'.
114 Farquharson, 'Wilson'; Miller, 'Crawford'.

as a steward.[115] Eggleston's family were not able to afford his university education at either Melbourne or Cambridge, so he trained as a lawyer before his career in politics.[116]

Wartime transition

World War II 'galvanised' university campuses.[117] Students enlisted in staggering numbers, campus grounds and facilities were used for training, research funds were funnelled towards relevant work, and academics were seconded to public service roles planning for the war effort and recovery.[118] Several Australian economic historians were temporarily moved from their university posts to various departments focused on education, training and managing resources during the war effort. Hancock was overseas at the time and was recruited into British home front service, including as editor of the civil series on the official history of Britain in World War II. Roberts remained within the university, but was focused on public communication, writing an almost-daily column for the *Sydney Morning Herald* called 'Our War Correspondent'.[119] Some, like Crawford, transitioned into the Department of Postwar Reconstruction, developing strategies for rebuilding Australia's society after the war.[120] This was also a training ground for prominent postwar economic historian Noel Butlin, with his integration with the public reconstruction effort crucial for his intellectual and professional development.

The total war developed a partnership between public and academic work, as well as the imperative for integrated, 'useful' knowledge. University silos, already porous, were almost entirely dismantled during the war. Academics were not only removed from the university space, but worked alongside policymakers and across paradigms to 'equip and maintain armed forces fighting in the tropics, make good the shortages of advanced manufactures that could no longer be imported, and expand primary production to sustain the Allies'.[121] These were life-or-death

---

115 Serle, 'Fitzpatrick'.
116 Osmond, 'Eggleston'.
117 Forsyth, *Modern Australian University*.
118 Forsyth, *Modern Australian University*; Stuart Macintyre, *The Poor Relation* (Melbourne: Melbourne University Press, 2010).
119 Davidson, 'Hancock'; Schreuder, 'Roberts'.
120 Miller, 'Crawford'.
121 Macintyre, *The Poor Relation*, 19.

problems that required an interdisciplinary effort to resolve. When it came to reconstruction, the problems were equally complex – refitting munitions factories, re-establishing and finding new patterns of trade and production, and finding employment for thousands of ex-service men and women. The challenges of war made most Western societies not only want to return to 'normal', but also to make the new world better. Universities and the development of 'useful' knowledge was seen as an important source of renewed equality and prosperity, reflecting and reinforcing postwar optimism.[122]

---

122 Macintyre, *The Poor Relation*; Forsyth, *Modern Australian University*.

3

The big bang

> Noel was this Moses, bringing these two books – 'here are the tablets, this is going to take the discipline forward'.
>
> David Merrett, March 2015[1]

In 1949, while sharing a house together in Hurstville in Sydney's south, economics lecturers Noel G. Butlin and Heinz Arndt won permission from the New South Wales statistician to examine Coghlan's papers, sources long since forgotten in the bottom of an inner-city basement. As Arndt recalled, 'for three days, stripped to the waist, we worked in indescribable grime, sorting thousands of volumes on to shelves'.[2] They eventually found the needle in the haystack: handwritten notes of Coghlan's estimates of aggregate output in colonial New South Wales. The result was an article where the two young scholars interrogated the nature of Coghlan's estimates and compared them with contemporary national income accounting frameworks. While Arndt quickly moved on to other work in economics, this project was the start of Butlin's pre-eminence in Australian economic history.

---

1   Merrett interview with author. Unless otherwise specified, interviews cited are those conducted by the author: see Appendix for details.
2   Heinz W Arndt, *A Course through Life: Memoirs of an Australian Economist* (Canberra: ANU, 1985), 16; see also Graeme Snooks, '"In My Beginning Is My End": The Life and Work of Noel George Butlin, 1921–1991', *Australian Economic History Review* 31, no. 2 (1991): 12, doi.org/10.1111/aehr.312001.

Noel Butlin is Australia's most influential economic historian. Contemporary colleagues argued his writings 'dominate' the field,[3] and that his work was instrumental in developing the 'intellectual identity' of members.[4] To this day Butlin has been praised as the source of the 'orthodox' reorientation of Australian economic history.[5] He is also remembered at an annual lecture at the Economic History Society of Australia and New Zealand, with his life and achievements introduced in well-worn reverential phrases. In this chapter, the focus is on a more complex story of Butlin's legacy – embedding his contributions within his professional context, and recognising the broader structural and social forces that enabled this intellectual movement. Doing so incorporates a greater understanding of the labour of producing great works, as well as revealing the ways that universities can encourage and support the production of interdisciplinary knowledge.

The words and the numbers

The 'orthodox school' – a term coined by economic historian Chris Lloyd and adopted for the remainder of this book – refers to the body of work in Australian economic history that emerged alongside, or was inspired by, Butlin's two influential volumes, colloquially termed 'the numbers' and 'the words': *Australian Domestic Product, Investment and Foreign Borrowing 1861–1938/9* (1962) and *Investment in Australian Economic Development, 1861–1900* (1964).[6] In the former, Butlin compiled Australian historical national statistics within a national income accounting framework. In the latter, Butlin used these statistics to describe the sector-by-sector

---

3   William Angus Sinclair, 'Economic History', in *Australians: A Guide to Sources*, ed. DH Borchardt (Sydney: Fairfax, Syme & Weldon, 1987), 245–51, 245.
4   C Boris Schedvin, 'Midas and the Merino: A Perspective on Australian Economic Historiography', *Economic History Review* 32, no. 3 (1979): 542–56, 548, doi.org/10.1111/j.1468-0289.1979.tb02058.x.
5   See William Coleman, 'The Historiography of Australian Economic History', in *Cambridge Economic History of Australia*, ed. Simon Ville and Glenn Withers (Melbourne: Cambridge University Press, 2015), 11–28, doi.org/10.1017/CHO9781107445222.004; Christopher Lloyd, 'Analytical Frameworks of Australia's Economic History', in Ville and Withers, *Cambridge Economic History of Australia*, 52–69; Christopher Lloyd, 'Economic History and Policy: Historiography of Australian Traditions', *Australian Journal of Politics and History* 41, no. 3 (1995): 61–79; Schedvin, 'Midas and the Merino'; Sinclair, 'Economic History'.
6   Noel G Butlin, *Australian Domestic Product, Investment and Foreign Borrowing 1861–1938/9* (London: Cambridge University Press, 1962) and Noel G Butlin, *Investment in Australian Economic Development, 1861–1900* (London: Cambridge University Press, 1964), doi.org/10.1017/CBO97813 16530160. See also Lloyd, 'Analytical Frameworks'.

mechanism of growth in the latter half of the nineteenth century. These two books were built on over a decade of research, with preliminary estimates published in the mid-1950s, and two articles published in *Economic Record* in 1958 and 1959.[7]

Figure 2: Professor Noel G. Butlin, ANU, 10 October 1989
Source: ANU Archives, ANUA 225-168.

Butlin's big statement, and arguably the feature that he has been best known for, was that the Australian economy was an important and interesting thing to study – not as a footnote to the industrial revolution; not as a British outpost; not as subject to the vicissitudes of international trade. In this he differed fundamentally from both Shann and Fitzpatrick's discussions of externally led economic development and exploitation, respectively. In 'the words', Butlin argued that urbanisation and domestic manufacturing (rather than export markets) were the dominant industries in Australia from the 1870s. When he first stumbled across this evidence in the mid-1950s, he and research assistant and later population expert,

---

7   Noel G Butlin and Henry de Meel, *Public Capital Formation in Australia: Estimates 1860–1900*, Social Science Monographs 2 (Canberra: The Australian National University, 1954); Noel G Butlin, *Private Capital Formation in Australia: Estimates 1861–1900*, Social Science Monographs 5 (Canberra: Australian National University, 1955); Noel G Butlin, 'The Shape of the Australian Economy, 1861–1900', *Economic Record* 34, no. 67 (1958): 10–29, doi.org/10.1111/j.1475-4932.1958.tb01312.x; Noel G Butlin, 'Some Structural Features of Australian Capital Formation, 1861–1938/39', *Economic Record* 35, no. 72 (1959): 389–415, doi.org/10.1111/j.1475-4932.1959.tb00480.x.

H. de Meel, seemed surprised. They initially thought that Australia's 'intimate links with the British economy' would suggest that domestic economic activity should move with Britain's.[8] However, they found no consistent relationship between the two, and speculated that comparable increases in the value of exports and imports over this period meant that trade may have played a minor role in determining growth.

Butlin's second key internalist conclusion was that structural disequilibrium from speculation on the real estate market and inefficiencies in railway construction caused an initial downturn before the 1890s depression.[9] In 1955, Butlin argued that the willingness of Britain to invest was important for Australia's economic progress in the nineteenth century, though he was adamant that this was only part of the story, and 'in some respects, not the most interesting part'.[10] He argued that Australia sought out British investment in this period, and that although railway building was made possible by the increased supply of overseas funds, it was 'more importantly' possible through rising local revenues.[11] Butlin's agenda was clear: although he acknowledged important external factors, they were, in his mind, not the 'most important' or 'most interesting' factors.

Butlin is famous for his approach as well as his interpretation. Taking cues from Coghlan's proto-national income accounting, Butlin set out without a theoretical framework, arguing instead that the 'whole approach has been framed with the particular circumstances of the Australian economy [...] in mind'.[12] He made some manipulations to the data, such as interpolation, extrapolating from small samples, and applying ratios between variables across time and place. However, he built his narrative of economic growth inductively by applying concepts to the trends found in his evidence. Butlin took Coghlan's work very seriously, with W. A. 'Gus' Sinclair recalling that Noel 'didn't have time for anyone else who had written on Australian economic history apart from Coghlan'.[13] Having said that, Butlin was cautious not to make the same mistakes Coghlan did, criticising the latter's lack of source information and description of

---

8   Butlin and de Meel, *Public Capital Formation*, 11.
9   See, in particular, Butlin, *Investment*, 351.
10 Butlin, *Private Capital Formation*, 2.
11 Butlin, *Private Capital Formation*, 14.
12 Butlin and de Meel, *Public Capital Formation*, 1.
13 Sinclair interview.

methods and the resulting 'tragedy' that the work had been disregarded by some in the economic history community.[14] As such, Butlin included an immaculate description of the way his statistics were compiled.

Although there was no explicit theoretical basis, implicitly Butlin's logic was a mix of neoclassical individualism and Keynesian macroeconomics. Regarding the former, he emphasised market signals and the decision-making of rational economic actors. To the latter, Keynes was introduced through Butlin's emphasis on the duality of the public and private spheres, a focus on the macroeconomy, his acceptance of capital formation as a key engine of growth and the use of quantitative measurement as the basis for public policy intervention. Although his focus on market signals was neoclassical, arguing that instability was due to non-rational responses to market signals was reminiscent of Keynes's contribution on herd behaviour. Keynesianism of a similar flavour dominated the economics discipline at the time, particularly in the policy circles through which Butlin was mentored. He was 'manpowered into the [...] Department of Post-War Reconstruction' as soon as he finished his undergraduate degree in 1942.[15] He spent about a year working for the department, before being sent to Washington and then to London as a public servant. The latter role involved 'virtually a six-month continuous seminar from John Maynard Keynes telling the assembled company from the Dominions and colonies how economics should be handled'.[16]

Many at the time recognised that Butlin was on a good wicket. Adelaide economist H. F. Lydall explicitly likened Butlin's work to other prominent national income accounting historians, arguing that 'what [Simon] Kuznets did for the United States, and Phyllis Deane and others for Britain, has now been done by Noel Butlin for Australia'.[17] Melbourne economic historian Ernst A. Boehm agreed that the work was significant through 'the stimulus [...] given to economists and historians to contribute with Professor Butlin to a more definitive Australian historiography'.[18] Labour economist Keith Hancock attributed the maturation of the field

---

14 Butlin, *Investment*, xv.
15 Stephen G Foster, 'Interview with Emeritus Professor Noel George Butlin' (Canberra: ANU Oral History Archive, 1991).
16 Foster, 'Interview with Noel George Butlin'; Maggie Shapley, 'Butlin, Noel George (1921–1991)', *Australian Dictionary of Biography* (hereafter *ADB*), adb.anu.edu.au/biography/butlin-noel-george-184/text26845, published online 2014.
17 HF Lydall, 'N.G. Butlin's Anatomy of Australian Economic Growth', *Business Archives and History* 3, no. 2 (1963): 204, doi.org/10.1111/aehr.32005.
18 Ernst A Boehm, 'Measuring Australian Economic Growth, 1861 to 1938–39', *Economic Record* 41, no. 94 (1965): 232, doi.org/10.1111/j.1475-4932.1965.tb02879.x.

in the 1960s to Butlin's work, arguing he had made the subject 'one of the most fruitful fields of research at the ANU'.[19] Oral history sources have also largely confirmed the prominence of Butlin's approach, arguing that it came from providing innovative interpretations of Australia's development, and the determination and stamina to unearth a wealth of primary quantitative data.[20] Fitzpatrick, eloquently as always, passed the torch to a new generation of economic historians:

> It is immaterial that our much-read Australian theses are qualified and corrected and transformed, that Shann climbs over Coghlan and Fitzpatrick over Shann and a whole formidable family over Fitzpatrick. It is enough for any sensible, conscientious tradesman, having that touch of creative imagination without which nobody can contribute to the advancement of knowledge of history, that he won, and for a time held, a place in the procession.[21]

Butlin's 'revolution' was hard to pull off without ruffling a few feathers. Criticism centred on the construction of the statistics, with some urging caution due to the occasional use of small samples and filling back from census data taken every 10 years.[22] Fitzpatrick gently questioned the validity of statistics collected by government statisticians, on which Butlin's work was based.[23] Boehm criticised the aggregation of statistics across Australia, arguing that there was quantitative and qualitative evidence to suggest economic development fluctuated between each colony.[24] There was also criticism of Butlin's underestimation of some elements of private investment,[25] and of the limited, cursory price index.[26]

Wool values generated a bit of a nasty exchange with Alan Beever at the University of Melbourne. In *Economic Record*, Beever acknowledged that Butlin's work was an 'invaluable pioneering study of Australian social accounts', but that the use of pre-Federation trade statistics overvalued

---

19   Keith Hancock, 'Review: Butlin, *Investment*; Forster, *Industrial Development*', *American Economic Review* 55, no. 3 (1965): 571.
20   Boot; Dingle/Davison; Gregory; Macintyre; Pincus; Sinclair; Troy interviews.
21   Brian Fitzpatrick, 'Counter Revolution in Australian Historiography?', *Meanjin Quarterly* 22, no. 2 (1963): 197–213, 213.
22   Lydall, 'Anatomy'; Boehm, 'Australian Economic Growth'.
23   Fitzpatrick, 'Counter Revolution', 211.
24   Boehm, 'Australian Economic Growth', 230.
25   Boehm, 'Australian Economic Growth', 213.
26   In reference to *Domestic Product*, see Boehm, 'Australian Economic Growth'. In reference to the 1954/1955 monographs, see Raymond W Goldsmith, 'Review: Butlin and De Meel, *Public Capital Formation in Australia*; Butlin, *Private Capital Formation in Australia*', *Journal of Economic History* 18, no. 1 (1958): 112–14, doi.org/10.1017/S0022050700089166.

wool by a considerable margin.[27] Butlin defended the use of trade statistics, arguing that Beever proposed a 'tantalizingly simple solution' to the very complex issue of wool values.[28] When Beever gave very little ground, Butlin's final reply has become infamous with members of the community.[29] In the first page and a half, Butlin argued that Beever was 'wrong' on no less than 25 separate issues, and remarked to the *Record*'s editor that he did not wish to continue the discussion.[30]

Some also criticised Butlin's focus on internal determinants of growth. Economist Colin G. F. Simkin was surprised by how little attention exports received within Butlin's overall narrative of growth, arguing that exports were a major determination of output for any small open economy such as Australia.[31] Keith Hancock similarly criticised Butlin's internalist interpretation of the 1890s depression, arguing it was 'less satisfactory than many of the subsidiary hypotheses which Butlin develops'.[32] Some reacted by publishing their own, contra research. Boehm, following his critique of Butlin's estimates, published new research arguing that the 1890s depression was caused by a combination of internal structural distortions such as land speculation, as well as British inability to lend to Australia.[33] In 1963, The Australian National University (ANU) economist and economic historian Alan Hall published his PhD thesis as a monograph. He argued that his motivation for publishing the work more than a decade after its completion was because it 'differed from Noel's view of the world'.[34] Hall traced the factors that influenced the flow of funds to Australia, concluding that it was the interaction of events in London and Australia that explained the pattern of capital flow in this period.[35]

---

27 E Alan Beever, 'The Australian Wool Clip 1861–1900', *Economic Record* 39, no. 88 (1963): 437, doi.org/10.1111/j.1475-4932.1963.tb01500.x. Beever recommended non-government sources, expressing the value of the wool clip in terms of the price they received at London auction houses.
28 See Noel G Butlin, 'A Problem in Prices and Quantities', *Economic Record* 40, no. 90 (1964): 233, doi.org/10.1111/j.1475-4932.1964.tb02151.x.
29 Merrett; Dingle/Davison; Hutchinson interviews.
30 Noel G Butlin, 'A Tangled Web', *Economic Record* 40, no. 90 (1964): 255–56, doi.org/10.1111/j.1475-4932.1964.tb02153.x.
31 CGF Simkin, 'Review: Butlin, *Investment in Australian Economic Development, 1861–1900*', *Business Archives and History* 5, no. 1 (1965): 68, doi.org/10.1111/aehr.51br1.
32 Hancock, 'Review: Butlin; Forster', 573.
33 Boehm, 'Australian Economic Growth'.
34 Hall interview. See Alan R Hall, *The London Capital Market and Australia 1870–1914* (Canberra: Australian National University Press, 1963), which was based on his 1951 PhD thesis: Alan R Hall, 'The London Capital Market and the Flow of Capital to Australia 1870–1914' (PhD thesis, London School of Economics, 1951).
35 Hall, *London Capital Market*. Although Hall since conceded that it is understandable to emphasise internal factors if you are embedded in the Australian data, he has argued that the bigger picture of Australia is certainly of an open economy. See Hall interview.

Orthodox recruitment

Butlin's contribution to understanding Australian economic history was remarkable. However, the institutional context enabled not only the production of the work itself, but also its promotion as an intellectual movement. In particular, 'the words' and 'the numbers' were only possible within the 'golden era' of higher education expansion. Many Western nations, including Australia, heavily invested in higher education after World War II. It was seen as the key to postwar nation-building and to ushering in a new era of prosperity and equality.[36] In Australia, this occurred on two fronts, with different rationales. The first implicitly invoked the Scottish enlightenment ideal of the university, with the expansion of sandstone universities and establishment of new tertiary institutions in the 1960s and 1970s largely with the aim of a mass-educated population trained in the professions (see Chapter 4). The Butlin revolution, on the other hand, was driven by an emphasis on research. World War II demonstrated the usefulness of basic scientific and social science research, as well as the importance of interdisciplinary, publicly engaged knowledge. The government invoked the German model of higher education, with scientific training and research focusing on new frontiers of knowledge, and university professors developing new research programs and guiding graduate students.[37] Under this rationale, the interwar Council for Scientific and Industrial Research (CSIR) was reconstructed to form the Commonwealth Scientific and Industrial Research Organisation (CSIRO), and was given an expanded role in basic research and integration with new secondary industries.[38] The federally funded Australian Research Grants Commission was also established to fund the creation of new, academic knowledge. Universities introduced PhD programs, attempting to stem the flow of graduate students

---

36 DS Anderson and E Eaton, 'Part 1: Post-War Reconstruction and Expansion 1940–1965', *Higher Education Research and Development* 1, no. 1 (1982): 8–93, doi.org/10.1080/0729436820010102; Hannah Forsyth, *A History of the Modern Australian University* (Sydney: University of New South Wales Press, 2014); Simon Marginson, *Monash: Remaking the University* (St Leonards: Allen & Unwin, 2000); Stuart Macintyre, *The Poor Relation* (Melbourne: Melbourne University Press, 2010).
37 John C Smart, Kenneth A Feldman and Corinna A Ethington, *Academic Disciplines: Holland's Theory and the Study of College Students and Faculty* (Nashville: Vanderbilt University Press, 2000).
38 Macintyre, *The Poor Relation*; C Boris Schedvin, *Shaping Science and Industry: A History of Australia's Council for Scientific and Industrial Research, 1926–49* (Sydney: Allen & Unwin, 1987), doi.org/10.1071/9780643101326.

overseas.[39] The compact between universities and governments, in both instances, was for knowledge and education to be deployed for the benefit of Australian society.

The Australian National University (ANU) was the centrepiece of the Commonwealth government's research-led university expansion. Established in 1946, the new national university was a unique blend of a national research agency like the CSIRO, and a university with its own academic priorities.[40] As was ideal under the German model, scholars were appointed to research positions, and supervision of graduate students was the only 'teaching' requirement. Compared to the short-staffing and deteriorating teaching loads elsewhere, ANU was an oasis for scholars. Migration to Canberra meant a substantial pay increase, as well as financial support and the time to devote oneself to research. It was an attractive offer: although Canberra was still more or less a big paddock in those days, ANU managed to attract the best and brightest – including Noel Butlin.[41]

The research-led ANU was amalgamated with Canberra University College (CUC) in the late 1950s. CUC was established in 1930 as an outpost of the University of Melbourne, awarding degrees primarily to public servants engaged in part-time study. Between 1958 and 1960, CUC was combined with the research university, with what was now called ANU having two 'arms': the Institute of Advanced Studies (the 'Institute'), and the School of General Studies (the 'Faculties'). There was a division of responsibility, with those in the research schools of the Institute focusing entirely on research and PhD supervision. The Faculties resembled the sandstone universities, with members teaching undergraduates and with some, but less, onus on research output.[42] There was some tension between the two groups – even in name, a hierarchy was established between the 'advanced' work of the Institute and the 'general' knowledge of the Faculties. Additionally, the curious dual structure – the 'maze' as Faculties economic historian R. V. 'Bob' Jackson has called it – led to the only instance in Australia, and probably the world, where

---

39   Forsyth, *Modern Australian University*; Marginson, *Monash*.
40   Macintyre, *The Poor Relation*.
41   Foster, 'Interview with Noel George Butlin'.
42   Stephen G Foster and Miriam M Varghese, *The Making of the Australian National University* (Sydney: Allen & Unwin, 1996).

two separate departments of economic history coexisted within the same university. As a result, Canberra became home to the largest, most stable group of economic historians in the country.

Economic historians started arriving in Canberra from the late 1940s, and were generally appointed to economics groups. Interwar economic historian Herbert Burton came up from Melbourne in 1948, as Australia's first professor of economic history at CUC. He stayed on after the amalgamation, but moved on to management roles from the late 1950s before retiring in 1965.[43] After a few years in his brother's department at the University of Sydney, and a Rockefeller fellowship at Harvard, Noel Butlin was appointed as senior research fellow in the Institute's Research School of Social Sciences (RSSS) economics department in 1951. Research assistants, including de Meel, Sinclair, John D. Bailey, Garry G. Pursell and Ruth Inall, each assisted Butlin with his efforts throughout the 1950s before further careers in academia or the public service. Alan Barnard and Colin Forster completed PhDs in the RSSS group, and were appointed to permanent positions in the Institute and Faculties, respectively, in the late 1950s.

These junior scholars were crucial for Butlin's contribution. De Meel was specifically appointed to the RSSS to assist with compiling statistical material, and as a result he and Butlin co-authored some of the very early orthodox estimates.[44] Pursell, Inall, Sinclair and Bailey also worked on the project in the 1950s, with Butlin repeatedly acknowledging their important role for developing the 'numbers'.[45] Sinclair has argued that he helped with the residential and public construction estimates, joining Butlin on trips to 'badger' agricultural companies to allow them access to records.[46] Sinclair's work during this time was the first explicitly in the orthodox image. He published a series of public capital formation estimates, deliberately mirroring the procedure in Butlin and de Meel's

---

[43] Selwyn Cornish, 'Burton, Herbert (Joe) (1900–1983)', *ADB*, adb.anu.edu.au/biography/burton-herbert-joe-180/text22025 (published first in hardcopy 2007).
[44] Australian National University, *Report of the Interim Council for the Period 1 January 1950 to 30 June 1951* (Canberra: Commonwealth of Australia, 1952), 11; Butlin and de Meel, *Public Capital Formation*.
[45] In particular: Butlin, 'The Shape of the Australian Economy', 10; Butlin, 'Some Structural Features', 389; Butlin, *Domestic Product*, preface; Butlin, *Investment*, preface.
[46] Sinclair interview.

1954 monograph. The two series were directly comparable, and Sinclair argued that, like Butlin, his quantitative and inductive approach aimed to provide 'grist to the theorists' mill'.[47]

Barnard and Forster trained for their PhDs under Noel's supervision in the 1950s, and they both complemented Butlin's initial orthodox work. Butlin's macroeconomic emphasis on business cycles required understanding capital formation at the industry and firm level, contributing to the collection of extensive business archives, and to Forster and Barnard's emphasis on the progress of individual firms. Forster examined manufacturing, and Barnard the wool industry, using a combination of statistical material and qualitative case studies. Forster's initial aim was to build detailed statistics for manufacturing, as Butlin had done for the pastoral and construction sectors, but as the project progressed he found the raw statistics had limited range and accuracy. He incorporated more case studies, as he was worried that quantification alone may be 'unrepresentative'.[48] Similarly, Barnard used aggregated quantitative material, incorporating case studies of local selling firms after recognising that the statistics were inadequate on their own.[49] Barnard and Forster both acknowledged Butlin's role in guiding these projects.[50]

Butlin's research in the RSSS was supported by the economics group. Butlin had the indulgence of the head of the RSSS economics department, Trevor Swan, who had worked with him in the Department of Postwar Reconstruction and was similarly influenced by Keynesian economics. Although Swan moved on to more advanced theoretical work throughout his career, he and Butlin co-supervised students, and maintained a professional collegiality. Swan has been credited with enabling Butlin's ambitious research agenda, allowing him to hire research assistants, recruit PhD students and eventually establish the RSSS economic history department.[51] More broadly in the economics group, Butlin's research program was strengthened by his leadership of regular seminars that

---

47   William Angus Sinclair, 'Public Capital Formation in Australia: 1919–20 to 1929–30', *Economic Record* 31, no. 61 (1955): 300; William Angus Sinclair, *Economic Recovery in Victoria 1894–1899* (Canberra: ANU, 1956), 2.
48   Colin Forster, *Industrial Development in Australia 1920–1930* (Canberra: Australian National University Press, 1964), viii.
49   Barnard commented that 'any effective analysis must await the completion of a great deal more statistical work'. See Alan Barnard, *The Australian Wool Market, 1840–1900* (Melbourne: Melbourne University Press, 1958), xvii, and similar mentions on 181, 199.
50   Forster, *Industrial Development*, ix; Barnard, *Australian Wool Market*, vi.
51   Hall; Troy; Gregory; Schedvin interviews.

included economists and economic historians from Canberra, Sydney and Melbourne, including Burton, La Nauze, Syd Butlin, R. M. 'Max' Hartwell, Edgars Dunsdorfs, Jules Ginswick and C. B. 'Boris' Schedvin.[52] Not only was the Butlin revolution in line with economics best practice, but also, institutionally, it was largely developed within the ANU economics group.

Butlin had some links with the RSSS history department, particularly those interwar economic historians who moved into the humanities. La Nauze had been in economics, economic history and history positions since the 1930s, though in the post–World War II period he 'found the increasingly mathematical orientation of economics uncongenial'.[53] He accepted Melbourne's Scott Chair of History in 1956, and in 1961 he moved to Canberra to the history department in the RSSS. La Nauze and Butlin had a relationship before the former arrived at ANU, with Butlin acknowledging his assistance with various matters throughout in the 1950s and early 1960s.[54] Sir W. Keith Hancock hired La Nauze to the RSSS, and had also favoured the humanities in his approach to economic history. Hancock helped to establish ANU in the late 1940s, and after some to-ing and fro-ing over whether he would work for the university moving forward, he was appointed director of the RSSS in 1957. He quickly established a seminar on wool – a multidisciplinary initiative despite its 'home' within the history group.[55] Barnard was heavily involved, handling much of the organisational work, and editing the volume of proceedings that would become *The Simple Fleece*.[56] The Wool Seminar was an avenue through which the orthodox contribution was promoted to a wide audience. Key economic historians presented work

---

52   ANU Archives (ANUA): ANU Department of Economic History administrative files, research material and publications, AU ANUA 230, item 294. Also, The Australian National University, *Report of the Council, 1 January 1952 – 31 December 1952* (Canberra: Commonwealth of Australia, 1953), 20; Australian National University, *Annual Report for 1958* (Canberra: Commonwealth of Australia, 1959), 47; Schedvin interview.
53   Stuart Macintyre, 'La Nauze, Andrew John (1911–1990)', *ADB*, adb.anu.edu.au/biography/la-nauze-andrew-john-575/text25044 (published first in hardcopy 2012).
54   Noel G Butlin, 'Colonial Socialism in Australia', in *The State and Economic Growth: Papers of a Conference Held on October 11–13, 1956 under the Auspices of the Committee on Economic Growth*, ed. HGJ Aitken (New York: Social Science Research Council, 1959), 42; Butlin, *Domestic Product*.
55   Research papers on wool industry, AU ANUA 377, item 1. See also Butlin's recollection of Hancock in Foster, 'Interview with Noel George Butlin'.
56   Alan Barnard, ed., *The Simple Fleece: Studies in the Australian Wool Industry* (Melbourne: Melbourne University Press, 1962). See also Geoffrey Bolton, 'Rediscovering Australia: Hancock and the Wool Seminar', *Journal of Australian Studies* 23, no. 62 (1999): 159–70, doi.org/10.1080/14443059909387515.

similar to their orthodox contributions at the same time.[57] Discussions focused on methodology, with scholars from different disciplines solving problems and imagining different lines of enquiry for each paper.[58] Butlin has recalled that while he was not terribly excited by the idea of research into wool, the seminar gave him the opportunity to interact with scientists from CSIRO.[59] His chapter on the biology of pastures and noxious scrubs indicates some cross-disciplinary (and cross-institutional) influence.[60]

The orthodox school was thus initially developed through a generous university environment and advocacy from both economists and historians. Just as the 'numbers' were published, Swan granted Butlin's petition for a separate department in economic history, matching the department in the Faculties that had come to life shortly beforehand. This changed the nature of professional interactions, moving the ANU group from the development of the agenda, to the recruitment of others to the orthodox approach.

Departments in postwar Australian universities were hierarchical, with the 'God Professor' at the top of the food chain. The God Professor was, at once, the group's most senior scholar and the administrator, meaning they had power by virtue of seniority, as well as control over hiring, teaching, graduate supervision, and funding.[61] At ANU, Noel Butlin was God Professor of the RSSS group. He had a fairly forceful personality,[62] and had established his scholarly pre-eminence in the field through 'the words' and 'the numbers'. His influence or control over the RSSS department is well-known, with Stephen Nicholas arguing that 'he ran the place as a little emperor'.[63] In the 1960s and early 1970s, the department had four or five ongoing members of staff and several graduate students who interacted regularly through seminars, supervision and joint projects.

---

57 Cain's chapter in the volume was more or less the same as his earlier article in *Economic Record*, and Barnard presented elements of his wool marketing thesis. See Barnard, *Australian Wool Market*; Neville Cain, 'Companies and Squatting in the Western Division of New South Wales 1896–1905: "It Is Not a Black Prospect; It Is a Black Past"', *Economic Record* 37 no. 78 (1961): 183–206, doi.org/10.1111/j.1475-4932.1961.tb01370.x.
58 Minutes from Wool Seminar discussions show participants highlighting potential profitable methodologies. See AU ANUA 377, item 1.
59 Foster, 'Interview with Noel George Butlin'.
60 Noel G Butlin, 'The Growth of Rural Capital', in Barnard, *The Simple Fleece*.
61 Forsyth, *Modern Australian University*; Geoffrey Serle, 'God-Professors and Their Juniors', *Vestes* 6, no. 1 (1963): 11–17.
62 Cornish; Gregory; Macintyre; Merrett; Pincus; Schedvin interviews.
63 Nicholas interview.

Graduate supervision was a primary method through which the orthodox approach was refined and promoted. Within the RSSS department, close supervision by Butlin was common, with other members of the department, including Barnard, Neville 'Nev' Cain, Bryan Haig and Jonathan Pincus also supervising students. Cooperation with economists in the RSSS was common, with Tom Sheridan supervised by economist Helen Hughes in the Research School of Pacific Studies (RSPacS), and Reverend A. M. C. Waterman supervised by Butlin and Trevor Swan in RSSS economics. Regardless of supervisor, Butlin's presence was certainly felt. He was acknowledged in all theses produced in the department at this time. Some, such as Susan Bambrick and David Pope, acknowledged his role as God Professor in addition to their main supervisors.[64] Others simply acknowledged his guidance throughout the process. For example, Ian McLean began his DPhil in 1968, and although Cain was his supervisor, he remembered Butlin as the dominant force. As McLean recalled, 'there was no doubt who exercised intellectual and supervisory clout in the department'.[65] Sheridan acknowledged the 'continued interest' that Butlin and Barnard took in his work.[66] J. A. Dowie, who had migrated to work with Butlin on a comparable study for the New Zealand economy, argued that 'without the benefit of his experience the task of compiling the capital formation estimates would probably have been insuperable'.[67] Graeme Snooks similarly acknowledged the 'important influence' that Butlin had on his project on Hume Enterprises in the first half of the twentieth century.[68]

In addition to the supervisory environment, students were also integrated into the normal activities of the RSSS economic history group. PhD students in the 1960s and 1970s regularly presented seminars on their thesis topic,[69] with some, like the 1966 series, almost entirely dedicated to graduate student presentations.[70] McLean, Sheridan, Snooks and Dowie

---

64 Susan Bambrick, 'Australian Price Indexes' (PhD thesis, The Australian National University, 1968); David Pope, 'The Peopling of Australia: United Kingdom Immigration from Federation to the Great Depression' (PhD thesis, The Australian National University, 1976).
65 McLean interview.
66 Tom Sheridan, 'A History of the Amalgamated Engineering Union: Australian Section, 1920–1954' (PhD thesis, The Australian National University, 1967), iv.
67 JA Dowie, 'Studies in New Zealand Investment 1871–1900' (PhD thesis, The Australian National University, 1965), iii.
68 Graeme Snooks, 'Hume Enterprises in Australia, 1910–1940: A Study in Micro-Economic Growth' (PhD thesis, The Australian National University, 1971), v.
69 AU ANUA 230, items 297, 305, 306, 307, 308, 309.
70 AU ANUA 230, item 307. The 1966 series (in order): Keating, Bambrick, Macarthy, Haig, Waterman, Keating, Sheridan, Macarthy, Cornish, Sheridan, Waterman. Haig was the only staff member to present in this year.

each acknowledged their integration with the wider economic history department at ANU,[71] and most continued their association with the institution throughout their careers. As Waterman acknowledged:

> One of the many advantages of preparing a thesis in the Australian National University is the opportunity of frequent discussion both in seminars and in private meetings, with many experienced research workers in one's own field.[72]

Most of these junior scholars adopted a similar approach to the orthodox school, specifically addressing criticisms levelled against 'the words' and 'the numbers'. McLean was dissuaded from his original thesis topic to a production function analysis of the Victorian economy.[73] He adopted the orthodox method, and addressed an important criticism – that by aggregating nationwide, Butlin missed important variations in growth between colonies.[74] Snooks, similarly, came to ANU to work with Butlin following his contribution on Western Australia's experience of the Great Depression.[75] Snooks deliberately set his Masters thesis, and subsequent publications, within what he referred to as the 'Butlin method'. Bambrick's thesis analysed the development of Australia's historical price series, providing a guide for analysing economic growth in real terms, as '"deflated by the wholesale price index" is, unfortunately, rarely good enough'.[76] This addressed the criticism of Butlin's cursory price series.[77] Michael Keating, after a Bachelor of Commerce at the University of Melbourne, moved to ANU to work on a historical time series of the workforce that he hoped would 'complement the series of gross product provided by

---

71   Ian W McLean, 'Rural Output, Inputs and Mechanisation in Victoria 1870–1910' (PhD thesis, The Australian National University, 1971), iii; Snooks, 'Hume Enterprises in Australia', v; Sheridan, 'Amalgamated Engineering Union', iv; Dowie, 'New Zealand Investment', iii.

72   AMC Waterman, 'Fluctuation in the Rate of Growth: Australia 1948–49 to 1963–64' (PhD thesis, The Australian National University, 1967), v–vi.

73   McLean interview; McLean, 'Mechanisation in Victoria'.

74   Boehm, 'Australian Economic Growth', 230.

75   Snooks completed this work initially as a University of Western Australia Masters thesis. It was then published as a monograph and a series of articles. Graeme Snooks, *Depression and Recovery in Western Australia 1928/29–1938/39* (Nedlands: University of Western Australia Press, 1974); Graeme Snooks, 'Regional Estimates of Gross Domestic Product and Capital Formation: Western Australia, 1923–1938-39', *Economic Record* 48, no. 124 (1972): 536; Graeme Snooks, 'Depression and Recovery in Western Australia, 1928–29 to 1938–39: A Deviation from the Norm', *Economic Record* 49, no. 127 (1973), doi.org/10.1111/j.1475-4932.1973.tb02280.x: 420; Graeme Snooks, 'The Arithmetic of Regional Growth: Western Australia 1912/13 to 1957/8', *Australian Economic History Review* 19, no. 1 (1979): 63–74, doi.org/10.1111/aehr.191004.

76   Bambrick, 'Australian Price Indexes', preface.

77   In particular Boehm, 'Australian Economic Growth'. For a similar critique of the 1954/1955 monographs, see Goldsmith, 'Review: Butlin and de Meel; Butlin'.

Professor N. G. Butlin and the Commonwealth Statistician'.[78] Dowie did not address a specific criticism, but attempted to do for New Zealand what Butlin had done for Australia.[79]

Bob Jackson was a unique case of recruitment. Jackson studied at the University of Sydney in the 1960s. Compared to the hands-on approach at ANU, Jackson was left to his own devices at Sydney, recalling he probably only saw his supervisors twice in the time he completed the thesis. This provided space for other intellectual influences, particularly Butlin's orthodox work on residential ownership. At the time 'everyone was studying Noel's book', and Jackson took umbrage with Butlin's assertion that Australian cities were majority owner-occupied in the nineteenth century. Jackson then went through Sydney's city rate books, and found that there were more renters than previously thought. Jackson's thesis was sent to Butlin to examine, and although he took some convincing, the thesis was passed and Jackson then went on to have a long career in the ANU Faculties from 1969.[80] Jackson's work with undergraduates in the 1970s demonstrated the need to synthesise the wealth of orthodox literature, and he wrote *Australian Economic Development*, published in 1977, as a remedy to students' confusion when confronted with Butlin's dense volumes.[81] Similar to the work of the other disciples, Jackson's book, Schedvin has argued, was crucial for promoting and 'giving shape' to Noel's initial contribution.[82]

Once the group was recruited, other key activities facilitated connections among the 'tribe'. After the establishment of separate departments in the early 1960s, seminars changed from broad gatherings to closed meetings. Economic history seminars occurred regularly throughout the 1960s, with 14 seminars per year in 1964 and 1965, 11 in 1966 and 16 in 1967–68.[83] Participants were either staff members or graduate students of the department. These specialised meetings encouraged collaboration among economic historians and were an important way for scholars to disseminate the findings of the orthodox school. However, this came at

---

78   Michael Keating, 'The Growth and Composition of the Australian Work Force, 1910–11 to 1960–61' (PhD thesis, The Australian National University, 1967), preface.
79   Dowie, 'New Zealand Investment', i–ii.
80   Jackson interview.
81   Robert V Jackson, *Australian Economic Development in the Nineteenth Century* (Canberra: Australian National University Press, 1977).
82   Schedvin interview.
83   AU ANUA 230, items 297, 305, 306, 307, 308.

the cost of connections to other groups, with economic historians no longer engaging with economists, historians or interdisciplinary audiences similar to the 'Wool Seminar'. There were some exceptions – including Hughes from the RSPacS economics group, and Graeme Davison who was, at the time, a graduate student in history – but otherwise there is very little to indicate involvement from scholars in other disciplines. For example, Hall decided to remain in Swan's economics department after the 'split' in the early 1960s. He has recalled that the economic history and economics groups both scheduled their seminars at the same time, on Friday afternoons. As a result, he rarely interacted with economic historians after the establishment of the separate department.[84]

Collaboration also reflected and reinforced the orthodox professional community. In the late 1960s, the ANU economic history group produced an edited volume that analysed the development of the Australian economy over the twentieth century. By this time Forster, the editor of the book, was in the Faculties, though he had strong professional connections to the RSSS, to Butlin and to the orthodox school. Contributors were also members of the orthodox 'tribe', including Sinclair, Cain, Hughes, Dowie and Butlin himself. The book reinforced the existing professional structures of the ANU economic history group, with contributors presenting draft chapters as part of the RSSS seminar from 1965 onwards.[85] Butlin, as the group's God Professor, has been remembered as asserting himself fairly substantially during these discussions, and contributors largely acknowledged each other for assistance and feedback.[86] Authors adopted the orthodox methodology in their contributions, examining an aspect of the macroeconomy using quantitative, statistical sources. Their approach was inductive, describing trends in the quantitative material rather than testing particular statistical relationships. However, contemporary economic theory, concerning industrial development and the trade cycle, was incorporated in most chapters. Butlin's emphasis on internal determinants of growth was also largely adopted, with chapters on non-export sectors – Forster on manufacturing, Hughes on iron and steel, and Dowie on services – accounting for half the volume. To compare, rural or

---

84 Hall interview.
85 This included Brown and Hughes' presentation on 'Business Organisation and Market Structure' in 1965, and Cain's presentation 'Trade and Structure at the Periphery' in 1967–68. See AU ANUA 230, items 305 and 308, respectively. The ANU annual report in 1966 also mentions collaboration on the volume, see Australian National University, *Annual Report, 1966* (Canberra: Commonwealth Government of Australia, 1967), 62.
86 Sinclair interview.

export industries were almost entirely omitted. This volume was the most consistent collective expression of the orthodox school, and represented the peak of ANU 'recruitment' of economic historians.

The revolution

Rather than the lone genius, it was a combination of Butlin, the community of like-minded scholars and the ANU environment that produced the orthodox approach in Australian economic history. While this was undoubtedly a major 'moment' for the field, it is worth interrogating the degree to which it was a 'revolution'. As in all intellectual revolutions, Butlin made his contribution by bracing against those who came before. He dismissed the interwar scholars – particularly Shann and Fitzpatrick – for their emphasis on external determinants of growth, as well as their general scholarship. He argued that Shann 'does little more than summarise Coghlan', and that although Fitzpatrick defined the basics of Australian economic history in the minds of recent graduates, it was not suitable for 'more advanced practitioners'.[87] Butlin took Coghlan, particularly his quantitative approach and the 'grandeur' of his mind, more seriously, but even so argued that the lack of source information made it easy to disregard the statistician's contribution.[88]

In defining his research as something 'new', Butlin may have overplayed his hand. Australian economic history had a long quantitative–inductive tradition, through the collection of colonial statistics and culminating in Coghlan's efforts towards the quantitative collection and description of economic matters. Shann and Fitzpatrick both employed substantial quantitative material, and Clark and Crawford continued to refine Coghlan's national income accounting efforts in the interwar period (see Chapter 2). The quantitative nature of the orthodox school was thus its least surprising feature, with Butlin's contribution simply the stamina to marshal the necessary source material.[89] Some within Butlin's circle have identified this, with Sinclair, in summarising the achievements of the orthodox school, arguing that the postwar 'new generation' of researchers were more like a 'repair gang than a team of wreckers, their main contribution being to make important alterations and additions to the

---

87 Butlin, *Investment*, 407; Butlin, 'The Shape of the Australian Economy', 10.
88 Butlin, *Investment*, xv.
89 Maddock; Schedvin; McLean interviews.

3. THE BIG BANG

existing structure'.[90] Colleague Rod Maddock has agreed, commenting that Butlin's legacy was 'the work he did himself […] that huge slog of just getting out a basic set of numbers […] that huge piece of infrastructure that we all use regularly'.[91]

The orthodox school was also consistent with the dominant paradigm in postwar economics. National income accounting, in particular, was a global phenomenon, encouraged by the dominance of Keynesianism and its focus on sectoral growth and long-term business cycles.[92] Simon Kuznets first formalised this technique through his work in the 1930s at the US National Bureau of Economic Research, a non-university institution focused on statistical and quantitative research.[93] Inspired in particular by Coghlan's work, Kuznets built estimates of income created by each industry.[94] Collection and use of national income estimates expanded in France, the UK, Spain, Belgium, India and elsewhere in the post–World War II decades.[95] In Australia, the economics discipline was also dominated by Keynesianism in the postwar period, while also demonstrating an enduring interest in deploying quantitative material for the purposes of nation-building.[96] Members of the economics discipline were particularly receptive to the work Butlin had done, with Arndt working with Butlin to develop the national income estimates for

---

90 William Angus Sinclair, *The Process of Economic Development in Australia* (Melbourne: Cheshire, 1976).
91 Maddock interview.
92 Francesco Boldizzoni and Pat Hudson, eds, *Routledge Handbook of Global Economic History* (London: Routledge, 2015), doi.org/10.4324/9781315734736.
93 John S Lyons, Louis P Cain and Samuel H Williamson, eds, *Reflections on the Cliometrics Revolution: Conversations with Economic Historians* (New York: Routledge, 2008), doi.org/10.4324/9780203799635.
94 Heinz W Arndt, 'A Pioneer of National Income Estimates', *Economic Journal* 59, no. 236 (1949): 616–25, doi.org/10.2307/2226600.
95 Erik Aerts and Ulbe Bosma, 'The Low Countries, Intellectual Borderlands of Economic History', in Boldizzoni and Hudson, *Global Economic History*, 175–92, doi.org/10.4324/9781315734736; Pat Hudson, 'Economic History in Britain: The "First Industrial Nation"', in Boldizzoni and Hudson, *Global Economic History*, 17–34, doi.org/10.4324/9781315734736; Naomi Lamoreaux, 'Beyond the Old and the New: Economic History in the United States', in Boldizzoni and Hudson, *Global Economic History*, 35–54, doi.org/10.4324/9781315734736; Lyons et al., *Reflections*; Herman Van Der Wee, 'Economic History: Its Past, Present and Future', *European Review* 15, no. 1 (2007): 33–45, doi.org/10.1017/S106279870700004X; Iñaki Iriarte-Goñi, 'Spanish Economic History: Lights and Shadows in a Process of Convergence' in Boldizzoni and Hudson, *Global Economic History*, 160–74, doi.org/10.4324/9781315734736; Prasannan Parthasarathi, 'The History of Indian Economic History', in Boldizzoni and Hudson, *Global Economic History*, 281–92, doi.org/10.4324/9781315734736.
96 Alex Millmow, *A History of Australasian Economic Thought* (London: Taylor & Francis, 2017), doi.org/10.4324/9781315716152.

New South Wales; Swan funding and endorsing the mammoth orthodox effort in the 1950s; and ANU economists such as Helen Hughes and Alan Hall working or collaborating with the economic history group.

Butlin's work also spoke to intellectual trends in vogue in the history discipline. Globally, the postwar focus on material matters was mirrored by members of the Australian discipline negotiating a 'national character' in light of new social movements, through labour, social, women's and Indigenous histories.[97] Thus, rather than dominated by a single paradigm as the economists were, the plurality of the history discipline from the 1950s to the 1970s provided points of discussion between Australian historians and orthodox economic history. Orthodox work was published in key history journals, with adjacent interdisciplinary outlets such as *Labour History* holding a primary place in Australian historiography in the 1970s (see Chapter 4). Prominent postwar historians Graeme Davison and Stuart Macintyre have similarly noted the synergy between their practice and that of the orthodox school.[98] By virtue of its alignment with global and national trends in economic historical work, the orthodox school was so successful partly because it was unsurprising. To speculate the counterfactual, it could easily have been imported through other avenues.

To demonstrate this, there were several Australian orthodox-style contributions that emerged on trajectories unconnected to ANU. For example, Max Hartwell completed his study of the Van Diemen's Land economy a decade before Butlin published *Investment*. Hartwell grew up in country New South Wales, before being educated at the Armidale Teachers' College and New England University College, the latter of which was affiliated with the University of Sydney. His Masters degree, also completed through Sydney, was published in 1954 as *The Economic Development of Van Diemen's Land*. Hartwell was influenced by interwar economic historians La Nauze and Hancock, whom he commented

---

97   Kenneth Lipartito, 'Reassembling the Economic: New Departures in Historical Materialism', *American Historical Review* 121, no. 1 (2016): 101–39, doi.org/10.1093/ahr/121.1.101; Mark McKenna, 'The History Anxiety', in *The Cambridge History of Australia*, ed. Alison Bashford and Stuart Macintyre, vol. 2 (Melbourne: Cambridge University Press, 2013), 561–80, doi.org/10.1017/CHO9781107445758.055; Hannah Forsyth and Sophie Loy-Wilson, 'Seeking a New Materialism in Australian History', *Australian Historical Studies* 48, no. 1 (2017): 169–88, doi.org/10.1080/1031461X.2017.1298635.

98   Dingle/Davison; Macintyre interviews. See also Geoffrey Serle, 'The State of the Profession in Australia', *Australian Historical Studies* 15, no. 61 (1973): 686–702, doi.org/10.1080/10314617308595499.

'taught me much about history, and also the importance of good writing for good history'.[99] Despite this emphasis on the humanities, Hartwell adopted an approach similar to the orthodox school, utilising a vast quantity of previously neglected official quantitative material for the colony, supplementing this with qualitative data such as newspapers and parliamentary debates.[100] His analysis was macroeconomic and built on a production function, incorporating Frederick Jackson Turner's 'frontier thesis' to examine economic expansion and the influx of labour and capital pivoted towards a marketable export surplus (particularly wool). After a DPhil in Oxford in the late 1940s, Hartwell returned to the University of New South Wales as the foundation chair of economic history in the 1950s. In 1956 he left Australia permanently, taking up an ongoing academic post at Nuffield College, Oxford.

Hartwell's back-and-forth to the UK betrays an important source of orthodox-style writings. In the 1950s, economic history in Britain developed into a more formal theoretical style that took cues from the economics discipline. British economic historians Alec Cairncross, Brinley Thomas, Robin Matthews and others began using a 'quantitative–historical' approach, which included theoretical reasoning, economic models and the analysis of extensive quantitative information.[101] As in the interwar period, the global hierarchy of academic knowledge largely demanded overseas education, and many of the young Australian postwar scholars took degrees in Britain before returning to substantive positions at home. Boehm, for example, spent several years working at the University of New England in Armidale in the 1950s, before working with Hartwell and John Wright in Oxford. In the book published from his thesis, Boehm examined Australia's experience in the 1890s depression. The approach was quantitative, drawing heavily on the primary statistics of Coghlan and Butlin, and on the statistical framework of interwar scholars Clark and Crawford. He was also staunchly inductive, tailoring the statistics to the 'peculiar features of Australia' and making claims only from what was

---

99   R Max Hartwell, *The Economic Development of Van Diemen's Land, 1820–1850* (Melbourne: Melbourne University Press, 1954), viii.
100 Coleman has argued that 'perhaps the feature that seemed most noticeable about Butlin's history to non-economists – its quantitative character – was the least distinguishing feature from other contemporary economic historians […] Max Hartwell had already taken care to delineate the quantitative profiles of his subjects'. Coleman, 'Historiography', 19.
101 Hudson, 'Economic History in Britain'; Van Der Wee, 'Economic History'.

directly observable from the quantitative material.¹⁰² Economic theory was incorporated, though it was used to furnish 'a logical basis' for the analysis, and explain the trends found in the empirical data. While Boehm's approach was consistent with the orthodox school, he attributed this to the British economic history community, rather than to Canberra.¹⁰³

Hall and Hughes experienced a similar trajectory. Although both worked within the ANU economic history group, their main contributions were initially written as theses in the UK. Hughes studied for her DPhil at the London School of Economics, returning to Australia to positions at the universities of New South Wales and Queensland from the late 1950s, before an appointment in the ANU RSPacS economics group from 1963. The book published from her PhD was released the following year, and she demonstrated the statistical and inductive tendencies of the orthodox approach. However, given the timing, and her acknowledgment of London School of Economics supervisor William Ashworth and Sydney colleagues Schedvin and John W. McCarty, it is unlikely her approach came from ANU.¹⁰⁴ Hall also graduated from the London School of Economics, completing his PhD thesis in 1951. This was well before any sort of economic history community had gathered in Canberra. Hall thanked his supervisors, British economic historians R. S. Sayers and T. S. Ashton, as well as acknowledging the assistance of Swan for the theoretical postscript.¹⁰⁵ For Hartwell, Boehm, Hughes and Hall, what might appear on the surface as the orthodox school was actually the outcome of substantial professional connections between Australia and Britain.

Conclusions

In the past, Noel Butlin has been praised as the seemingly sole source of the quantitative, macroeconomic reorientation of Australian economic history in the 1950s and 1960s.¹⁰⁶ He made a substantial contribution

---

102 Ernst A Boehm, *Prosperity and Depression in Australia, 1887–1897* (Oxford: Clarendon Press, 1971), 25.
103 Boehm, *Prosperity and Depression*, 1.
104 Helen Hughes, *The Australian Iron and Steel Industry 1848–1962* (Melbourne: Melbourne University Press, 1964), vii.
105 Hall, *London Capital Market*, preface, 192.
106 See Coleman, 'Historiography'; Lloyd, 'Analytical Frameworks'; Lloyd, 'Economic History and Policy'; Schedvin, 'Midas and the Merino'; Sinclair, 'Economic History'.

to the field's quantitative infrastructure, and made the 'loud, emphatic statement' that Australia's economic past mattered.[107] However, responsibility for the emergence of the orthodox approach cannot be wholly placed on Butlin's shoulders. The 'big bang' was the outcome of a confluence of individual effort, institutional support and professional connections. A favourable higher education environment, particularly the generous conditions at ANU, gave Butlin and his colleagues the space and resources to conduct the labour-intensive work of 'the words' and 'the numbers', and provided him a platform through which he could recruit colleagues and students to this intellectual movement. Its endurance was further assisted by its similarity (rather than distinctiveness) to global intellectual trends, and its ability to speak to the interests of both parent disciplines and to the growing global community of economic historians. Although Butlin was a remarkable scholar, he was also someone in the right place at the right time.

---

107 Merrett interview.

4

A moment in the sun

> If you get six people together and make them work together for
> 30 years and not talk to anybody except each other, they'll go mad.
>
> Rod Maddock, December 2015[1]

The 'big bang' provided a boost of innovation for, and interest in, Australian economic history. The development of quantitative infrastructure provided material to work with, and the 'new' orthodox interpretations left plenty to debate and refine. At the same time, the expansion of Australia's university sector, endorsement of the subject within economics, and the administrative fragmentation of universities led to the establishment of new departments of economic history. Each of these departments was kitted out with a small group of scholars, and their professional lives began to revolve around frequent interactions within their silo. This contributed to distinctive communities of economic history in each place, with collaboration and intellectual trends broadly following geographic lines in the 1960s, 1970s and 1980s.

Intellectual communities are rarely thought of in terms of place. Historians of education have analysed the production of knowledge in single universities, though rarely use cities or regions as frames to understand ideas.[2] Existing work on Australia's economic history field

---

1   Maddock interview with author. Unless otherwise specified, interviews cited are those conducted by the author: see Appendix for details.
2   William James Breen and John A Salmond, *Building La Trobe University: Reflections on the First 25 Years 1964–1989* (Melbourne: La Trobe University Press, 1989); Peter Groenewegen, *Educating for Business, Public Service and the Social Sciences: A History of the Faculty of Economics at the University of Sydney 1920–1999* (Sydney: Sydney University Press, 2009), doi.org/10.2307/j.ctv1wmz4h4; Ross Williams, *Balanced Growth: A History of the Department of Economics, University of Melbourne*

has aggregated the approach nationwide, examining individual scholars and their texts largely independent of the communities in which they existed.[3] Departments for economic history (in Australia or elsewhere) have rarely been interrogated for their impact.[4] The logic is generally that more money is good, so more departments – and thus more students and funding – must be good. The focus of this chapter is the 'departmental era' of Australian economic history, examining the way departments reinforced a spatial placement of ideas and restricted the field's core function of mediating the interdisciplinary space. This interpretation of departments and place provides guidance for both interdisciplinary practitioners and university managers on the way to encourage integrated cross-disciplinary knowledge.

Growth

The 'golden era' of higher education expansion

Until the 1960s, post–World War II expansion of higher education was the domain of older sandstone universities, and The Australian National University (ANU). Student numbers grew through government returned servicemen schemes, the professionalisation of many occupations and the growing perception that tertiary education was necessary for social

---

(Melbourne: Australian Scholarly Publishing, 2009); Fay Anderson and Stuart Macintyre, eds, *The Life of the Past: The Discipline of History at the University of Melbourne* (Melbourne: RMIT Publishing, 2006); WGK Duncan and RA Leonard, *The University of Adelaide, 1874–1974* (Adelaide: Rigby Ltd, 1973); Stephen G Foster and Miriam M Varghese, *The Making of the Australian National University* (Sydney: Allen & Unwin, 1996).

3   William Coleman, 'The Historiography of Australian Economic History', in *Cambridge Economic History of Australia*, ed. Simon Ville and Glenn Withers (Melbourne: Cambridge University Press, 2015), 11–28, doi.org/10.1017/CHO9781107445222.004; C Boris Schedvin, 'Australian Economic History', *Economic Record* 65, no. 190 (1989): 287–90, doi.org/10.1111/j.1475-4932.1989.tb00938.x; Christopher Lloyd, 'Analytical Frameworks of Australia's Economic History', in Ville and Withers, *Cambridge Economic History of Australia*, 52–69; David Meredith and Deborah Oxley, 'The Rise and Fall of Australian Economic History', in *Routledge Handbook of Global Economic History*, ed. Francesco Boldizzoni and Pat Hudson (London: Routledge, 2015), 73–94, doi.org/10.4324/9781315734736.

4   For exceptions, see Claire EF Wright and Simon Ville, 'The University Tea Room: Informal Public Spaces as Ideas Incubators', *History Australia* 15, no. 2 (2018): 236–54, doi.org/10.1080/14490854.2018.1443701; Claire EF Wright and Simon Ville, 'Visualising the Interdisciplinary Research Field: The Life Cycle of Economic History in Australia', *Minerva* 55, no. 3 (2017): 321–40, doi.org/10.1007/s11024-017-9319-z; Claire EF Wright and Simon Ville, 'The Evolution of an Intellectual Community through the Words of Its Founders: Recollections of Australia's Economic History Field', *Australian Economic History Review* 57, no. 3 (2017): 345–67, doi.org/10.1111/aehr.12110.

and economic advancement.⁵ University and teacher's college enrolments doubled between 1945 and 1950, and this growth rate was sustained throughout the next two decades.⁶ Governments also paid greater attention to research, with opportunities for funding and the introduction of domestic PhD programs. As discussed in Chapter 3, ANU was the centrepiece of the new emphasis on university research. Elsewhere, general growth in student numbers in the 1940s and 1950s increased the pressure on the state-based sandstone universities. Many experienced deteriorating teaching loads, and needed to hire younger and less experienced staff. The New South Wales University of Technology (1949) and the Newcastle University College (1951) were established, in part, to meet this demand. In 1957, the Commonwealth Government's Murray Report recommended the establishment of several new universities, and a closer relationship between universities, public needs and the government.⁷ Monash University, Wollongong University College, Flinders University and La Trobe University were established in the decade following the Murray Report. ANU was amalgamated with Canberra University College (CUC) in 1960, and New South Wales University of Technology was transformed into the University of New South Wales (UNSW) in 1958. The 'golden era' of higher education expansion had begun.

This expansion created enormous opportunities for most disciplines and fields, including economic history. In the university market, students mean money, and money means power. As new universities were established and existing ones expanded their offerings, they hired young scholars to teach in all sorts of areas. Total university staff expanded by an outrageous 19 per cent in the 1960s, dropping back down to about 6 per cent in the 1970s, and 2.5 per cent in the 1980s.⁸ Business and commerce instruction was a particularly fruitful area of expansion. Prior to World War II, university education for business professionals was uncommon,

---

5   DS Anderson and E Eaton, 'Part 1: Post-War Reconstruction and Expansion 1940–1965', *Higher Education Research and Development* 1, no. 1 (1982): 8–93, doi.org/10.1080/0729436820010102; Hannah Forsyth, *A History of the Modern Australian University* (Sydney: University of New South Wales Press, 2014); Simon Marginson, *Monash: Remaking the University* (St Leonards: Allen & Unwin, 2000); Stuart Macintyre, *The Poor Relation* (Melbourne: Melbourne University Press, 2010).
6   Anderson and Eaton, 'Post-War Reconstruction'; Andrew Norton and Ittima Cherastidtham, *Mapping Australian Higher Education 2018* (Melbourne: Grattan Institute, 2018), grattan.edu.au/wp-content/uploads/2018/09/907-Mapping-Australian-higher-education-2018.pdf.
7   Keith A Murray et al., *Report of the Committee on Australian Universities* (Canberra: Commonwealth Government, September 1957.
8   Graeme Hugo, 'Demographic Trends in Australia's Academic Workforce', *Journal of Higher Education Policy and Management* 27, no. 3 (2005): 327–43, doi.org/10.1080/13600800500283627.

indeed even for entrenched professions such as accounting, people were trained 'on-the-job' by serving articles with their employer. From World War II, university education became the norm for many white-collar business professions, including accounting, banking and economics.[9] The number of students in business and economics degrees grew fivefold in a decade, from about 7,000 in 1964, to over 40,000 in 1974. This number doubled again to about 92,000 students in 1989. Of course, university education grew in general over this time, but business education managed to take an increasingly large slice of this pie, attracting 11.6 per cent of students in 1964, 15.7 per cent of students in 1974 and up to 20.8 per cent of students in 1989.[10]

The expansion of economic history was driven through the expansion of economics and commerce degrees. Economics, at the time, was largely consumed by Keynesianism, which was predisposed towards the long-run, contextual approaches that characterise economic history. The field was thus broadly accepted as a key part of understanding the economy. The premier Australian economics journal, *Economic Record*, indicates growing acceptance of historical research over the postwar period, with the number of articles published increasing from seven in the 1940s to 26 in the 1970s. While some of this was published by mainstream economic historians such as Noel Butlin, Sinclair, Boehm and McLean, a substantial amount was also produced by members of the broader discipline. For example, historian and political scientist Lloyd G. Churchward examined Australia's international trade since 1791; Ronald Lawson focused on Brisbane's economic development during the 1890s depression; and economist Brian L. Bentick the long-run quantitative series on foreign borrowing.[11] These scholars weren't appointed to economic history

---

9   Claire EF Wright and Hannah Forsyth, 'Managerial Capitalism and White-Collar Professions: Social Mobility in Australia's Corporate Elite', *Labour History* 121, no. 1 (2021): 99–127, doi.org/10.3828/jlh.2021.20.
10   Malcolm Abbott and Chris Doucouliagos, 'The Changing Structure of Higher Education in Australia, 1949–2003' (School of Accounting, Economics and Finance Working Paper Series, Deakin University, 2003). See also Philip Maxwell, 'The Rise and Fall (?) of Economics in Australian Universities', *Economic Papers: A Journal of Applied Economics and Policy* 22, no. 1 (2003): 79–92, doi.org/10.1111/j.1759-3441.2003.tb00338.x.
11   LG Churchward, 'Australian–American Trade Relations, 1791–1939', *Economic Record* 26, no. 50 (1950): 69–86, doi.org/10.1111/j.1475-4932.1950.tb01250.x; Ronald Lawson, 'Brisbane in the 1890s: The Economic Shape of a Key Decade', *Economic Record* 47, no. 4 (1971): 568–78, doi.org/10.1111/j.1475-4932.1971.tb00776.x; Brian L Bentick, 'Foreign Borrowing, Wealth, and Consumption: Victoria 1873–93', *Economic Record* 45, no. 3 (1969): 415–31, doi.org/10.1111/j.1475-4932.1969.tb00180.x.

positions, they didn't necessarily participate in the main professional structures; instead, a historical approach was considered a key component of mainstream economic analysis.

Most business, commerce and economics degrees required broad introductory courses in the first year, with specialised instruction later. At the same time, the field of play was relatively uncluttered, with disciplines like marketing, management and finance not yet divided into separate areas within commerce education.[12] Faculty deans thus wanted to provide good introductory instruction, as well as ways to 'fill out' their new commerce and economics degrees. Economic history's entrenched position within economics made it seem like a suitable option. Bachelor of Commerce or Economics degrees in the 1960s, 70s and 80s generally included accounting, economics, econometrics, industrial relations (maybe) and economic history.[13] UNSW economic historian Barrie Dyster has recalled that economic history commanded a quarter of the first year commerce instruction. Quite a few of these students flowed on to upper-level courses, partly because there was not 'a great deal of competition'.[14] Similarly, supported by Professor James Belshaw, who had 'pioneered both Economics and History' at the University of New England (UNE), in 1965 the formation of a new Faculty of Economics included two departments: Economics and Economic History. Both had required subjects in the undergraduate economics degree.[15] Even in places where there were no departments in the subject, economic history was a requirement in commerce or economics degrees. At the University of Adelaide, McLean has recalled that economic history instruction was valued within economics, with at least one compulsory course in the first year, and another two or three options at upper levels.[16]

This confluence of intellectual and institutional factors gave economic history a relatively strong position within post–World War II economics and commerce faculties. Separate departments in the subject followed,

---

12   Robert B Ellis and David S Waller, 'Marketing Education in Australia before 1965', *Australasian Marketing Journal* 19, no. 2 (2011): 115–21, doi.org/10.1016/j.ausmj.2011.03.003; Roy Green, Marco Berti and Nicole Sutton, 'Higher Education in Management: The Case of Australia', in *The Future of Management Education*, ed. Stéphanie Dameron and Thomas Durand (London: Palgrave Macmillan UK, 2017), 117–37, doi.org/10.1057/978-1-137-56091-9_4.
13   Dingle/Davison interview.
14   Dyster interview.
15   Matthew Jordan, *A Spirit of True Learning: The Jubilee History of the University of New England* (Sydney: UNSW Press, 2004), 117–18.
16   McLean interview.

assisted by general university expansion and fragmentation of large, complex faculties into smaller autonomous groups.[17] Noel Butlin was the sole example of an individual petitioning for a separate department. Hall has recalled that Noel 'pestered' Trevor Swan (then ANU Research School of Social Sciences [RSSS] Head of Economics) to set up a department of economic history, and because of the university's expansionary mood and Swan's indulgent attitude towards the subject, Noel's request was granted. Even he was relatively late to the game: Melbourne had a department since 1947, CUC (which became the ANU Faculties) from 1957, and the rest were established gradually between 1960 and 1975. In all other cases, faculty or university management created the group. For some, the department was built around a new chair, including John McCarty at Monash, Gordon Rimmer at UNSW and Seymour A. Broadbridge at Flinders. In other cases, scholars were gathered in a separate group, with the chair drawn from their ranks a few years later.[18] La Trobe established a department comparatively late, in the late 1980s. Eric Jones was already a professor of economics, and those who became members of the new department were in the economics group. It was entirely a bureaucratic decision, with a review of La Trobe's broader 'schools' structure recommending the establishment of departments, including economic history.[19] Separate departments were thus a decision made much further up the chain than individual scholars, reflecting the institutional environment rather than the success (or otherwise) of Australia's economic history field.

Recruitment

Compulsory economic history subjects, and the departments that followed, meant that the number of dedicated economic history staff in Australia grew from 12 in 1960, to 30 in 1970, to a peak of about 50 in 1980s.[20] Staff numbers at economic history's entrenched institutions – ANU and the universities of Sydney and Melbourne – stabilised in the 1970s and 1980s, with expansion of the domain of newer universities

---

17 Groenewegen, *Educating for Business*; Jordan, *A Spirit of True Learning*; Dingle/Davison interview.
18 Mac Boot and Ron Neale were initially the members of the economic history group at UNE, with Neale listed as the professor from 1974. At Sydney, Syd Butlin was initially the professor (in 1970), but the following year he went to ANU in quasi-retirement. See Appendix.
19 Frost interview.
20 This includes those appointed to separate departments in the subject, not counting the many economic historians based in economics or history groups.

such as UNSW, Monash, Flinders, UNE and La Trobe. To meet the new demand for economic history staff, the field's leaders had two options: either train the next generation of Australian economic historians themselves, or recruit from overseas. As such, graduate training expanded, with government policy increasingly directed towards research and training PhD students at home.[21] Most graduate students were trained at ANU in the 1950s, 1960s and 1970s, with others at the universities of Sydney, Melbourne, Monash and Western Australia. Some of these PhD students left the main Australian economic history community, though not for lack of available positions.[22] Those who remained found ongoing positions relatively easily, with the surplus of vacant positions filled by overseas recruits from the UK and the US.

By virtue of the university sector's rapid expansion, Australian economic historians were, on average, very young. At the same time, the model of the 'God Professor' demanded that each new department have a senior scholar as its head. Home-grown leadership had not quite developed to the point where there were enough suitable scholars to fill these new chairs, so universities looked to the metropole. Gordon Rimmer at UNSW, Eric Jones at La Trobe, Derek Aldcroft and Stephen Salsbury at the University of Sydney, and Ron Neale and Malcolm Falkus at UNE were brought to Australia from the UK or the US in the 1960s and 1970s.[23] Other postwar leaders followed the 'interwar model', with Syd Butlin, John McCarty, Gus Sinclair and ANU Faculties Professor Graham S. L. Tucker completing their Masters or PhD theses in the UK.[24] Even the staunchly Australianist Noel Butlin spent two years at Harvard in the 1950s, as he believed that 'was where the real *economist*-historians were'.[25]

---

21   Forsyth, *Modern Australian University*; Marginson, *Monash*.
22   Waterman, Peter Macarthy and Neil de Marchi accepted positions overseas, Pursell and Bambrick moved into the economics discipline and Keating left academia for a career in the public service.
23   Michael J Oliver, ed., *Studies in Economic and Social History: Essays in Honour of Derek H. Aldcroft* (Aldershot, UK: Ashgate, 2002); 'Obituary: Salsbury, Prof. Stephen Matthew', *Sydney Morning Herald*, 5 March 1998; GR Henning, 'RS Neale, 1927–85', *Australian Economic History Review* 26, no. 2 (1986): 91–95, doi.org/10.1111/aehr.262001; Matthew Cawood, 'Malcolm Falkus Obituary', *Pulse News*, 1 March 2018, blog.une.edu.au/pulsenews/2018/03/01/malcolm-falkus-obituary/ (site discontinued).
24   As in the interwar period, this was generally seen as an 'interlude' – as necessary to legitimise the scholar's pedigree, but with minimal ongoing impact on their collaborations or career. See Sinclair interview.
25   Stephen G Foster, 'Interview with Emeritus Professor Noel George Butlin' (Canberra: ANU Oral History Archive, 1991), emphasis mine.

This created a culture of legitimacy from the metropole that structured hiring and training. Privilege accrued to those trained in the US or UK, with scholars such as McCarty or Tucker offered chairs relatively early in their careers, on the basis of a small amount of published work but perceived exemplary training at Oxbridge. In interviews, scholars similarly noted the 'quality' of a colleague's Oxbridge degree, independent of the work that was produced from it.[26] In many cases, senior scholars encouraged mentees to study overseas, reinforcing this model intergenerationally. Melbourne economic historian David Merrett has commented that McCarty encouraged others to study at Cambridge, his alma mater. Similarly, Chris Lloyd has recalled that encouragement from Ron Neale formed part of his decision to study in the UK:

> If you were wanting a career as an academic, Britain was the place to go [...] and the thinking was, that this gave you an advantage in the Australian job market [...] Of course, Ron Neale, my professor [at UNE], was English and he was very pleased for me to be going back.[27]

God Professors also reinforced colonial structures of privilege through their hiring practices. During the period of recruitment, overseas-trained God Professors hired a greater proportion of scholars from their country of origin, often with an informal hiring process. For example, at UNSW, Head of Economic History Gordon Rimmer was born and educated in the UK, and purposefully recruited from UK universities.[28] Peter Shergold studied at Hull and Illinois, and was supervised by Professor Charlotte Erickson at the London School of Economics for his DPhil. Erickson and Rimmer knew each other, and so Shergold was recruited without a completed thesis, an application or an interview.[29] Stephen Nicholas studied for his undergraduate degree in North America, and at Hull for his (incomplete) doctorate. John Perkins also attended Hull, and Ian Inkster the University of East Anglia. David Meredith trained at the University of Exeter, and was hired on the basis of a phone call between Rimmer and the head of the Exeter Department of Economic History.[30] Wray Vamplew, who was born in Yorkshire and completed his

---

26 Interviews: Sinclair and Boot for Tucker; Dingle and Dingle for McCarty; Nicholas for Rimmer; Hall for Hartwell; Merrett for Sinclair; Sinclair for Beever.
27 Lloyd interview.
28 Shergold; Hutchinson interviews.
29 Shergold interview.
30 Oxley/Meredith interview.

DPhil at Edinburgh, has similarly recalled the informal hiring process at Flinders. British-trained Graham Tucker had already offered Vamplew a job in the ANU Faculties prior to his PhD, which he turned down. Later he accepted an offer from the Flinders economic history department, which came from a chance meeting with British-born Flinders historian Eric Richards. Much like members of the UNSW department, Vamplew has recalled there was no formal application, simply the submission of a CV.[31] At the ANU RSSS, internationalisation was determined by Noel Butlin's training at Harvard, favouring those from the US. Glenn Withers completed his PhD at Harvard, Rod Maddock at Duke University and Jonathan Pincus at Stanford. Ian McLean was trained at ANU, though held several visiting positions at Yale and Harvard throughout the 1970s and 1980s.

From 1980, the bottom fell out of the job market: universities and enrolments had expanded to a point of saturation, the underlying rhetoric of governments shifted from Keynesianism to neoliberal austerity, and academic positions had been filled by young scholars likely to kick around for decades. There is a clear distinction between the job market fortunes of students who graduated before and after 1980, with Andrew Wells, who trained at ANU, Lionel Frost from Monash, Martin Shanahan from Flinders, Greg Whitwell and Tim Duncan from Melbourne, and Diane Hutchinson and Deborah Oxley from UNSW, having a much harder time of it. For example, Frost has recalled that when he submitted his thesis in the early 1980s, 'there were literally no jobs'. He then completed teaching qualifications, and taught high school for several years before being hired by Eric Jones at La Trobe.[32] Oxley and Hutchinson, although separated by a decade, had similar experiences. They were both appointed to several short-term contracts or fellowships at universities interstate, which was more or less 'all there was going at the time'.[33] Hutchinson was then awarded tenure at the University of Sydney in late 1980s, and Oxley was appointed to the University of Oxford in 2007.[34] Shanahan has recalled the 'pretty depressing' job market in the late 1980s, taking a job at the South Australian parliamentary library as 'there didn't seem to be any positions available'. A short time later, he was appointed as

---

31   Wray Vamplew, 'Count Me In: Reflections on a Career as a Sports Historian', *Sport in Society* 19, no. 3 (2016): 297–312, doi.org/10.1080/17430437.2015.1056573.
32   Frost interview.
33   Hutchinson interview.
34   Oxley/Meredith; Hutchinson interviews.

an economics lecturer at the South Australian Institute of Technology.[35] Although this was not a uniquely Australian problem, nor one special to economic history, it was a very challenging environment.[36]

Departments as silos

The expansion of domestic training, and the scramble for new recruits from overseas meant that from about 1980 there was a 'full suite' of departments of economic history. While departments have been seen as the field's prime marker of success, they came with their own set of problems for interdisciplinary research. The professional architecture of departments is designed to funnel communication and ideas inwards, with appointments, collaboration, teaching, seminars and even the physical space all designed to develop appropriate teams for disciplinary teaching and frontier knowledge (see Chapter 1). In Australian economic history, departments were generally small, with no more than a dozen appointments at any one time. The workforce was also stable – scholars obtained tenure at a young age during the sector's expansion. After this, there very few new appointments, and very little mobility between groups. Each department had a God Professor, who was able to exert influence over the teaching and research program, and the physical space along a single floor or corridor encouraged close connections among the 'tribe'. Activities associated with departments – teaching, joint projects, seminars and training of graduate students – helped to reinforce these connections and created a sense of joint endeavour among members of each group.

Small departments can have two main impacts. The first, common to any field or discipline, is that long-term dense connections risk stifling innovation.[37] Particularly in Australia's case, where the higher education sector expanded very rapidly, and then almost overnight went into a hiring

---

35 Shanahan interview.
36 Ville, for example, has recalled a challenging job market in Thatcher-era Britain. Ville interview.
37 JS Coleman, *Foundations of Social Theory* (Cambridge: Harvard University Press, 1990); JT Klein, *Interdisciplinarity: History Theory, and Practice* (Detroit: Wayne State University, 1990); JT Klein, *Crossing Boundaries: Knowledge, Disciplinarities, and Interdisciplinarities* (Charlottesville: The University of Virginia Press, 1996); Richard Whitley, *The Intellectual and Social Organisation of the Sciences* (Oxford: Clarendon, 1984); Robert Frodeman and Carl Mitcham, 'New Directions in Interdisciplinarity: Broad, Deep, and Critical', *Bulletin of Science, Technology and Society* 27, no. 6 (2007): 506–14, doi.org/10.1177/0270467607308284; Jerry A Jacobs and Scott Frickel, 'Interdisciplinarity: A Critical Assessment', *Annual Review of Sociology* 35, no. 1 (2009): 43–65, doi.org/10.1146/annurev-soc-070308-115954.

freeze, the same small group, all of whom were a similar age, worked in departments together for a very long time. As Maddock has argued for ANU, departments had a deeply flawed 'social psychology', as he put it:

> If you get six people together and make them work together for 30 years and not talk to anybody except each other, they'll go mad. [laughs] I don't mean to suggest in that direct sense that my colleagues were mad, but they certainly heard every idea that the others had – in some sense they get bored with each other. So I don't think there was any meaningful dialogue, really, amongst the older colleagues in those departments.

Departments also represented a fundamental trade-off for interdisciplinary scholars like economic historians. The choice on offer was the chance to develop greater professional identity, institutional space, resources and recognition, at the cost of a restricted ability to develop broader connections. Economic history departments generally held their own seminars, and as a result, members rarely went to seminars in history, economics, politics and so on. Economic historians had their own courses, which meant they rarely (if ever) gave guest lectures in economics or history subjects. Departments also trained their own PhD students, rather than engaging with a mix of complementary supervisors. Some practitioners found departments uncongenial to their style of work. Pincus, for example, has 'never been a fan' of separate departments.[38] McLean has similarly recalled the 'horribly fragmented' institutional structure at ANU. Division of scholars into small groups, in his words, restricted the flow of people and ideas, and led to poorer grounding in either economics or history. Part of the reason that McLean accepted an appointment at the University of Adelaide was because there was no separate economic history group.[39]

Enclaves

The departmental era, and the associated professional architecture of these groups, created several professional and intellectual enclaves. The development of research clusters is, of course, inevitable and good. However, the strength of ties in each department created a fragmented institutional and intellectual structure, with economic historians at each

---

38 Pincus interview.
39 McLean interview.

university or in each city seeing themselves as their own 'tribe'. This contributed to a lack of integration, and hostility, between different traditions.

Antipodean cliometrics

ANU continued to be a primary centre for Australian economic history research throughout the 1970s and 1980s. The School of General Studies – the 'Faculties' – focused on teaching, and with the expansion of student numbers, hired quickly from the UK. By contrast, members of the RSSS more or less maintained a similar staff list from the Butlin boom, hiring new researchers in small numbers over the next two decades. Jonathan Pincus was hired in 1972, and was one of a small number of new RSSS recruits. The RSSS also trained some of the next generation of economic historians, including David Pope, Graeme Snooks and Andrew Wells. Between the two departments, Canberra hosted the largest group of economic historians in the country, and the largest number of those interested in Australian research topics. Although there were newer communities in Melbourne and Sydney, ANU continued to be a major hub. Adelaide can also be considered an outpost of ANU at this time, with economic historians at the University of Adelaide – such as Ian McLean and Tom Sheridan – having been trained at ANU in the 1960s, and McLean particularly maintaining his professional connections to Canberra. McLean commented that:

> My links were with ANU […] and then I forcibly established my links with the US […] If I was going to maintain basic enthusiasm for my field, there wasn't all that much on offer in Australia.

Flinders had a small but talented group of economic historians in the 1970s and 1980s. Gus Sinclair led the group throughout the 1970s, and Pincus took over in 1985. Sinclair appointed Snooks, Vamplew and Ralph Shlomowitz in the mid-1970s, and this group was stable throughout the next two decades. Sinclair, Snooks and Pincus were all members of Butlin's circle, maintaining contact and collaborative relationships with other orthodox scholars. Although Vamplew's research interests lay elsewhere, his main contribution to Australian economic history was to edit the statistical volume for the 1988 bicentennial series on Australian history.[40] He was awarded a summer fellowship to ANU, which enabled him to

---

40   Wray Vamplew, *Australians, Historical Statistics* (Broadway: Fairfax, Syme and Weldon Associates, 1987).

bring on several ANU economic historians as authors.[41] Although it was ostensibly a national project, Vamplew's connections within economic history were embedded in the Canberra–Adelaide community.

ANU developed a shared vision for economic history. Within each group there was potential for friendships, with Jackson recalling a vibrant social community in the Faculties.[42] Similarly, Butlin had a 'shack' at Guerilla Bay on the New South Wales South Coast, and his son Matthew has remembered him often inviting colleagues and visiting scholars.[43] Seminars involved cooperation between economic historians in the Faculties and the RSSS, with Rod Maddock and John Gage, Kosmas Tsokhas and Colin Forster, and Bob Jackson and David Pope among the pairs who organised the series throughout the 1980s.[44] Although this encouraged a sense of joint endeavour, it also created tension between the 'spoilt' RSSS scholars, and those considered the 'workers' in the Faculties.[45]

International visitors, particularly from the US, were a distinctive aspect of the ANU community. RSSS economist R. G. 'Bob' Gregory has argued that in the 1980s ANU was the centre of economic history in the world 'as a place to come to'.[46] Consistent with the global hegemony of knowledge, 'the world' in this case meant the US, with the group favouring US cliometricians in the visiting scholars program. Cliometrics became the dominant intellectual trend in US and Canadian economic history from the 1960s, with scholars combining neoclassical economic theory, counterfactual reasoning and econometric techniques to challenge conventional wisdom about long-run economic progress. The 'revolution' is generally traced to a gathering of the US Economic History Association in Williamstown in 1957. Here, Alfred H. Conrad and John R. Meyer presented pioneering papers on the use of statistics and economic theory, and slavery in the antebellum south. Although Conrad and Meyer received a polarised reaction from the Williamstown audience, the 'boldly innovative' research program appealed to younger scholars, and eventually

---

41 Vamplew correspondence, 19 October 2019.
42 Jackson interview. He has recalled playing football with John Gage, and helping Mac Boot build his house.
43 Matthew Butlin; Troy interviews.
44 Cornish; McLean; Statham interviews. See memos about changes to seminar programs in ANU Archives (hereafter ANUA), ANU Department of Economic History files, teaching materials and publications, AU ANUA 62, item 115.
45 Maddock interview.
46 Ville has similarly argued that ANU was a bit like Piccadilly Circus – at some point everyone passes through. See Gregory; Ville interviews.

became the dominant intellectual tradition in North American economic history. The approach was also adopted by some in the UK and Europe, though they remained in the minority.[47] Closer to home, Maddock has argued that his cohort – Pincus, McLean, Withers and himself – brought back the techniques and attitudes of US economic history to work on Australian topics. Pincus has attributed his interest in hypothesis testing to his time at Stanford,[48] and McLean has commented that the US scene in the 1970s and 1980s was exciting, and that his connections there gave him 'a completely expanded view of the discipline'.[49] Pincus and Butlin aimed to inject these new ideas and methods into the ANU community, inviting cliometricians such as Barry Eichengreen, Mark Thomas, Mary McKinnon, Tim Hatton and Dierdre McCloskey throughout the 1980s.[50] Visitors collaborated on research, and seminars and conferences were arranged to align with US visitors.[51]

These distinctive professional networks developed the group's intellectual character. In short, most members of this enclave used economic historical data to contribute to mainstream economics. The orthodox approach, inherited from ANU in the 1950s and 1960s, was already aligned with the dominant Keynesian paradigm of the post–World War II decades. The nature of orthodox research encouraged a transition towards the new frontiers of economics from the 1970s, which incorporated neoclassical theory, hypothesis testing and advanced mathematical techniques.[52] In the 1960s, Butlin himself foreshadowed the connection between orthodox work and this frontier economics research, noting his intention to write a third analytical essay to sit alongside 'the words' and 'the numbers'.[53]

---

47 John S Lyons, Louis P Cain and Susan H Williamson, eds, *Reflections on the Cliometrics Revolution: Conversations with Economic Historians* (New York: Routledge, 2008), doi.org/10.4324/9780203799635; Boldizzoni and Hudson, *Global Economic History*.
48 Pincus interview.
49 McLean interview.
50 Pincus; Gregory interviews.
51 Gregory interview. See also acknowledgments in Robert G Gregory and Noel G Butlin, eds, *Recovery from the Depression: Australia and the World Economy in the 1930s* (Cambridge: Cambridge University Press, 1988), doi.org/10.1017/CBO9780511597206.
52 Alex Millmow, *A History of Australasian Economic Thought* (London: Taylor & Francis, 2017), doi.org/10.4324/9781315716152; Peter Groenewegen and Bruce McFarlane, *A History of Australian Economic Thought* (London: Routledge, 1990).
53 Noel G Butlin, *Investment in Australian Economic Development, 1861–1900* (London: Cambridge University Press, 1964), xiv, doi.org/10.1017/CBO9781316530160. 'The words' and 'the numbers' refer to Butlin's seminal works, respectively Noel G Butlin, *Australian Domestic Product, Investment and Foreign Borrowing 1861–1938/9* (London: Cambridge University Press, 1962) and Butlin, *Investment*.

Although this volume never appeared, he clearly thought this would be a good thing to do. In the 1980s Butlin was still very active, extending his quantitative estimates back to 1788, and compiling the statistical base for key edited works.[54] Although he did not personally engage in so-called 'analytical' or cliometric work, he was supportive of such efforts.

The orthodox tradition of collecting and describing national income data was, as McLean put it, 'inherently temporary', before the analytical step.[55] Much like their colleagues in the US, the younger generation of scholars in Canberra and Adelaide spent time augmenting or improving Butlin's original statistics, and then using these data to test the validity of economic models. For example, with Pincus and Adelaide economist Sue Richardson, McLean adjusted Butlin's statistics (which demonstrated stagnating living trends between 1900 and 1939) to include a wider variety of social indicators such as income inequality, physical infrastructure, education, life expectancy and length of the working week. Inferring inductively from these various trends, they argued that there was no indication of stagnating living standards over this period, but that there was greater income inequality during the depression.[56] McLean also attempted to improve the standard balance of payments and rural workforce estimates, synthesising work from Butlin and Roland Wilson in the former, and workforce estimates from Butlin and Dowie, and Michael Keating in the latter.[57] McLean's deductive work used his orthodox statistics on rural production in Victoria to demonstrate the Solow economic growth model of technological change; and with Maddock he used quantitative material to examine the Dutch disease model of economic growth for

---

54 Noel G Butlin, 'Contours of the Australian Economy 1788–1860', *Australian Economic History Review* 26, no. 2 (1986): 96–125, doi.org/10.1111/aehr.262002; Noel G Butlin and William Angus Sinclair, 'Australian Gross Domestic Product 1788–1860: Estimates, Sources and Methods', *Australian Economic History Review* 26, no. 2 (1986): 126–47, doi.org/10.1111/aehr.262003; Gregory and Butlin, *Recovery*; Noel G Butlin, Jonathan J Pincus and Alan Barnard, *Government and Capitalism: Public and Private Choice in Twentieth Century Australia* (Sydney: George Allen & Unwin, 1982).
55 McLean interview.
56 Ian W McLean and Jonathan J Pincus, 'Did Australian Living Standards Stagnate between 1890 and 1940?', *Journal of Economic History* 43, no. 1 (1983): 193–202, doi.org/10.1017/S002205070002917X; Ian W McLean and Susan Richardson, 'More or Less Equal? Australian Income Distribution in 1933 and 1980', *Economic Record* 62, no. 176 (1986): 67–81, doi.org/10.1111/j.1475-4932.1986.tb00883.x.
57 Ian W McLean, 'The Australian Balance of Payments on Current Account 1901 to 1964–65', *Australian Economic Papers* 7, no. 10 (1968): 77–90, doi.org/10.1111/j.1467-8454.1968.tb00153.x; Ian W McLean, SF Molloy and P Lockett, 'The Rural Workforce in Australia 1871–1911', *Australian Economic History Review* 22, no. 2 (1982): 172–81, doi.org/10.1111/aehr.222004.

Australia's gold discoveries in the 1850s.[58] Research into Australia's labour market also used orthodox school statistics to test whether minimum wage regulations increased unemployment during the Great Depression.[59] Forster adopted the orthodox approach to examine the impact of the minimum wage on unemployment, while also writing a more deductive piece that tested the relationship between various socio-economic factors and the fertility rate.[60]

David Pope was particularly influenced by the intellectual combination of Butlin and Pincus. He completed his DPhil on early twentieth-century British migration under the supervision of Pincus and ANU economic historian Nev Cain, while acknowledging the substantial influence of Butlin (see Chapter 3). He also noted his debt to the economic history joint departmental seminar, and his colleagues in both economics and economic history.[61] As a result, Pope's thesis was a marriage of orthodox and cliometric approaches. Part I was orthodox, sketching the contours of the Australian economy, the labour market, government policy and, ultimately, the quantitative material on British migration to Australia. Part II devised a model of UK immigration, and subjected the quantitative material to various empirical tests. From this thesis, Pope published an article in the *Australian Economic History Review* that used the orthodox approach to outline trends found in Australian immigration

---

58 Ian W McLean, 'Growth and Technological Change in Agriculture: Victoria 1870–1910', *Economic Record* 49, no. 128 (1973): 560, doi.org/10.1111/j.1475-4932.1973.tb01956.x; Ian W McLean, 'The Analysis of Agricultural Productivity: Alternative Views and Victorian Evidence', *Australian Economic History Review* 21, no. 1 (1981): 6–28, doi.org/10.1111/aehr.211002; Rod Maddock and Ian W McLean, 'Supply-Side Shocks: The Case of Australian Gold', *Journal of Economic History* 44, no. 4 (1984): 1047–67, doi.org/10.1017/S0022050700033088.
59 They used either Peter Macarthy, 'The Harvester Judgment – An Historical Assessment' (PhD thesis, The Australian National University, 1967); Noel G Butlin and John A Dowie, 'Estimates of Australian Work Force and Employment, 1861–1961', *Australian Economic History Review* 9, no. 2 (1969): 138–55, doi.org/10.1111/aehr.92003; or Michael Keating, *The Australian Workforce, 1910–11 to 1960–61* (Canberra: Australian National University Press, 1973). See David Pope, 'Wage Regulation and Unemployment in Australia: 1900–1930', *Australian Economic History Review* 22, no. 2 (1982): 103–26, doi.org/10.1111/aehr.222001; William Angus Sinclair, 'Was Labour Scarce in the 1830s?', *Australian Economic History Review* 11, no. 2 (1971): 115–32, doi.org/10.1111/aehr.112001; Tom J Valentine, 'A Model of the Australian Labour Market in the Interwar Period', *Australian Economic History Review* 20, no. 1 (1980): 46–63, doi.org/10.1111/aehr.201003.
60 Colin Forster, 'An Economic Consequence of Mr Justice Higgins', *Australian Economic History Review* 25, no. 2 (1985): 95–111, doi.org/10.1111/aehr.252001; Colin Forster, 'Aspects of Australian Fertility, 1861–1901', *Australian Economic History Review* 14, no. 2 (1974): 105–22, doi.org/10.1111/aehr.142001.
61 David Pope, 'The Peopling of Australia: United Kingdom Immigration from Federation to the Great Depression' (PhD thesis, The Australian National University, 1976), xiii.

data.[62] Additionally, by himself and with colleague Glenn Withers, Pope published cliometric work that deductively tested the motivations and effects of immigration.[63]

The group's US connections reflected and reinforced their intellectual orientation towards the economics discipline. ANU scholars regularly contributed to Australia's key economics journal, *Economic Record*, publishing a mix of orthodox research and cliometric approaches.[64] Large collaborative projects also engaged with economics. In the 1980s, Butlin apparently decided that 'he was going to advise the [RSSS] director to close economic history down unless the department agreed on a joint project'.[65] Staff pitched ideas, and Pincus suggested examining political institutions and twentieth-century Australian capitalism. Butlin agreed, and launched the 'Government and Capitalism' project. He established a common statistical series, and hired Rod Maddock to work on taxation. There were a number of subsidiary articles among members, and it culminated in a large co-authored work by Butlin, Barnard and Pincus.[66] Each author essentially tossed a coin to decide which section they were to write, and they circulated drafts prior to publication.[67] The method was largely orthodox, but the analysis of the interaction between the public and private sectors of the macro-economy was done with the explicit aim

---

62 David Pope, 'Contours of Australian Immigration, 1901–30', *Australian Economic History Review* 21, no. 1 (1981): 29–53, doi.org/10.1111/aehr.211003.
63 Glenn Withers, 'Immigration and Economic Fluctuations: An Application to Late Nineteenth-Century Australia', *Australian Economic History Review* 17, no. 2 (1977): 131–49, doi.org/10.1111/aehr.172003; Glenn Withers and David Pope, 'Immigration and Unemployment', *Economic Record* 61, no. 2 (1985): 554–64, doi.org/10.1111/j.1475-4932.1985.tb02010.x; David Pope, 'Some Factors Inhibiting Australian Immigration in the 1920s', *Australian Economic History Review* 24, no. 1 (1984): 34–52, doi.org/10.1111/aehr.241003; David Pope, 'The Push-Pull Model of Australian Migration'. *Australian Economic History Review* 16, no. 2 (1976): 144–52. doi.org/10.1111/aehr.162004.
64 Graeme Snooks, 'Regional Estimates of Gross Domestic Product and Capital Formation: Western Australia, 1923–1938-39', *Economic Record* 48, no. 124 (1972): 536, doi.org/10.1111/j.1475-4932.1972.tb00399.x; McLean, 'Growth and Technological Change'; Withers and Pope, 'Immigration and Unemployment'; McLean and Richardson, 'More or Less Equal?'; Glenn Withers, 'Economic Influences Upon Marriage Behaviour: Australia, 1954–1984', *Economic Record* 55, no. 149 (1979), doi.org/10.1111/j.1475-4932.1979.tb02211.x: 118; Alan Barnard and Noel G Butlin, 'Australian Public and Private Capital Formation, 1901–75', *Economic Record* 57, no. 4 (1981): 354–67, doi.org/10.1111/j.1475-4932.1981.tb01071.x; David Pope, 'Price Expectations and the Australian Price Level: 1901–30', *Economic Record* 58, no. 4 (1982): 328–38, doi.org/10.1111/j.1475-4932.1982.tb00383.x; Michael Keating, 'Relative Wages and the Changing Industrial Distribution of Employment in Australia', *Economic Record* 59, no. 167 (1983): 384–98, doi.org/10.1111/j.1475-4932.1983.tb00828.x.
65 Pincus interview. See also Graeme Snooks, '"In My Beginning Is My End": The Life and Work of Noel George Butlin, 1921–1991', *Australian Economic History Review* 31, no. 2 (1991): 3–27, 20, doi.org/10.1111/aehr.312001.
66 Butlin et al., *Government and Capitalism*.
67 Pincus interview.

of providing background to contemporary economists and policymakers. Further, as with Butlin's earlier work, the statistical database was produced with the aim of 'testing' their conclusions down the road.[68]

Maddock and McLean's *The Australian Economy in the Long Run*, published in 1987, involved several younger members of the ANU economic history community such as Pincus, Withers, Pope and Matthew Butlin. Other contributors were largely Australian economists such as Tom Valentine, Adrian Pagan, John Freebairn, Kym Anderson and Michael Carter. Most contributors had spent some time working at ANU during the 1970s and 1980s, and many had co-authored with other contributors throughout this period. The group met at ANU on four separate occasions to discuss the book, and for the final meeting they invited a number of discussants (most of whom were also members of economics or economic history at ANU).[69] The editors commented that they 'relied mainly though not exclusively on the methods employed and questions posed by economists', analysing a standard economics framework over time.[70] The volume was divided into chapters on the factors of production, the internal/external sector, and the private/public sector, providing an *analysis* of the components of the economy, rather than a narrative of overall economic change. Gregory and Butlin's *Recovery from the Depression* (hereafter *Recovery*) was also deeply embedded in the economics discipline. Overseas cliometricians participated through the RSSS visiting scholars program, and contributions used both orthodox and cliometric methods.[71] Economist Bob Gregory co-edited the volume, and he argued that 'we [...] believed that it would be useful to bring together economists and economic historians to a conference to discuss the recovery process from the depression'.[72]

---

68   Butlin et al., *Government and Capitalism*, ix.
69   Rodney Maddock and Ian W McLean, eds, *The Australian Economy in the Long Run* (Cambridge: Cambridge University Press, 1987), ix.
70   Rod Maddock and Ian W McLean, 'The Australian Economy in the Very Long Run', in *The Australian Economy in the Long Run*, ed. Rod Maddock and Ian W McLean (Melbourne: Cambridge University Press, 1987), 5–29, 5. Maddock has also argued that they set the volume within a 'standard economists' framework', see Maddock interview.
71   See Tom J Valentine, 'The Depression of the 1930s', in Maddock and McLean, *The Australian Economy in the Long Run*, 61–77.
72   Gregory and Butlin, *Recovery*, preface.

Melbourne interdisciplinarity

Those in Melbourne developed an interdisciplinary vision of economic history. Although teaching in the subject was largely based within economics and business degrees, the history discipline's research program from the 1950s to the 1980s welcomed economic matters as a part of their diverse thematic and methodological foci.[73] Key history journals such as *Historical Studies* and *Labour History* frequently published economic history research, and although administratively separate, historian Geoffrey Serle included economic historians in his survey of the discipline in the 1970s.[74] It was thus largely through research, rather than teaching, that economic historians in Melbourne were able to bridge the interdisciplinary space. Melbourne was home to the field's oldest economic history department, with the University of Melbourne establishing the group in 1945. The department enjoyed steady growth, from an average of about six staff in the 1950s, to between 10 and 13 members throughout the 1960s, 1970s and 1980s. Monash University opened its doors in 1961, and had five dedicated economic history appointments by 1970. This increased to an average of about eight staff members throughout the 1970s and 1980s. La Trobe was the smallest community of economic historians in Melbourne, and was home to around three or four dedicated staff from the late 1960s.

Although it will make any Melburnian's blood boil, the story of economic history in Victoria really begins at the University of Sydney with its pre-eminent postwar economic historian Sydney James Butlin. Noel's elder brother by 11 years, Syd was already an established scholar at the University of Sydney when his younger brother arrived in the late 1940s. Syd became the head of the Butlin household in 1926, at the age of 16, when his father was killed by a hit and run diver near their home in Singleton. He studied for an economics degree at the University of Sydney, and was then awarded several travelling scholarships to attend Trinity College, Cambridge, in the 1930s. There he was immersed in the Keynesian revolution, as well as gaining an interest in monetary economics. He returned to Sydney

---

73 See Chapter 3. Mark McKenna, 'The History Anxiety', in *The Cambridge History of Australia*, ed. Alison Bashford and Stuart Macintyre, vol. 2 (Melbourne: Cambridge University Press, 2013), 561–80, doi.org/10.1017/CHO9781107445758.055; Hannah Forsyth and Sophie Loy-Wilson, 'Seeking a New Materialism in Australian History', *Australian Historical Studies* 48, no. 1 (2017): 169–88, doi.org/10.1080/1031461X.2017.1298635.
74 Dingle/Davison; Macintyre interviews. Geoffrey Serle, 'The State of the Profession in Australia', *Australian Historical Studies* 15, no. 61 (1973): 686–702, doi.org/10.1080/10314617308595499.

in 1934, and was appointed lecturer at the University of Sydney in the following year. As was typical at the time, Syd had an interlude in public service during World War II, as director of the economic division of the Department of War Organisation and Industry. From 1946, Butlin was Chair of Economics and, for much of what remained of his career, was dean of the Faculty of Economics. He retired from Sydney in late 1971, and spent his final years in Canberra as an independent professor in his brother's department in the RSSS.[75]

Like Noel, Syd was an empiricist, marshalling incredible volumes of data to understand a topic comprehensively. Syd was preoccupied with the Australian monetary system for much of his career, inspired by his contact with British monetary theorist Sir Dennis Robertson during his time in the UK, and by the Australian Royal Commission into monetary and banking systems in the 1930s.[76] Syd found that contemporary interest in money and banking lacked historical background, and so he set about providing it. The outcome, *Foundations of the Australian Monetary System*, published in 1953, compiled a statistical appendix for data relating to banking operations, and interpreted it in the context of early British-Australian settlement. He argued that at each stage 'monetary organisation repeated in miniature the larger story', with the development of a fully-fledged monetary system alongside a fairly modern economy in a short space of time. Syd's approach was staunchly inductive, refusing to speculate on any issues not explicitly covered by his evidence. He justified this approach as follows:

> I have elected to give my version in full detail, partly to make it unnecessary for others to rediscover the facts, but mainly because my object has been to display a set of institutions coming into being and in operation, and, on first telling, that story requires detail.[77]

---

75 Judy Butlin correspondence, 30 June 2021; C Boris Schedvin, 'Butlin, Sydney James (Syd) (1910–1977)', *Australian Dictionary of Biography* (hereafter *ADB*), adb.anu.edu.au/biography/butlin-sydney-james-syd-9647/text17017 (first published in hardcopy 1993); Noel G Butlin, 'A Fraternal Farewell: Tribute to S.J. Butlin', *Australian Economic History Review* 18, no. 2 (1978): 99–108, doi.org/10.1111/aehr.182001.
76 Schedvin, 'Butlin, Sydney James'.
77 Syd J Butlin, *Foundations of the Australian Monetary System 1788–1851* (Melbourne: Melbourne University Press, 1953), v.

Figure 3: Professor Syd Butlin, University of Sydney, 1960
Source: University of Sydney Archives, G3_224_2636.

Syd's *Foundations* quickly became a standard text in Australian economic history, and was reviewed as a 'definitive' and 'enduring' work in Australian history.[78] Syd's work also aged well, with Boris Schedvin describing it as 'rigorous in the use of evidence and theory, comprehensive and imaginative in scope, bold and elegant in structure'.[79] Alan Hall referred to *Foundations* as 'the best economic history that has yet been produced in terms of scholarship'. David Merrett similarly commented that 'before Noel's "two books", there was Syd's "book", and it is the perfect research monograph. It is still probably unrivalled. It is awe-inspiring and terrifying'.[80]

In certain circles, Syd Butlin is remembered with as much reverence as his brother. He has been remembered by his colleague, collaborator and, ultimately, biographer Schedvin, as:

> quiet, shy and deeply private […] a gifted conversationalist and raconteur, and inveterate tea-drinker and chain-smoker, as well as a courteous and kindly man who delighted in the achievements of his family.[81]

The connection between Syd and Noel is obvious, and even when prompted to talk about the former, interviewees couldn't help but compare them. They have been remembered with contrasting personalities: Noel was 'loose', 'fun', 'bohemian' and 'affable',[82] whereas Syd was 'uptight', 'fastidious', 'precise' and a 'perfectionist'.[83] Although Schedvin has recalled that Noel became critical of Syd's style of scholarship, Noel's obituary of Syd was respectful of his brother's detailed analysis of his subjects.[84]

Leaders of the Melbourne community were mentored by Syd Butlin in the 1950s and 1960s. Boris Schedvin completed his PhD at the University of Sydney in the early 1960s, and returned to a lectureship there after a brief stint in the UK. John McCarty had a Melbourne undergraduate degree, and a DPhil from Cambridge. He then spent a small amount of time lecturing in the economics department at UNSW and working for Syd Butlin as a research assistant, before he was appointed to a lectureship

---

78 Allan Shaw, 'Review: Butlin, *The Foundations of the Australian Monetary System*', *Australian Quarterly* 26, no. 1 (1954): 102–4, doi.org/10.2307/20633421; CGF Simkin, 'Review: Butlin, *The Foundations of the Australian Monetary System*', *Historical Studies* 6, no. 22 (1954): 226.
79 Schedvin, 'Butlin, Sydney James'.
80 Hall; Merrett interviews.
81 Schedvin, 'Butlin, Sydney James'.
82 Pincus; Gregory; Blainey interviews.
83 Gregory; Hall; Schedvin; Blainey interviews.
84 Butlin, 'A Fraternal Farewell'; Schedvin interview.

at the University of Sydney.[85] McCarty and Schedvin worked closely together, and with Syd, throughout the 1960s. In particular, Schedvin and McCarty jointly edited the *Australian Economic History Review* in its fledgling era. In 1968, McCarty was appointed to Monash University, and in 1972 became the inaugural chair of the newly created economic history department. McCarty brought Schedvin into the Monash department in the following year. Boris maintained contact with Syd after he left Sydney, collaborating on the second volume of the *War Economy* in the 1970s.[86]

Schedvin adopted elements of Syd Butlin's scholarship, and said that 'Noel [...] might have claimed that I was infected by Syd's empirical descriptivism'.[87] To compare their prominent works of the time – Syd's *Foundations* and Schedvin's *Australia and the Great Depression* – both marshalled large amounts of data to comprehensively understand their topic. They treated each case chronologically, accounting with impressive detail all or most of the relevant factors in a particular event. They took institutions, policymakers and rhetoric seriously, with Syd incorporating profiles of prominent bankers and quotations from contemporary editorials, and Schedvin including lively reconstructions of the political institutions, policies and policymakers, to argue that internal determinants such as poorly designed public investment programs were crucial for the extent, timing and shape of the Great Depression in Australia.[88] This differed markedly from the approach of the ANU enclave. Rather than explaining their primary material using contemporary business cycle or sectoral growth theory, Syd Butlin and Schedvin instead focused on detailed, contextual reconstructions of historical events.[89] Integration between economic analysis and historical narrative was present in

---

85 Tony Dingle, 'John William McCarty, 1931–1998', in *1999 Annual Report* (Canberra: Academy of the Social Sciences in Australia, 1999), 74. See also acknowledgments in Syd J Butlin, *Australia and New Zealand Bank: The Bank of Australasia and the Union Bank of Australia Limited, 1828–1951* (London: Longmans, 1961), viii.
86 Syd J Butlin and C Boris Schedvin, *The War Economy: 1942–1945* (Canberra: Australian War Memorial, 1977). The first volume was published in 1955 and, as Boris recalls, Syd had simply 'run out of steam' on the second half. They divided the work down the middle, and Syd apparently gestured to the archive of World War II records, asking Schedvin to 'go to it'. Schedvin has argued that there was very little intellectual collaboration on this book, that instead he spent a lot of time editing Syd's 'complex', 'parenthetical' writing. See Schedvin interview.
87 Schedvin interview. See also Tony Dingle, who argued that Schedvin was 'an extension of Syd's historical approach'; and David Merrett who agreed that McCarty and Schedvin 'both had more links to the Syd Butlin work, rather than Noel'. Dingle/Davison; Merrett interviews.
88 C Boris Schedvin, *Australia and the Great Depression: A Study of Economic Development and Policy in the 1920s and 1930s* (Sydney: Sydney University Press, 1970).
89 Indeed, Kuznets or other business cycle theorists do not emerge at all, explicitly or implicitly, in either Schedvin or Syd's work.

these works, with Heinz Arndt reviewing Schedvin's contribution as 'historian's rather than economist's economic history'.[90] Reviews of Syd's work similarly identified that his approach was at home with historical tradition, with economist Colin Simkin arguing that *Foundations* was a 'comprehensive, reliable, detailed, and fully documented *account*' of the Australian monetary system.[91]

Although McCarty was professionally connected to Syd and Boris, his research deviated from their empirical, contextual reconstructions. In 1964, while they were working at the University of Sydney, McCarty published an article in the *Australian Economic History Review* that applied staples thesis to the study of Australian economic development in the first half of the nineteenth century. Initially developed in the interwar period to explain Canada's economic history, staples thesis argues that growth stems from the export of a series of key commodities to industrialised 'Mother countries'.[92] External demand for primary exports sets the pace of expansion, but local production sets the pattern of growth and the distribution of income.[93] McCarty adopted this framework, concluding that the pace and pattern of Australian economic growth in the early period of British settlement was determined externally through a staple export – in this case the private sector production of food for the colonial government to feed the convict workforce.[94] McCarty's grounding in economic theory was complemented by engagement with a range of political, social and historical themes. For example, historian Donald Denoon acknowledged that McCarty had contributed to reintegrating Australian *history* with broader global conversations.[95] Similarly, Tony Dingle remembered McCarty as the 'quintessential social scientist', occupying a special place in Australian economic history by bridging the 'widening gap between the disciplines of economics and history'.[96]

---

90   Heinz W Arndt, 'Review: Schedvin, *Australia and the Great Depression*', *Australian Quarterly* 43, no. 2 (1971): 121–25, doi.org/10.2307/20634446.
91   Simkin, 'Review: Butlin, *Foundations*', 226. Emphasis mine.
92   For Canada, fur, cod fishing, timber, wheat and minerals were exported firstly to France, then Britain, then the US.
93   Douglas McCalla, 'Making a Country (and an Economy): Economic History in Canada', in Boldizzoni and Hudson, *Global Economic History*, 55–72, doi.org/10.4324/9781315734736; MH Watkins and HM Grant, *Canadian Economic History: Classic and Contemporary Approaches* (Ottawa: Carleton University Press, 1993).
94   John W McCarty, 'The Staple Approach in Australian Economic History', *Business Archives and History* 4, no. 1 (1964): 1–22, doi.org/10.1111/aehr.41001.
95   Donald Denoon, 'The Isolation of Australian History', *Australian Historical Studies* 22, no. 87 (1986): 252–60, doi.org/10.1080/10314618608595747. Emphasis mine.
96   Dingle, 'John William McCarty', 74.

While McCarty's approach was interdisciplinary, by attempting to fit Australia's experience within a theory developed for another context he differed fundamentally from his Sydney colleagues. His article was influential, remaining one of the highest-cited pieces in the *Australian Economic History Review*, though criticism centred on its deductive approach.[97] The journal ran a series of follow-up articles from a diverse range of contributors. Noel Butlin criticised McCarty's approach for being 'deliberately abstract'; Melbourne historian Geoffrey Blainey, although he reviewed the externalism of the piece largely favourably, commented that a North American approach may not be 'entirely fit for export'; and UNSW economic historian Graham J. Abbott commented that the application of a ready-made theory to a situation from which it was not derived was to 'abandon historical methods altogether'.[98] Schedvin has similarly reflected that although an externalist interpretation was appropriate, the staples thesis was not the right vehicle.[99] While McCarty's interpretation of Australian economic history was not in line with vogue scholarship, staples thesis was a broader, more interdisciplinary version of economic history than the sectoral analysis of national income accounting. It was an alternative way of approaching the subject – one that incorporated a range of economic, social and historical elements.

As elsewhere, the university structures in Melbourne did their best to quash interdisciplinary knowledge. Melbourne was home to three major universities with economic history groups, all within close proximity. Melbourne and Monash both had separate departments within economics throughout the 1970s and 1980s, with La Trobe, curiously, following suit in the early 1990s. As elsewhere, separate departments fostered links among economic historians at the expense of broader connections. Departments were located in economics and commerce faculties, structuring the curriculum around the professional needs of economists. Collaborative ties were dense in each group, with members co-editing and co-authoring papers and books, and frequently offering each other feedback prior to publication. Seminars were held within each group, as well as joint events

---

97 Andrew J Seltzer, 'Publication Trends and Future Challenges for the Australian Economic History Review: A Bibliometric Analysis', *Australian Economic History Review* 58, no. 2 (2018): 112–33, doi.org/10.1111/aehr.12143.
98 Noel G Butlin, 'Growth in a Trading World: The Australian Economy, Heavily Disguised', *Australian Economic History Review* 4, no. 2 (1964): 138–58, 158, doi.org/10.1111/aehr.42003; Geoffrey Blainey, 'Technology in Australian History', *Business Archives and History* 4, no. 2 (1964): 117–37, 126, doi.org/10.1111/aehr.42002; Graham J Abbott, 'Staple Theory and Australian Economic Growth, 1788–1820', *Business Archives and History* 5, no. 2 (1965): 142–154, 153, doi.org/10.1111/aehr.52004.
99 Dingle/Davison; Schedvin interviews.

with groups elsewhere in Melbourne. Doctoral supervision similarly created a sense of professional identity, with students integrated into each department's professional network.

While departments in Melbourne, as elsewhere, encouraged professional silos, the difference in this case was that those leading the group were committed to diverse, interdisciplinary research. Those prominent in the interwar period gave the University of Melbourne department its start, with Herbert Burton the first professor from 1944, and John La Nauze taking over in 1949. As part of the interwar group, both balanced between humanities and social science paradigms in their careers. Schedvin and McCarty, as above, both adopted a broad approach to the subject, influenced by Syd Butlin's narrative account of systems, institutions and individuals. Geoffrey Blainey also worked in both economics and history. After undergraduate studies in history at the University of Melbourne, history Chair Max Crawford encouraged Blainey to pursue a career in the subject. He worked as a freelance writer throughout the 1950s, and during this time penned *Peaks of Lyell*, a pioneering foray into Australian business history.[100] In 1961 he returned to the University of Melbourne, as a member of the economic history department, leading the group from 1968 to 1976. Blainey's written work reflected the potential for economic history to engage with interdisciplinary practice, with *The Rush That Never Ended*, the *Tyranny of Distance* and *A Land Half Won* engaging with economists' questions on the nature of Australia's sectoral growth and export industries, and historians' interest in land, labour and colonisation.[101] During the 1960s and 1970s, Blainey was professionally connected to various groups, contributing regularly to the *Australian Economic History Review*, *Historical Studies* and *Economic Record*. However, like La Nauze before him, Blainey gradually left behind his connections to economics from the 1970s, finding the plurality of the history discipline, which welcomed the study of material matters, more amenable to his style of work. Formalising this transition, Blainey was appointed to the University of Melbourne's Ernest Scott Chair of History in 1978.

---

100 Blainey interview; Geoffrey Blainey, *The Peaks of Lyell* (Melbourne: Melbourne University Press, 1954).
101 Geoffrey Blainey, *The Tyranny of Distance* (Melbourne: Sun Books, 1966); Geoffrey Blainey, *The Rush That Never Ended: A History of Australian Mining* (Melbourne: Melbourne University Press, 1963); Geoffrey Blainey, *A Land Half Won* (South Melbourne: Macmillan, 1980).

W. A. 'Gus' Sinclair skilfully mediated the interdisciplinary space. Born in Scotland but raised in Albury, Sinclair's interest in economic history was piqued by John La Nauze's lectures at the University of Melbourne from the late 1940s. La Nauze then supervised Sinclair's Masters thesis, and put him in touch with Noel Butlin at ANU to work on the orthodox data collection in the 1950s.[102] Moving between professional tribes, Sinclair used this broad experience to unify the post–World War II literature and describe Australia's 'continuing process of economic development' since 1788.[103] This book, in his own words, was an attempt to reconcile Butlin's orthodox work with McCarty's staples interpretation.[104] Rather than attributing everything to the development of export industries (as McCarty attempted to do), Sinclair utilised orthodox school statistics to argue that export industries were the starting point from which other, internalist development occurred.[105] Sinclair also used his work to communicate between parent disciplines. Articles by Sinclair were a regular fixture in *Economic Record*, and he used these to promote both his own orthodox and cliometric work, and the contributions of Melburnians to the economics discipline.[106] As an example, Sinclair used quantitative material to test a theoretical model of female workforce participation in a piece for *Economic Record*. The following year, in an article for *Historical Studies*, he used a combination of qualitative and quantitative methods to understand the reasons for the decline in women's workforce participation in the decades prior to World War I. Sinclair's aim with these two articles was specifically interdisciplinary: to demonstrate that 'the insights of the economist can yield relevant findings' to historical questions, and that historical data could yield useful theoretical knowledge on the labour market.[107]

---

102 Sinclair interview.
103 Sinclair worked for Butlin at ANU in the 1950s; at Melbourne, Monash and La Trobe from 1958 to 1973; was the head of the Flinders economic history group from 1973 to 1982; then returned to Monash as dean of their Economics and Politics Faculty from 1983. See Appendix. William Angus Sinclair, *The Process of Economic Development in Australia* (Melbourne: Cheshire, 1976), foreword.
104 Sinclair interview.
105 Sinclair interview; Sinclair, *Process of Economic Development*, 4.
106 For example, he went in to bat for Schedvin on the matter of Boehm's review of *Australia and the Great Depression*. See Ernst A Boehm, 'Economic Development and Fluctuation in Australia in the 1920s: A Reply', *Economic Record* 51, no. 135 (1975): 414–20, doi.org/10.1111/j.1475-4932.1975.tb00270.x; William Angus Sinclair, 'Economic Development and Fluctuation in Australia in the 1920s', *Economic Record* 51, no. 135 (1975): 409–13, doi.org/10.1111/j.1475-4932.1975.tb00269.x.
107 William Angus Sinclair, 'Women at Work in Melbourne and Adelaide since 1871', *Economic Record* 57, no. 4 (1981): 344–353, 352, doi.org/10.1111/j.1475-4932.1981.tb01070.x; William Angus Sinclair, 'Women and Economic Change in Melbourne 1871–1921', *Historical Studies* 20, no. 79 (1982): 278–291, 278, doi.org/10.1080/10314618208595684.

Figure 4: Professors Gus Sinclair (left) and Allan Fels from the Monash Faculty of Economics and Politics
Source: Photograph taken by Richard Crompton, held at Monash University Archives.

As a result of robust professional structures, younger members of the Melbourne group absorbed this interdisciplinary approach to economic history. Members were, for the most part, trained at Melbourne and Monash, by the eclectic group of senior economic historians in those departments. David Merrett, for example, was supervised for his Masters degree by Gus Sinclair, and was the youngest member of the Monash department from the early 1970s. During his postgraduate work, David was sent up to ANU to talk to Noel Butlin. Noel suggested Merrett examine GDP fluctuations for Victoria, which resulted in, in Merrett's words, a 'poor imitation of what Snooks did for Western Australia'.[108] Although the thesis was never published, Merrett's engagement with the orthodox school continued. In the 1970s he and Tony Dingle (who had arrived at Monash from the London School of Economics in 1967) had a 'dalliance in urban history', writing two articles on nineteenth-century home ownership in Melbourne.[109] They essentially replicated Bob Jackson's work on Sydney to contend with Butlin's conclusion that tenancy levels in Melbourne increased as a result of the 1890s depression.[110] At the same time, Merrett also worked on business history and economic policy.[111] Frost has recalled complementary supervision by McCarty and Merrett at Monash, commenting that McCarty was an excellent sounding board, and that Merrett provided 'fantastic [...] searching' written critique.[112] Frost's thesis examined rural development in Victoria, a topic that spoke to Frost's interest in rural industries, McCarty's work in exports and comparative development, and Merrett's abilities in the orthodox school.[113] Schedvin and Whitwell have both recalled ongoing interactions during Whitwell's DPhil, which began at Monash, but moved to the University of Melbourne when Schedvin accepted the Chair in Economic History in 1979.[114] Whitwell has commented that

---

108 Merrett interview.
109 Merrett interview.
110 Anthony E Dingle and David T Merrett, 'Home Owners and Tenants in Melbourne 1891–1911', *Australian Economic History Review* 12, no. 1 (1972): 21–35, doi.org/10.1111/aehr.121002; Anthony E Dingle and David T Merrett, 'Landlords in Suburban Melbourne, 1891–1911', *Australian Economic History Review* 17, no. 1 (1977): 1–24. doi.org/10.1111/aehr.171001.
111 David T Merrett, *ANZ Bank: An Official History* (Sydney: Allen & Unwin, 1985); David T Merrett, 'The Victorian Licensing Court 1906–1968: A Study of Role and Impact', *Australian Economic History Review* 19, no. 2 (1979): 123–50, doi.org/10.1111/aehr.192002.
112 Frost correspondence, 3 January 2017.
113 Lionel Frost, 'Victorian Agriculture and the Role of Government, 1880–1914' (PhD thesis, Monash University, 1982). See also Frost interview; Lionel Frost, 'A Reinterpretation of Victoria's Railway Construction Boom of the 1880s', *Australian Economic History Review* 26, no. 1 (1986): 40–55, doi.org/10.1111/aehr.261003.
114 Schedvin; Whitwell interviews.

Schedvin was his 'towering intellectual influence', and that 'he and I got on very well [...] He asked me if I would do a PhD, and I didn't hesitate for a moment'.[115] The book from Whitwell's thesis, *The Treasury Line*, analysed the foundations of Australia's economic policy, particularly the ideas of Treasury policymakers.[116]

Alan Beever and Katrina Alford also worked within orthodox and broader interdisciplinary frames. Beever was appointed to the University of Melbourne department in the late 1950s. He engaged with both the economics and history discipline in his work, writing for *Economic Record* an article critiquing Noel Butlin's 'numbers', and contributing to *Historical Studies* on archival sources for business history.[117] In his work for the *Australian Economic History Review*, Beever integrated different types of sources, drawing on official statistics as well as qualitative material in company reports and magazine articles.[118] Katrina Alford was supervised by the 'thoroughly scholarly' Beever for her DPhil in the late 1970s, recalling the 'relatively interdisciplinary perspective' of economic history in Melbourne as motivating her choice of specialty.[119] Alford's work on feminist economic history utilised qualitative sources such as correspondence, reports and images, and she illustrated her arguments through case studies of women's importance for the public and private labour force.[120] Alford engaged extensively with historians, acknowledging, in particular, assistance from members of the University of Melbourne history department. Alford was also competent in the work of the orthodox school, critiquing biased labour force estimates from colonial statisticians, and using this grounding through work as a research fellow in Butlin's economic history department in the 1980s (see Chapter 5).

---

115 Whitwell interview.
116 Greg Whitwell, *The Treasury Line* (Sydney: Allen & Unwin, 1986). Whitwell has argued that Boris suggested he study the Australian Treasury, and influenced his approach to understanding the intellectual paradigms of policymakers. See Whitwell interview.
117 E Alan Beever, 'The Clyde Company Papers', *Historical Studies* 15, no. 61 (1973): 760–70, doi.org/10.1080/10314617308595504 ; E Alan Beever, 'The Australian Wool Clip 1861–1900', *Economic Record* 39, no. 88 (1963): 437, doi.org/10.1111/j.1475-4932.1963.tb01500.x.
118 See, for example, E Alan Beever, 'The Pre-Gold Economic Boom in Australia 1843–1851', *Australian Economic History Review* 19, no. 1 (1979): 1–25, doi.org/10.1111/aehr.191001.
119 Alford interview.
120 Alford interview; Katrina Alford, *Production or Reproduction? An Economic History of Women in Australia, 1788–1850* (Melbourne: Oxford University Press, 1984).

Historian Graeme Davison also connected mainstream economic history to the history discipline. Davison trained as a historian, with a philosophy, politics and economics degree from Oxford, then attended ANU for his doctorate in urban history. When he arrived, La Nauze – who was by that stage the head of the RSSS history department – took him to the tea room to meet Noel Butlin:

> What I hadn't realised was that there had been a discussion beforehand of whether I really belonged under Butlin's supervision, or with La Nauze – Butlin had a strong claim for saying he was the urban man [...] So we went down and Butlin began in his abrupt way by saying 'now what are you interested in? Are you interested in people or things?' [...] I then probably eventually said something like 'well I'm sort of interested in both, but when it comes down to it, I am probably interested in people'. And after that he sort of haruffed and said 'well I guess you'd better stay with La Nauze'.[121]

Davison retained his engagement in economic history throughout his career, collaborating with economic historians from within the history departments at the universities of Melbourne and Monash. Davison attended the Monash economic history seminars, and several scholars remembered interactions despite him being in a different department.[122] His primary foray into economic history was *The Rise and Fall of Marvellous Melbourne* – a book loosely based on his ANU thesis, in which he, like Merrett, Dingle and Jackson, critiqued Butlin's orthodox work regarding home ownership and urbanisation.[123] Davison has since recalled (with Dingle's agreement) that his thesis was quantitative and statistical, being influenced by the orthodox school environment in which it was completed.[124] While the monograph that emerged a decade later toned down the statistics, its place in the Australian history canon demonstrates the importance of economic and social history for the discipline at this time.

John P. Fogarty was hired to the University of Melbourne in the 1960s, and in the 1980s he led a comparative approach to Australian economic history. Fogarty co-supervised Tim Duncan in the early 1980s (alongside

---

121 Dingle/Davison interview.
122 Schedvin; Dingle/Davison; Merrett interviews.
123 Graeme Davison, *The Rise and Fall of Marvellous Melbourne* (Melbourne: Melbourne University Press, 1978).
124 Dingle/Davison interview.

Argentinian historian Ezequiel Gallo at the Instituto Torcuato di Tella in Buenos Aires), and in 1984 they published *Australia and Argentina: On Parallel Paths*. The book aimed to represent the 'current state of a scholarly relationship between the two countries', with the authors adopting a broad socio-political interpretation.[125] Rather than applying economic theory to understand comparative development, the authors used secondary and qualitative sources to argue that different political systems – Australia with a stable democratic government and Argentina with an unstable totalitarian government – encouraged a divergence in their progress. Their approach was seen as 'interesting and informative' by McCarty, though was not to the taste of those based within economics, such as Maddock, who dismissed the volume as 'not to be read closely for its economics or economic history'.[126] Prompted by their connections to Fogarty in Melbourne, the following year Dingle and Merrett (on behalf of the Economic History Society of Australia and New Zealand) edited a collection of essays comparing economic development in Australia and Argentina. The volume emerged from a 1982 symposium organised in conjunction with British economist Kenneth Boulding's visit to the University of Melbourne.[127] Boulding outlined a theoretical framework of possible reasons for divergence between the two countries; Fogarty compared Australia and Argentina on the basis of rural export industry productivity; and Duncan argued that differences in the party system in each nation created divergences in performance.[128] Schedvin finally commented that while there were differences in resource endowments and political relationships between the two countries from 1930, it was cultural norms (which may have then manifested as policy) that was

---

125 Tim Duncan and John Fogarty, *Australia and Argentina: On Parallel Paths* (Melbourne: Melbourne University Press, 1984), xiii.
126 Rod Maddock, 'Review: Duncan and Fogarty, *Australia and Argentina*', *Economic Record* 61, no. 174 (1985): 685, doi.org/10.1111/j.1475-4932.1985.tb02022.x; John W McCarty, 'Review: Duncan and Fogarty, *Australia and Argentina*', *Australian Economic History Review* 26, no. 2 (1986): 196, doi.org/10.1111/aehr.262br10.
127 Anthony E Dingle and David T Merrett, eds, *Argentina and Australia: Essays in Comparative Economic Development* (Clayton: Economic History Society of Australia and New Zealand, 1985), iii.
128 Specifically, nationalism and isolationism in Argentinian politics (with no institutional political checks) led to, at different times, creative or destructive outcomes for the economy. In Australia, bureaucracy and interest-based parties led to steady but mildly disappointing economic performance. John Fogarty, 'The Role of the Export Sector in Industrialisation: The Australian and Argentine Experience Compared', in Dingle and Merrett, *Argentina and Australia*, 19–36. See also Kenneth E Boulding, 'Internal and External Influences on Development', in Dingle and Merrett, *Argentina and Australia*, 1–18; Tim Duncan, 'Australia and Argentina: A Tale of Two Political Cultures', in Dingle and Merrett, *Argentina and Australia*, 37–56.

the deciding factor.¹²⁹ In each contribution, the approach was broad – authors engaged with orthodox aggregated quantitative material, as well as extensive case studies of political figures, institutions and culture.

The field's main professional structures were populated with Melbourne scholars, and they used this as an avenue to develop interdisciplinary connections. The *Australian Economic History Review* was established in 1956 as the *Bulletin of the Business Archives Council of Australia*. It was an attempt to 'form a bridge between business people and the academic researcher interested in the development of Australian business and the economy'.¹³⁰ The name changed to *Business Archives and History* in 1962, at which time the scope of the journal widened, and editorship passed from Alan Birch to John McCarty, both then at the University of Sydney. From 1966, the journal was formally transferred to the Department of Economics at the University of Sydney, and the name was changed to the *Review*. Boris Schedvin, also then at the University of Sydney, joined McCarty as editor, and they noted that the name change was, in part, because the journal had developed as 'the specialist journal of economic history in Australia'.¹³¹ In 1974 ownership and management of the journal was again transferred, this time from the University of Sydney to the newly formed Economic History Society of Australia and New Zealand. The EHSANZ now owned the publication: they used its pages to report on meetings, and the editors used the society's annual conference to solicit articles. The *Review* was thus largely seen as the 'military arm' of EHSANZ activities. Scholars in Melbourne – including Schedvin, McCarty, Sinclair, Merrett and Dingle – took charge of the journal throughout the 1970s and 1980s, with other editors spread across Australia.¹³²

Those in Melbourne used the *Review* to advance their idea of what economic history should be. McCarty and Schedvin forged the intellectual character of the journal in the 1960s, encouraging a mixture of approaches, from more general historical discussions, to traditional accounts of the development of industries, through to quantitative approaches concerning

---

129 C Boris Schedvin, 'Australia and Argentina: Responses to Instability and Industrialisation 1930–1960', in Dingle and Merrett, *Argentina and Australia*, 57–76.
130 Stephen Morgan and Martin Shanahan, 'The Supply of Economic History in Australasia: The *Australian Economic History Review* at 50', *Australian Economic History Review* 50, no. 3 (2010): 217–39, 217, doi.org/10.1111/j.1467-8446.2010.00303.x.
131 'Editorial Note', *Australian Economic History Review* 6, no. 2 (1966): 203.
132 Ginswick and Rimmer in Sydney, Pincus in Adelaide, and Snooks in Adelaide and Canberra.

sources of growth.[133] Sinclair, for the 1970s, similarly argued that he did not encourage any particular 'style' of economic history, and Merrett for the 1980s reflected that the journal was particularly important for 'experimentation' in the field as it emerged.[134] A number of minor edited collections reflected the group's research interests and approach, including the socio-political interpretation in Dingle and Merrett's collection on Australia and Argentina (see above). In the 1970s, McCarty and Schedvin also edited two collections on Australian urban history. The first was a reprint of the September 1970 issue of the journal, at which time McCarty and Schedvin were editors.[135] The second, in 1978, reprinted the essays by McCarty, Davison and Sydney-based urban historian Max J. Kelly. They also added several 'urban biographies', as well as new essays by Merrett and Meredith Thomas.[136] Melbourne economic historians represented most contributors, with essays diverse in approach through the use of orthodox quantitative statistics and qualitative sources such as newspapers and city council reports. Although the diverse remit of the journal and society made for connections across the interdisciplinary divide, it faced criticism with, for example, Schedvin recalling that Adelaide economic historian Ralph Shlomowitz 'used to get stuck into us, saying "this is a dreadful journal, it should all be like [Robert] Fogel"'.[137]

Global Sydney

The tendency to hire from overseas in the 1970s, particularly in New South Wales (University of Sydney, UNSW and UNE), created a separate enclave of expats in the field. Although the shared experience of immigrating to Australia as young men bonded those at UNSW,[138] as with the other enclaves the trade-off was that members had comparatively little interest contributing to the research or professional structures of the Australian

---

133 Morgan and Shanahan, 'Supply of Economic History'; Jonathan Pincus and Graeme Snooks, 'The Past and Future Role of the *Australian Economic History Review*: Editorial Reflections and Aspirations', *Australian Economic History Review* 28, no 2 (1988): 3–7, doi.org/10.1111/aehr.282001.
134 Sinclair; Merrett interviews.
135 C Boris Schedvin and John W McCarty, eds, *Urbanization in Australia: The Nineteenth Century* (Sydney: Sydney University Press, 1974). Other authors: Bob Jackson, Sean Glynn and Weston Bate represented ANU; Maurice T Daly and Max Kelly were from Sydney (Macquarie University and UNSW, respectively); and Davison, Schedvin and McCarty were from Monash University.
136 John W McCarty and C Boris Schedvin, eds, *Australian Capital Cities: Historical Essays* (Sydney: Sydney University Press, 1978).
137 Schedvin interview.
138 Shergold has recalled a lively social scene among the younger members of the department in the 1970s and 1980s. Shergold interview.

group. For example, UNSW hosted the largest single department of economic history in the country, and yet, with the exception of David Pope and Barrie Dyster, members rarely wrote Australian economic history. They contributed book reviews to the *Australian Economic History Review*, but wrote a grand total of three research articles for the field's flagship journal throughout the 1970s and 1980s.[139] Diane Hutchinson has commented that during her doctorate in the late 1970s, she was the sole representative at a conference held by the society at the University of Sydney only a few suburbs from their home base. At UNE, similarly, research interests were largely elsewhere, with economic historians R. A. Cage, Ron Neale and Graydon R. Henning regularly contributing book reviews, but only one research article each across the two decades.[140] Overseas hires at the University of Sydney similarly had no research articles in the *Review* over these two decades, though they were very productive in international professional communities.

While certainly clustered in Sydney, this phenomenon also occurred elsewhere. For example, Eric Jones at La Trobe had a prominent international reputation and was an encouraging colleague within his department, but rarely contributed to the *Review* or other professional structures such as the EHSANZ.[141] Vamplew, at Flinders, has similarly argued that, beyond editing the bicentennial statistical volume in the 1980s, he had 'little to do with [the *Review*] as I focussed my teaching and research on Britain and looked towards British and European journals'.[142] Reginald 'Reg' Appleyard was well placed to advocate for Perth's economic historians – he saw economic history as an essential part of economics education, and was both the head of economics and the foundational Chair in Economic History at the University of Western Australia. However, he was, in his own words, a 'fly in fly out Professor', often overseas advocating for the internationalisation of the academic

---

139 Peter R Shergold, 'The Walker Thesis Revisited: Immigration and White American Fertility, 1800–60', *Australian Economic History Review* 14, no. 2 (1974): 168–89, doi.org/10.1111/aehr.142005; John Perkins, 'German Shipping and Australia before the First World War', *Australian Economic History Review* 29, no. 1 (1989): 42–59, doi.org/10.1111/aehr.291003; John Perkins, 'Rehearsal for Protectionism: Australian Wool Exports and German Agriculture, 1830–80', *Australian Economic History Review* 25, no. 1 (1985): 20–38, doi.org/10.1111/aehr.251002.

140 RA Cage, 'The Origins of Poor Relief in New South Wales: An Account of the Benevolent Society, 1809–62', *Australian Economic History Review* 20, no. 2 (1980): 153–69, doi.org/10.1111/aehr.202004; RS Neale et al., 'Life and Death in Hillgrove 1870–1914', *Australian Economic History Review* 21, no. 2 (1981): 91–113, doi.org/10.1111/aehr.212001.

141 Nicholas interview.

142 Vamplew correspondence, 19 October 2019.

and student base, rather than developing research and teaching capacity among economic historians.¹⁴³ These scholars were all productive, but actively pursued professional communities elsewhere.

In Sydney, the UNSW 'Convict Workers' project was a turning point. Their attitude changed, with Shergold reflecting:

> it wasn't until you had a group of economic historians who clearly realised they were going to stay in Australia [...] that then you start to think 'well if I'm here, I'm going to start doing some Australian work'.¹⁴⁴

Nicholas and Shergold led the project, integrating the Australian archive into the very fashionable global slavery literature – particularly US cliometricians Robert Fogel and Stanley Engermann's *Time on the Cross*.¹⁴⁵ Their methodological choice was motivated by existing abilities, in addition to its recognition in the metropole if they decided to move on. Nicholas had trained in the 'new' economic history from his time at Toronto in the early 1970s, and Shergold had experience in the statistical analysis of wages and labour.¹⁴⁶ Shergold's wife was an archivist at the State Library of New South Wales, which held extensive convict indents. When one of the UNSW faculty members went on two years unpaid leave, the dean encouraged the group to spend the money on a project that included as many members as possible.¹⁴⁷ The result was digitised convict indents for the purposes of statistical economic analysis. *Convict Workers: Reinterpreting Australia's Past*, published in 1988, was grounded in the Australian context, though the authors rejected the 'curious insularity of much Australian history which treats transportation and convictism as peculiarly Australian'.¹⁴⁸ Nicholas, Shergold and Meredith's expertise on international slavery, immigration and British empire policy was combined with Dyster and DPhil student Deborah Oxley's Australian perspective. There were comparisons with both the experience

---

143 John Bannister, *Reginald Appleyard interview*, 13 December 2013, 2 January 2014, 8 January 2014 and 14 January 2014, University of Western Australia Historical Society, oralhistories.arts.uwa.edu.au/items/show/42.
144 Shergold interview.
145 Robert W Fogel and Stanley L Engerman. *Time on the Cross: The Economics of American Negro Slavery* (Boston: Little, Brown and Company, 1974).
146 Nicholas; Shergold; Dyster; Oxley/Meredith interviews.
147 Oxley/Meredith interview.
148 Stephen Nicholas and Peter R Shergold 'Unshackling the Past', in *Convict Workers: Reinterpreting Australia's Past*, ed. Stephen Nicholas (Melbourne: Cambridge University Press, 1988), 3–13, 4, doi.org/10.1017/CBO9781139084840.003.

of free workers in Britain, and with other forms of coerced labour such as Indian/Melanese bonded workers, American slaves, and other convicts. In particular, the authors argued that the aims of convict transportation, the characteristics of convicts, and the work done when they arrived, was similar across the British Empire, India and a number of other European powers at the time.[149] Although Shlomowitz – who had engaged with the slavery literature using a similar method – took umbrage with Nicholas's characterisation of class and the system of labour assignment, *Convict Workers* did much to engage Australian economic history with frontier global research.[150] In reflection of this, Oxley has remembered that, at the time, the team jokingly suggested they should call the volume *Time on the Southern Cross*.[151]

Heterodox perspectives

In addition to professional and intellectual disagreement between members of economic history departments based in different locations, longstanding interest in the subject from political economists and labour historians contributed to further diversity of members' efforts. Political economy and labour history have been adjacent interdisciplinary fields, managing their own relationships with parent disciplines. Both have sought to understand the structure of the economy from a heterodox or critical perspective, particularly the way that capitalism naturalises a potentially unhelpful set of ideologies and practices. Both fields grew out of the post–World War II expansion of higher education. Work in labour history had drawn from activism and the organised labour movement since the late nineteenth century, with the field institutionalised within burgeoning departments of Australian history from the 1960s to the

---

149 Stephen Nicholas and Peter R Shergold, 'Transportation as Global Migration', in Nicholas, *Convict Workers*, 28–41, 38–39, doi.org/10.1017/CBO9781139084840.005.
150 Ralph Shlomowitz, 'The Search for Institutional Equilibrium in Queensland's Sugar Industry 1884–1913', *Australian Economic History Review* 19, no. 2 (1979): 91–122, doi.org/10.1111/aehr.192001; Ralph Shlomowitz, 'The Profitability of Indentured Melanesian Labour in Queensland', *Australian Economic History Review* 22, no. 1 (1982): 49–67, doi.org/10.1111/aehr.221003. For his review of *Convict Workers*, see Ralph Shlomowitz, '*Convict Workers*: A Review Article', *Australian Economic History Review* 30, no. 2 (1990): 67–88, doi.org/10.1111/aehr.302005; Stephen Nicholas, 'Understanding *Convict Workers*', *Australian Economic History Review* 31, no. 2 (1991): 95–105, doi.org/10.1111/aehr.312005; Ralph Shlomowitz, 'Convict Transportees: Casual or Professional Criminals?', *Australian Economic History Review* 31, no. 2 (1991): 106–8, doi.org/10.1111/aehr.312006; Stephen Nicholas, 'Matters of Fact: Convict Transportees Were Not Members of the Criminal Class', *Australian Economic History Review* 31, no. 2 (1991): 109, doi.org/10.1111/aehr.312007.
151 Oxley/Meredith interview.

1980s.¹⁵² The Australian Society for the Study of Labour History was formed in 1961, with the journal *Bulletin for the Society of Labour History* (later *Labour History*) produced by this society from 1962. Although often drawing on similar archives and data sets as orthodox economic historians, labour historians were aligned with the core of the history discipline, particularly the 'new social history' in Australia and overseas, as well as activist-scholarship in political economy, industrial relations, sociology, politics and women's studies.¹⁵³

Along similar lines, Australian political economy research stemmed from increased interest in radical social science and the New Left from the early 1970s. Like labour historians, political economists were encouraged by the revitalisation of interest in Australian politics and class following the end of the postwar Menzies era and election of the progressive Whitlam government. This field did not experience a 'departmental era'; instead they found their way through a variety of disciplinary groups. In 1975, Wheelwright and Buckley lamented the lack of alternative economic thought, particularly Marxism, taught within economics degrees, and reflected on the 'years of struggle' within the Department of Economics at the University of Sydney to establish 'alternative' economics units. The 'volatile', hostile dispute between mainstream and radical members of the economics department at Sydney conceded space to the field within the curriculum, but this was largely the exception rather than the rule.¹⁵⁴ Members of the political economy tradition were drawn from politics, sociology, labour history, international relations and so on, with some – like Kenneth 'Ken' Buckley at the University of Sydney, Philip McMichael at UNE, Dave Clark at UNSW and Andrew Wells at ANU – working for a time within economic history departments. The *Journal of Australian Political Economy* was established in 1977 as a meeting place for these conversations.

---

152 Frank Bongiorno, 'Australian Labour History: Contexts, Trends and Influences', *Labour History* 100, no. 1 (2011): 1–19, doi.org/10.5263/labourhistory.100.0001; Ben Maddison, '"The Day of the Just Reasoner": TA Coghlan and the Labour Public Sphere in Late Nineteenth Century Australia', *Labour History* 77 (1999): 11–26, doi.org/10.2307/27516667.
153 Forsyth and Loy-Wilson, 'New Materialism'; Raelene Frances and Bruce Scates, 'Is Labour History Dead?', *Australian Historical Studies* 25, no. 100 (1993): 470–81, doi.org/10.1080/10314619308595930; Eric Fry, 'The Labour History Society (ASSLH): A Memoir of Its First Twenty Years', *Labour History* 77 (1999): 83–96, doi.org/10.2307/27516671.
154 A separate department in political economy was eventually established at the University of Sydney in 2008. See Groenewegen, *Educating for Business*; Gavan Butler, Evan Jones and Frank JB Stilwell, *Political Economy Now! The Struggle for Alternative Economics at the University of Sydney* (Sydney: Darlington Press, 2009). Schedvin interview.

Heterodox histories of the economy incorporated political, social and cultural perspectives with an understanding of economic forces. Scholars were explicit about the ideology that shaped economic analyses, incorporated the State as an actor in Australia's economic system, and had an interest in power relations and class conflict.[155] The key proponents of historical political economy were E. L. 'Ted' Wheelwright and Buckley, both of whom were at the University of Sydney throughout the 1970s and 1980s. In their co-edited *Essays in the Political Economy of Australian Capitalism*, published between 1975 and 1983, scholars from a range of disciplines examined the nature and progress of Australian capitalism. As with other intellectual movements, contributors sought to reappraise received wisdom from economists and economic historians on orthodox topics such as unemployment, wages, immigration, the role of the State, protectionist trade policies and the convict labour market. Dave Clark, a member of the UNSW economic history department from the early 1970s, worked in the orthodox space thematically by assessing Fitzpatrick and Noel Butlin's conclusions on the role of British capital and trade for the Australian economy. He argued that, although the 'Australian experience does not fit a vulgar model of imperialism', British capital and trade did contribute to some structural disadvantages.[156] These orthodox topics sat alongside labour, political and social history, including the progress of the labour movement, Australian imperialism in the Pacific, nationalism and regionalism, and issues relating to class, gender and ethnicity. Contributors did not seek to establish entirely new data series, but used a variety of intellectual frameworks, including Marxism, to reinterpret existing knowledge on their subject.

Wheelwright and Buckley then drew on these contributions in a more systematic and historical discussion, *No Paradise for Workers*, in which they analysed significant episodes in the history of the State's role within the economy. They accounted for Australian capitalism chronologically, with the underlying dialectic of class conflict between British capital and Australian labour, squatters and farmers, and trade unions and employees.

---

155 Ben Huf, 'Making Things Economic: Theory and Government in New South Wales, 1788–1863' (PhD thesis, The Australian National University, 2018).

156 David L Clark, 'Australia: Victim or Partner of British Imperialism', in *Essays in the Political Economy of Australian Capitalism*, Vol. 1, ed. Edward Lawrence Wheelwright and Kenneth D Buckley (Sydney: Australia and New Zealand Book Company, 1975), 47–71, 70; David L Clark, 'Unequal Exchange and Australian Economic Development: An Exploratory Investigation', in *Essays in the Political Economy of Australian Capitalism*, Vol. 3, ed. Edward Lawrence Wheelwright and Kenneth D Buckley (Sydney: Australia and New Zealand Book Company, 1978), 142–66.

Similar to orthodox scholars, Wheelwright and Buckley argued that the State had done more than just provide the legal and institutional framework through which producers and consumers operated, but was an economic actor in its own right.[157] Philip McMichael, a sociologist and lecturer in economic history at UNE in the late 1970s before a long and successful career in the US, also focused on the distinct way that settler capitalism emerged in Australia, through the lens of resource extraction and dispossession.[158] Much like Fitzpatrick in the 1940s, McMichael examined the uneven growth of the capitalist economy, particularly Britain's power over Australia's economic future. Historian Donald Denoon focused on the uneven balance of economic and political power in the global economy, with his *Settler Capitalism*, published in 1983, examining the development of settler societies – Australia, Argentina, Chile, New Zealand, Uruguay and South Africa – in the late nineteenth and early twentieth centuries. Denoon combined quasi-Ricardian international trade theory with Marxist socio-political analysis, examining both the role of staple exports and the 'relations between social classes as they interacted with political institutions'.[159] He accounted for differences between the tropical, non-white colonies in Africa, Asia and Latin America, and the largely temperate regions that became sites of mass European settlement.[160] Andrew Wells, in the book produced from his ANU thesis, examined the relationship between the market and the State. Wells adopted a Marxist frame to understand the formation of Australian capitalism, arguing that it was an uneven and gradual process of 'commodification' of societal relations.[161]

Although some of these heterodox scholars were based in departments of economic history, they were disconnected from the mainstream community. For example, although Buckley administered the *Australian Economic History Review* when it was based at Sydney in the 1960s, over

---

157 Kenneth D Buckley and Edward Lawrence Wheelwright, *No Paradise for Workers: Capitalism and the Common People in Australia, 1788–1914* (Melbourne: Oxford University Press, 1988).
158 Philip McMichael, *Settlers and the Agrarian Question: Capitalism in Colonial Australia* (Cambridge: Cambridge University Press, 1984), doi.org/10.1017/CBO9780511529139.
159 Donald Denoon, *Settler Capitalism: The Dynamics of Dependent Development in the Southern Hemisphere* (Oxford: Clarendon Press, 1983), 226.
160 Peter Beilharz and Lloyd Cox, 'Review Essay: *Settler Capitalism* Revisited', *Thesis Eleven* 88, no. 1 (2007): 112–24, doi.org/10.1177/0725513607072461.
161 Andrew Wells, *Constructing Capitalism: An Economic History of Eastern Australia, 1788–1901* (Sydney: Allen & Unwin, 1989); Huf, 'Making Things Economic'.

time he became less involved in mainstream structures.[162] Dave Clark, similarly, was a long-term member of the economic history department at UNSW, and although he attended the EHSANZ conferences, he never contributed to the *Review*. In *Settlers and the Agrarian Question*, McMichael acknowledged members of the Australian New Left scholarship such as Ken Buckley, Raewyn Connell and Terry Irving, rather than members of mainstream economic history.[163] Denoon worked at ANU in the 1980s and 1990s, although he was appointed to the Research School of Pacific Studies and did not integrate with the mainstream economic historians. Andrew Wells was trained in the ANU RSSS economic history group, under the supervision of Noel Butlin, Rod Maddock and labour historian Eric Fry. However, his collaboration and integration with the mainstream professional structures was limited.

When heterodox and mainstream economic historians did interact, it was often hostile. In 1975 and 1976, *Labour History* ran a series of articles where Snooks (representing mainstream economic history) went toe-to-toe with political economists Clark, Tim Rowse and Bruce McFarlane on the integration of Noel Butlin's work with a Marxist or heterodox socio-political frame.[164] Snooks argued that the New Left presented an inconsistency, as scholars rejected the models of mainstream economics, and yet based their own conclusions on orthodox economic history (which used Keynesian and neoclassical economic theory). Rowse, on the other hand, argued that Butlin's statistics could be accepted for their merits, while still applying a Marxist frame to interpret the evidence. Clark disagreed with both Snooks and Rowse, arguing that rather than accept or reject Butlin's conclusions, a radical challenge to Butlin's authority was necessary to write an authoritative Marxist economic history of Australia.[165] Clark, a self-confessed radical post-Keynesian, was a source of conflict between the two streams. While Hutchinson has recalled his 'refreshing' approach to research and teaching, for the most part he has been remembered as a

---

162 Buckley supervised Boris Schedvin's PhD, though Schedvin has recalled that he was only 'sort of' involved. He also hardly ever contributed to the journal.
163 McMichael, *Settlers*, xvi.
164 David L Clark, 'Marx Versus Butlin: Some Comments on the Snooks–Rowse Debate', *Labour History*, no. 30 (1976): 58–65, doi.org/10.2307/27508217; Graeme Snooks, 'Orthodox and Radical Interpretations of the Development of Australian Capitalism', *Labour History*, no. 28 (1975): 1–11, doi.org/10.2307/27508159; Tim Rowse, 'Facts, Theories and Ideology: A Comment on Graeme Snooks', *Labour History*, no. 28 (1975): 12–17, doi.org/10.2307/27508160; Bruce McFarlane, 'The Use of Economic Theory in History: Snooks Snookered', *Labour History*, no. 31 (1976): 83–85, doi.org/10.2307/27508240.
165 Clark, 'Marx Versus Butlin'.

very loud, very critical scholar, as someone who was difficult to get along with, and who 'impaired' or 'spoiled' the conferences for everyone else.[166] He also criticised the *Australian Economic History Review*, understandably, for not engaging with political economy approaches, and noted the 'limited utility' of most economic history research for understanding Australian capitalism.[167]

Ideological battlelines were also drawn around the role of the State. The Canberrans advocated mainstream economic theory in their institutional work. In the image of Schedvin's *Australia and the Great Depression*, contributors to Noel Butlin and Bob Gregory's *Recovery* adopted a Keynesian frame, assessing the extent to which government macro-economic management was successful in reducing the timing and extent of the depression, and the speed of recovery.[168] In *Government and Capitalism*, similarly, Butlin and Alan Barnard were both largely in favour of government intervention.[169] Maddock and McLean's edited work, on the other hand, had a neoclassical, *laissez faire* message, arguing that government policies either constrained private activity or made the private sector inefficient.[170] There was some conflict between mainstream institutional scholars based on their advocacy for a Keynesian or neoclassical message, with Pincus recalling that his collaboration with Butlin and Barnard on *Government and Capitalism* was not always a happy one.[171] While Butlin and Barnard saw government intervention as necessary and progressive, Pincus saw public enterprise as inefficient, monopolistic and semi-exploitative.[172] The latter garnered an apparently 'hysterical' reaction from the great sons of postwar reconstruction. Regardless, for those working in mainstream institutional economic history, the efficiency of the market was at the forefront of their analysis, and State action was seen as helping or hindering market operations. This primarily spoke to contemporary economic theory, which reflected the alignment of many economic historians in Canberra with the economics discipline.

---

166 Hutchinson; Schedvin; Dingle; Nicholas interviews. See also Peter Groenewegen and John Lodewijks, 'Dave Clark (1946–2008): Economist, Larrikin, "Critical Drinker" and Friend', *Agenda: A Journal of Policy Analysis and Reform* 15, no. 3 (2008): 101–4, doi.org/10.22459/AG.15.03.2008.08.
167 Clark, 'Marx Versus Butlin', 61; Clark, 'Unequal Exchange', 142.
168 Gregory and Butlin, *Recovery*, preface; Schedvin, *Australia and the Great Depression*.
169 Butlin et al., *Government and Capitalism*.
170 Maddock and McLean, *The Australian Economy in the Long Run*.
171 Pincus interview.
172 For Pincus's take, see Butlin et al., *Government and Capitalism*, 237–39. This was similar to his assessment in *The Australian Economy in the Long Run*. See Jonathan J Pincus, 'Government', in Maddock and McLean, *The Australian Economy in the Long Run*, 291–317.

Buckley and Wheelwright, on the other hand, advocated for a State that engaged in heavy redistribution of income and a deliberate agenda of improving the lives of common people. They criticised the State for granting monopolies in the economy and for adopting policies that were in neither the long-run economic interest of the nation, nor the interest of common people. Wheelwright outwardly objected to the mainstream institutional approach from the Canberrans, criticising the lack of theory of the capitalist state in *Government and Capitalism*. He commented that 'the deliberate neglect of Marxist approaches is both unscholarly and incredibly self-limiting'.[173] Similarly, Katrina Alford in Melbourne criticised Pincus's adherence to neoclassical economics and the lack of consideration given to the school's 'many substantial criticisms'.[174] From the mainstream economic historians, Schedvin has recalled that Wheelwright was 'trapped' in the Marxist frame of 'mocking the class system', while dismissing Buckley as an '*old fashioned* labour historian'.[175]

A fragmented community

The expansion of Australia's higher education sector – and the importance of both business education and compulsory subjects in economic history – created unprecedented institutional space for the field in the 1960s, 1970s and 1980s. Rather than being embedded in larger economics or history groups, members were instead placed in small, separate departments. This encouraged something akin to 'disciplinary' growth, with strong collaboration and the development of a similar approach within each enclave. These enclaves demonstrated different disciplinary affiliations, with tension between factions and very little sense of joint enterprise. Professional structures like the *Australian Economic History Review* and the Economic History Society of Australia and New Zealand provided communicating infrastructures between parent disciplines and the different communities, though commitment to these activities varied. Overall,

---

173 Edward Lawrence Wheelwright, 'Review: Butlin, Barnard and Pincus, *Government and Capitalism*', *Economic Record* 59, no. 167 (1983): 408.
174 Katrina Alford, 'Economy and State. A Review of N.G. Butlin, A. Barnard, and J.J. Pincus *Government and Capitalism: Public and Private Choice in Twentieth Century Australia*', *Journal of Australian Political Economy*, no. 14 (1983): 90.
175 Schedvin interview, emphasis mine.

there was uneven integration with parent disciplines, with the place of departments in economics groups encouraging most groups to resemble a subfield of that discipline rather than an interdisciplinary operation.

Rather than the 'rise' part of the traditional narrative of Australian economic history, understanding this era in terms of the sociology of university structures highlights the risk of disciplinary growth for interdisciplinary fields. The fragmented community and unbalanced nature of integration was encouraged by small departments and dense hierarchical connections. While these departments did contribute to the field's stability and command over resources, professional isolation was inappropriate for a connected domain of knowledge like economic history. As such, the field was vulnerable to the institutional, intellectual and leadership challenges that occurred in the 1990s, with *Review* editors Pincus and Snooks expressing a premonition that 'the future of economic history [...] may well depend upon whether we can present a united front to those who covet the resources we now control'.[176]

---

176 Pincus and Snooks, 'Editorial Reflections', 5.

5

The resistance

> It is a harrowing experience being in a tiny group whose survival is constantly threatened, and it is depressing when your audience – of students and colleagues – is perpetually small.
>
> Greg Whitwell, 1997[1]

In late 1997, authors for a special issue of the *Australian Economic History Review* mourned the death of Australian economic history. Stephen Nicholas, Greg Whitwell and Chris Lloyd discussed the current state and possible futures for the field. They were acutely aware of their status as the 'poor cousins' of business faculties, and that their careers were characterised by a 'vain quest for students and recognition'.[2] The future of teaching economic history was 'bleak', it was 'impossible' for economic history to attract students on its own, and it was altogether far too late to convince other disciplines of the subject's pedagogical relevance.[3] Members of the field have spoken like soldiers at war – they recalled fending off 'attacks', they were 'defeated in battle' and they felt they were the 'collateral damage' of the institutional changes around them.[4] Despite this, many still had fight left in them, acknowledging their role in, as Barrie Dyster put it, 'the resistance'.

---

1 Greg Whitwell, 'Future Directions for the *Australian Economic History Review*', *Australian Economic History Review* 37, no. 3 (1997): 275–81, doi.org/10.1111/aehr.373007.
2 Whitwell, 'Future Directions', 276.
3 Stephen Nicholas, 'The Future of Economic History in Australia', *Australian Economic History Review* 37, no. 3 (1997): 270–71, doi.org/10.1111/aehr.373006.
4 Dyster; Frost; Ville; Keneley interviews with author. Unless otherwise specified, interviews cited are those conducted by the author: see Appendix for details.

It was the end of economic history's moment in the sun. The field had had around 20 years of stability – between finalising the 'full suite' of departments in the early 1970s, to the contraction of appointments from the early 1990s. Within just over a decade there were no departments left: La Trobe added its department in 1990, but lost it again only two years later. Flinders lost their department the same year, Monash followed in 1993, Melbourne in 1995, the University of New South Wales (UNSW) in 1996, The Australian National University (ANU) Research School of Social Sciences (RSSS) and the University of New England (UNE) in 1998, the RSSS Faculties in 2000 and finally Sydney in 2003.[5] The loss of departments meant that vacant chairs and appointments went unfilled, and students were rarely exposed to economic history in the curriculum. This cut off the main pipeline for generational renewal. When elder members of the field moved on to larger governance roles, retired or, sadly, passed on, there were very few scholars coming through at the entry level to replace them.[6] There were small numbers hired from PhD programs, and some recruited from overseas, but the number of dedicated appointments in Australia declined from a peak of 56 in 1982, to seven at the end of the millennium and zero shortly after. As Alford has argued, economic history was 'declared effectively at the status of the yellow-bellied potoroo by the early 2000s'.[7]

The focus on departments and dedicated appointments as measures of economic history's progress has resulted in despondent reflections on this time. Whether writing or speaking during the 1990s or later, this period is generally considered 'the fall' part of the narrative.[8] Economic history has been seen as largely passive to institutional changes, unable to stem the tide of modern neoliberal universities. There is very little discussion of the challenges that the field, in part, created, and no systematic assessment of the extent of intellectual disconnect between economic history and its parent disciplines. This chapter reimagines this period of the field's history, seeing members as active participants rather than passive agents.

---

5   See Appendix, based on Commonwealth University Calendars. I have quoted a year range here, because the departments were closed or merged at some point between the survey for one Calendar and the next.
6   This issue, in part, preceded the loss of departments, with very few domestic postgraduate students, and a general hiring freeze from around 1980. See Chapter 4.
7   Alford interview.
8   David Meredith and Deborah Oxley, 'The Rise and Fall of Australian Economic History', in *Routledge Handbook of Global Economic History*, ed. Francesco Boldizzoni and Pat Hudson (London: Routledge, 2015), 73–94, doi.org/10.4324/9781315734736.

In examining the reasons for the crisis, it attends to the combination of intellectual and leadership factors that compounded the challenging Dawkins-era environment. It also assesses, for the first time, the initiatives taken by members of the field to ensure that, once the crisis had passed, there still was an economic history field in Australia. As with the period prior to the Butlin revolution, this chapter and the next encourages us to consider the success of interdisciplinary fields in broader terms than simply those dictated by disciplines.

The crisis in Australian economic history

Institutional

Economic history was one of many casualties of Australia's neoliberal higher education reform. John Dawkins was appointed the federal minister for education, employment and training in Bob Hawke's Labor government from 1987, and he swiftly set about seeking advice from a select group of higher education leaders about policy reform. Dawkins and his team published their green paper in the same year, and the 1988 white paper of proposed reform is 'memorialised by the higher education sector like a kind of perverted Bastille Day'.[9] The suite of policies was intended to increase capacity and upgrade the skills of the workforce, as the foundation for a flexible, innovative, resourceful knowledge economy. Similar trends were experienced in many other Western countries from the 1980s onwards, built on the principles of the 'New Public Management', which argued that academics, like other professionals, require monitoring and incentives to improve their performance.[10] The Dawkins reforms were

---

9   Hannah Forsyth, 'The Ownership of Knowledge in Higher Education in Australia 1939–1996' (PhD thesis, University of Sydney, 2012), 203; Stuart Macintyre, Andre Brett and Gwilym Croucher, *No End of a Lesson: Australia's Unified National System of Higher Education* (Melbourne: Melbourne University Press, 2017).
10 Peter Woelert and Lyn Yates, 'Too Little and Too Much Trust: Performance Measurement in Australian Higher Education', *Critical Studies in Education* 56, no. 2 (2015): 175–89, doi.org/10.1080/17508487.2014.943776; Jill Blackmore, Marie Brennan and Lew Zipin, *Re-Positioning University Governance and Academic Work* (Rotterdam: Sense Publishers, 2010), doi.org/10.1163/9789460911743; S Marginson and M Considine, *The Enterprise University: Power, Governance and Reinvention in Australia* (Cambridge: Cambridge University Press, 2000); Hugh Lauder et al., *Educating for the Knowledge Economy? Critical Perspectives* (London: Routledge, 2012); Evan Schofer and John W Meyer, 'The Worldwide Expansion of Higher Education in the Twentieth Century', *American Sociological Review* 70, no. 6 (2005): 898–920, doi.org/10.1177/000312240507000602.

also designed in an environment of neoliberal policy reform, dominant from the 1980s, which sought to make existing markets wider, and create new markets where they did not exist before.[11]

The Dawkins reforms introduced deregulation and competition, treating each university like any other trading entity in a free market. Institutions began to compete for student income through a new system of tertiary fees (Higher Education Contribution Scheme [HECS]), with Dawkins hoping that a competitive teaching environment would encourage institutions to diversify courses, respond to signals from the job market, and improve the quality, relevance and usefulness of their instruction. The result was a vastly different higher education sector. Smaller institutions were amalgamated, technical colleges were converted into universities, and student numbers almost doubled in the decade to 1996.[12] Universities also expanded their competition for federal research funds through the newly formed Australian Research Council (ARC). Formal measurement systems were used to evaluate performance and distribute funding based on alignment with national and market priorities, in the hope that it would encourage higher quality and more 'useful' research.[13]

These reforms moved universities towards commercial language and corporate techniques designed to make the most of these new 'markets' for students and research. Collegial structures gave way to the control of managers and executives, where power lay with those administering the budget rather than those conducting the university's core business. Students were paying for their education, so they became 'customers' or 'consumers' of the university 'product'; a product that now needed to be branded and valued on the market. Research was evaluated in terms of traditional peer review, inter- and intranational rankings, in addition to the new, literal dollar amount it was able to bring to the university's bottom line. Rather than the guardians of independent knowledge and the public good, universities came to resemble corporations.

Corporatised universities, particularly the competition for students, were hostile terrain for Australia's economic historians. Throughout the postwar period, scholars' research in economic history was largely supported by

---

11   Raewyn Connell, 'The Neoliberal Cascade and Education: An Essay on the Market Agenda and Its Consequences', *Critical Studies in Education* 54, no. 2 (2013): 99–112, doi.org/10.1080/175084 87.2013.776990.
12   Hannah Forsyth, *A History of the Modern Australian University* (Sydney: University of New South Wales Press, 2014); Schofer and Meyer, 'Worldwide Expansion'.
13   Woelert and Yates, 'Too Little and Too Much Trust'.

their teaching activities – by large introductory courses elected or required for economics and business degrees. Some of these first-year students flowed through to upper-level undergraduate and postgraduate education, maintaining the student base, and the steady generational renewal of economic historians (see Chapter 4). The introduction of student fee income meant that departments and faculties now actively competed for students. Previously, electives across faculties were encouraged, and provided a good space for economic historians to operate. They were able to leverage both the compulsory subjects within economics or commerce degrees, and the more casual interest from history or politics students.[14] Several economic historians identified the 'ideological shift' in university management towards efficiency, competition and market forces.[15] Electives across faculties were discouraged to maintain each group's income. Often these 'trade barriers' were subtle – faculties did not necessarily prevent students from taking certain subjects, but they changed the prerequisites or credit points to make it very inconvenient to take courses elsewhere.[16]

The Scottish model, already dominant within Australian universities, became more robust under Dawkins. The emphasis on vocational education encouraged degrees tied to professional accreditation, with students in accounting, management and finance expanding quickly, while subjects in economics suffered. For example, the number of business students in Australia trebled in the 1990s and 2000s, whereas economics enrolments consistently declined.[17] Further, much of the expansion of business enrolments at Australian universities was from international students, who paid higher fees.[18] In neoliberal universities, whoever has the students has the money, and whoever has the money has the power. Those in the newer business disciplines found themselves with the power to decide the curriculum of most commerce or business graduates.

---

14 Dyster interview.
15 Maddock; Lloyd; Dyster; Nicholas; Oxley/Meredith interviews.
16 Oxley/Meredith interview.
17 Roy Green, Marco Berti and Nicole Sutton, 'Higher Education in Management: The Case of Australia', in *The Future of Management Education*, ed. Stéphanie Dameron and Thomas Durand (London: Palgrave Macmillan, 2017), 117–37, doi.org/10.1057/978-1-137-56091-9_4; Alex Millmow, 'The Market for Economists in Australia', *Economic Papers* 14, no. 4 (1995): 83–96, doi.org/10.1111/j.1759-3441.1995.tb00110.x; Alex Millmow, 'Trends in Economic Degree Enrolments within Australia 1990–2004', *Australasian Journal of Economics Education* 3, no. 1 (2006): 111–24; Alex Millmow, 'The State We're In: University Economics 1989/1999', *Economic Papers* 19, no. 4 (2000): 43–51, doi.org/10.1111/j.1759-3441.2000.tb00974.x.
18 Green et al., 'Higher Education in Management'; Andrew Norton and Beni Cakitaki, *Mapping Australian Higher Education 2016* (Melbourne: The Grattan Institute, 2016), grattan.edu.au/wp-content/uploads/2016/08/875-Mapping-Australian-Higher-Education-2016.pdf.

Accounting and finance groups had very little interest in economics, and Nicholas rightly commented that 'economists will not protect us at the expense of their own discipline'.[19] Economic history became, partly, a pawn for economists to send to the front, to take the initial onslaught on budgets and student numbers. Lionel Frost has recalled the 'bitter divide' between members of the business faculty and the economists at La Trobe during the 1990s. The accountants apparently insisted that only a minimal amount of economics needed to be in the program. Under threat, and with their own challenges in attracting students, economists often responded first by removing first-year economic history requirements. At UNSW, the economic history group taught a quarter of compulsory first-year subjects in the Bachelor of Commerce throughout the 1970s and 1980s, along with several other second- and third-year courses. By the 1980s, Barrie Dyster has recalled, faculty management stripped away one of the compulsory subjects, and by 2000 students had a single (non-compulsory) economic history course.[20] In an exceptional case, members of the accounting discipline were allies for economic historians. Simon Ville, a British-born economic historian who, in 1991, migrated to Australia as the new head of the ANU Faculties department, has recalled making a deal with the accountants. The head of the Department of Accounting and Finance – accounting historian Russell Craig – was supportive of economic history, and Ville convinced him to support required first-year economics and economic history subjects. This essentially halved the compulsory economics students, and maintained those studying (and teaching) economic history. Apparently, the economists 'were just totally dumbstruck, they couldn't believe anybody could do something so wicked'.[21] This was the exception rather than the rule, with most compulsory economic history subjects squeezed out by new business courses and economics groups under threat, and alternative pathways through arts or social sciences degrees discouraged to maintain each group's budget.

New university structures also contributed to a reduction in the number of graduate students. This was, in part, through a lack of undergraduate subjects, with interest at the undergraduate level the way most entered the profession. Additionally, the territorial and increasingly credentialised nature of disciplines in Dawkins-era universities meant that students faced

---

19 Nicholas, 'The Future of Economic History', 268.
20 Dyster interview.
21 Ville interview.

new barriers to enrolling in an economic history doctorate from outside commerce or business faculties. Dyster has recalled that, although students would still find their way to his supervision through 'very circuitous routes', by the 1990s, the Commerce Faculty at UNSW would no longer accept them as graduate students, as they 'didn't have the prerequisites which the faculty now saw as crucial'.[22]

Research funding was a saving grace of Australian economic history at this time. During the Dawkins reforms, the government reduced the discretionary research funding given to universities, and increased funds allocated competitively through the ARC.[23] Although some ARC procedures reinforce disciplinary knowledge (see Chapter 6), funding played a major role in sustaining Australian economic history in the 1990s and 2000s. Ville has recalled that ARC funding allowed him to do most of his major research projects during the resistance.[24] ARC funding enabled Merrett and Ville's work on cartels and wool marketing, Frost's research on Australia's Inland Corridor, Andy Seltzer's research on labour markets, Nicholas's examination of foreign investment, and social and economic historian Hamish Maxwell-Stewart's work on convicts and anthropometric history. ARC projects also enabled major endeavours in Indigenous economic history at this time, as well as much of Oxley's early career work. For example, Oxley was awarded several ARC fellowships throughout the 1990s and 2000s, when there were very few lectureships advertised. Although Oxley identified the challenges of successive ARC positions – namely medium-term precarity and restricted career progression – it ultimately enabled her to develop a research profile through which she was awarded a post at Oxford in 2007.[25] The ARC was a lifeline for some, though on the whole the income generated by economic history departments was much less than required for academic salaries and administration costs. University managers – under their own pressure to balance budgets – saw 'deficit' departments such as economic history as non-essential and forced their closure.

---

22 Dyster interview.
23 The ARC was established in 1988. University medical research is funded separately through the National Health and Medical Research Council (the NHMRC).
24 Ville interview.
25 Oxley/Meredith interview.

Identity

The closure of departments was the most visible symptom of Dawkins-era change. It thus appeared to those observing that the poor fortunes of Australian economic history were primarily due to declining resources for higher education and the implementation of neoliberal policies. For example, in the 1997 special issue of the *Australian Economic History Review*, Nicholas argued that changes to universities meant there was no teaching future – and subsequently no departmental future – for economic history. Whitwell similarly invoked the funding gap between student income and staff costs as the primary reason for the closure of departments. Lloyd agreed that 'the crisis seems to be largely an institutional one', drawn from declining resources in the higher education sector and the politics of disciplinary rivalries.[26]

Members of the field had a short memory – in the late 1980s the editors of the *Review*, Pincus and Snooks, advocated for broader content and engagement as key to the field's future.[27] They were right to be concerned. As outlined in the previous chapter, with the exception of those in Melbourne, Australia's economic historians published work that was increasingly tied to the interests and methods of the economics discipline. Particularly in the 1980s, major joint projects out of ANU and UNSW adopted an economics framework, collaborated with economists and were designed with an economics audience in mind. Fewer key themes were represented, and there was tension with heterodox approaches from political economists and labour historians. The field was also largely isolated from global conversations on economic history, looking, for the most part, to the US for professional and intellectual connections. Pincus and Snooks identified issues with the *Review*'s geographic scope in the late 1980s, with the journal narrowing from a range of international contributors throughout the 1960s and 1970s to, in the 1980s, authors representing only New Zealand, the UK and the US.

---

26 Nicholas, 'The Future of Economic History'; Christopher Lloyd, 'Can Economic History Be the Core of Social Science? Why the Discipline Must Open and Integrate to Ensure the Survival of Long-Run Economic Analysis', *Australian Economic History Review* 37, no. 3 (1997): 256–66, doi.org/10.1111/aehr.373005; Whitwell, 'Future Directions'.

27 Jonathan Pincus and Graeme Snooks, 'The Past and Future Role of the *Australian Economic History Review*: Editorial Reflections and Aspirations', *Australian Economic History Review* 28, no. 2 (1988): 3–7, doi.org/10.1111/aehr.282001.

In the late 1990s there was only partial acknowledgment of the intellectual factors responsible for the status of Australian economic history. Whitwell identified that economic history needed to broaden its scope and readership (particularly towards business, management and marketing groups), but argued that this was 'born out of necessity' rather than a contributor to the crisis itself.[28] While Nicholas argued that scholars had 'failed to convince other disciplines that economic history is relevant', this was in the context of teaching. Regarding research, Nicholas was positive, quoting the external reviewers who had evaluated the University of Melbourne's economic history research profile as 'world class'.[29] Lloyd came closest to identifying the field's intellectual challenges, arguing that the crisis was due to the 'failure of economic history to entrench itself as an essential component of both economics and social science more generally'.[30] Even then, Lloyd's comments betray a social science aspiration for the field. A future for the field in the history discipline was not pursued nor even truly considered. Some were outright dismissive of economic history in the humanities, with Nicholas arguing that it was 'unlikely that historians can be convinced of the usefulness of economic history' due to the discipline's 'increasingly feminist, postmodern and deconstructionist approaches'.[31] Engagement with this parent discipline was also conspicuously absent from recommendations in the 2004 and 2007 reflections on the field's state of practice, with McLean and Shanahan reporting in 2007 that 'surprisingly, there was no discussion at the forum or in the essays about the relationship with the history discipline'.[32]

Internal disregard for connections with history was met with intellectual challenges from both economists and mainstream historians. By rights, economic history should have remained a core aspect of Australian economics. Economic historians had good relationships and patronage from economists since the interwar period, with postwar Keynesianism then providing methodological and intellectual congruence with Noel Butlin's orthodox school. Those in Canberra, and the group at UNSW, made the transition to cliometrics and the new neoclassical paradigm, incorporating frontier theories, data and mathematical techniques.

---

28 Whitwell, 'Future Directions', 276.
29 Nicholas, 'The Future of Economic History'.
30 Lloyd, 'Core of Social Science?', 256.
31 Nicholas, 'The Future of Economic History', 270.
32 Ian W McLean and Martin Shanahan, 'Australasian Economic History: Research Challenges and Big Questions', *Australian Economic History Review* 47, no. 3 (2007): 300–15, 309, doi.org/10.1111/j.1467-8446.2007.00214.x.

These scholars used similar techniques and frameworks as economists, but with a historical or long-run timescale. The economics discipline seemed supportive during the 1980s, indeed scholars like Bob Gregory co-edited economic history research, and in 1989 the *Economic Record* ran a special issue on new work in economic history. In 1993, the Nobel Prize for economics was won by two US economic historians, Robert Fogel and Douglass C. North, leading to unprecedented interest globally in cliometrics. Engagement between economists and economic historians on institutions, the environment, technological change, demography, path dependence and so on throughout the 1990s and 2000s provided plenty of common ground between the two groups.[33]

Despite these factors supporting the place of economic history in Australian economics, it became marginalised in the discipline. This was, in part, the result of a general narrowing of mainstream Australian economics, away from the study of context, business cycles and comparative economic systems, and towards a rigorous, mathematical neoclassical program.[34] Based on a survey of economics curricula at Australian universities between 1980 and 2011, Tim Thornton found 14 per cent growth in subjects classified as neoclassical economics, econometrics and mathematical methods, and a decline of almost 17 per cent in broader 'economics as a social science' subjects such as economic history, the history of economic thought, comparative economic systems, heterodox economics and so on.[35] Economic history experienced the largest decline of any of the categories, with 14.1 per cent fewer subjects in 2011 compared to 1980.[36] There was also a narrowing of work published in the key Australian economics journal, *Economic Record*. Using a fairly broad brush, there was a decline in the number of historical articles in the *Record*, from 25

---

33 Tirthankar Roy, 'Economic History: An Endangered Discipline', *Economic and Political Weekly* 39, no. 29 (2004): 3238–43.
34 Monica Keneley and Phil Hellier, 'A Market Oriented Approach to Australian Undergraduate Economics Education: Justification and Explanation', *Economic Papers* 20, no. 2 (2001): 81–94, doi.org/10.1111/j.1759-3441.2001.tb00283.x; Peter Docherty, 'The Role of Economic History and History of Economic Thought in Macroeconomics and Finance Courses after the Global Financial Crisis', *Australasian Journal of Economics Education* 11, no. 2 (2014):1–24; John Kees Lodewijks, 'The History of Economic Thought in Australia and New Zealand', *History of Political Economy* 34, no. 5 (2002): 154–64, doi.org/10.1215/00182702-34-Suppl_1-154.
35 Tim Thornton, 'The Economics Curriculum in Australian Universities 1980 to 2011', *Economic Papers* 31, no. 1 (2012): 103–13, doi.org/10.1111/j.1759-3441.2011.00163.x.
36 Thornton, 'Economics Curriculum'. To compare, the history of economic thought experienced a 1.4 per cent decline.

in the 1970s, to only 15 and 16 in the 1980s and 1990s, respectively.[37] Alex Millmow and Jacqueline Tuck found a similar trend, that although economic history featured relatively prominently in the *Record* between 1960 and 2009 (10.1 per cent of articles on average), in their most recent five years, only 2 per cent of articles were coded as economic history.[38]

It is difficult to pinpoint the reason for this narrowing. It was, in part, due to expectations set in the metropole, with similar trends experienced in US economics departments.[39] The 'philosophical overhang' of logical positivism within economics globally, which became increasingly influential in the latter half of the twentieth century, constructed an identity for economists as 'scientists' concerned with evidence-based explanations of observable phenomena, and the continual, linear improvement of practice and theory over time.[40] Logical positivism, by seeking the 'best' theory and method, is fundamentally antithetical to pluralism or interdisciplinarity, perceiving work that adopts different approaches as less 'scientific'. A positivist paradigm is also specifically antithetical to historical approaches such as economic history, as history looks backwards (rather than forwards) for its insights.[41]

This was probably a frustrating paradox. Those who did not adhere to the approach and methods of neoclassical economics were dismissed as less scientific or 'not real economists'.[42] However, those cliometricians who did meet the expectations of the economics discipline were tolerated, but not advocated for. Pincus, for example, has recalled that at one point during his tenure in Butlin's department at ANU, he tried to move to economics, only to be told by economist Fred Gruen that 'you contribute to my department, you write some economics, why would I move you over and have to pay for you?'.[43] Scholars were also met with the identity

---

37   Historical, in this case, means either a historical time period, or longitudinal work covering more than 20 years.
38   Alex Millmow and Jacqueline Tuck, 'The Audit We Had to Have: *The Economic Record*, 1960–2009', *Economic Record* 89, no. 284 (2013): 112–28, doi.org/10.1111/1475-4932.12003.
39   Keneley and Hellier, 'Market Oriented Approach'; Docherty, 'The Role of Economic History'.
40   Docherty, 'The Role of Economic History'; Tim Thornton, 'The Narrowing of the Australian University Economics Curriculum: An Analysis of the Problem and a Proposed Solution', *Economic Record* 89, Suppl. S1 (2013): 106–14, doi.org/10.1111/1475-4932.12035; Mark Blaug, 'No History of Ideas, Please, We're Economists', *Journal of Economic Perspectives* 15, no. 1 (2001): 145–64, doi.org/10.1257/jep.15.1.145.
41   Thornton, 'Narrowing'.
42   Alford interview.
43   A similar conversation apparently also occurred with Keith Hancock, the head of economics at Flinders while Pincus was there in the 1980s. See Pincus interview.

crisis of losing their distinctiveness. This was common in many contexts around the world, with scholars concerned that in their attempt to mimic neoclassical paradigms, cliometricians were perceived as simply a subset of applied economics.[44] For Australia, Nicholas has commented that:

> If [economic historians] are nothing more than economists, using bad data, you know, what sort of scope is there going to be for economists to find value?[45]

The Dawkins-era institutional structure compounded these identity issues, with many economic historians looking and sounding like economists, but administratively separate from the department and teaching structure. With the need for departments to be territorial over students and funding, economic history units were easy to jettison: they either closely overlapped with core economics units, or were not considered sufficiently rigorous for professional economics training. This 'same but separate' mentality, created by the departmental structure, explains the comparatively worse outcomes experienced by the Australian economic history curriculum, compared to history of economic thought, or economic historians in, say, the US, both of which were integrated into economics groups. Ian McLean identified the risks associated with separate departments, arguing that it was easier for members to 'fall through the cracks'.[46]

The outlook was frosty from historians as well. Historians had once engaged in genuine dialogue with economic historians, with interwar scholars moving between groups, and the postwar focus on urban, social and labour history providing good space for the inclusion of economic matters. From the late 1980s, the cultural turn opened a major interstice between economic history and history. As with the forces acting on the Australian economics discipline, this too was imported from the metropole, with postmodern transformations of Marxism and the *Annales* school combining with developments in poststructuralism, linguistics, literary criticism and anthropology. The result was the 'new cultural history' that moved many historians away from the large, often 'faceless' structures of economic, social and labour history, and towards the

---

44 Claudia Goldin, 'Cliometrics and the Nobel', *Journal of Economic Perspectives* 9, no. 2 (1995): 191–208, doi.org/10.1257/jep.9.2.191; Simon Ville and Claire EF Wright, 'Neither a Discipline nor a Colony: Renaissance and Re-Imagination in Economic History', *Australian Historical Studies* 48, no. 2 (2017): 152–68, doi.org/10.1080/1031461X.2017.1279197.
45 Nicholas interview.
46 McLean interview.

'investigation of the contextually situated production and transmission of meaning'.[47] For some, the previous Marxist focus on the proletariat subaltern expanded to include contextually contingent approaches to understanding gender, sexuality and ethnicity. For others, microhistories of single neighbourhoods or factories rejected the class metanarratives of labour and social history to examine the specificity of identity and power in that area. Adopting a cultural approach with a postcolonial lens lent itself to comparative studies of empire and colonial encounter, while maintaining a focus on contextual specificity and the use of cultural evidence such as discourse.[48] Although these intellectual trends were common, and influenced economic history in the US and Europe, Hannah Forsyth and Sophie Loy-Wilson have argued they had particular importance in Australian history, so much so that Richard White argued in the late 1990s that 'the study of culture was the study of Australia'.[49]

As historians lost confidence in materiality, their interest in the economy declined. The usefulness of structures such as work, occupation, industry, money and class was challenged in favour of other aspects of identity such as gender, sexuality, ethnicity and place. The poststructuralist approach – highlighting the interpretive and intertextual nature of evidence, and focusing on linguistic and discursive sources – also challenged the positivist and empirical methods favoured by economic historians.[50] Even though Australian economic history was comparatively less wedded to cliometrics, the orthodox use of quantitative data was seen as limited

---

47 Hannah Forsyth and Sophie Loy-Wilson, 'Seeking a New Materialism in Australian History', *Australian Historical Studies* 48, no. 1 (2017): 169–88, 171, doi.org/10.1080/103146 1X.2017.1298635. See also Kenneth Lipartito, 'Reassembling the Economic: New Departures in Historical Materialism', *American Historical Review* 121, no. 1 (2016): 101–39, doi.org/10.1093/ahr/121.1.101; John E Toews, 'Intellectual History after the Linguistic Turn: The Autonomy of Meaning and the Irreducibility of Experience', *American Historical Review* 92, no. 4 (1987): 879–907; Tom Mackay, 'Cultural Abundance, Economic Scarcity: Cultural Studies, Economics, and Contemporary Australian History', *Flinders Journal of History and Politics* 30, no. 1 (2014): 84–110; Ann Curthoys, 'Labour History and Cultural Studies', *Labour History*, no. 67 (1994): 12–22, doi.org/10.2307/27509272; Naomi Lamoreaux, 'The Future of Economic History Must Be Interdisciplinary', *Journal of Economic History* 75, no. 4 (2015): 1251–57, doi.org/10.1017/S0022050715001679; Ben Huf and Glenda Sluga, '"New" Histories of (Australian) Capitalism', *Australian Historical Studies* 50, no. 4 (2019): 405–17, doi.org/10.1080/1031461X.2019.1663773.
48 Hsu-Ming Teo and Richard White, *Cultural History in Australia* (Sydney: UNSW Press, 2003); Forsyth and Loy-Wilson, 'New Materialism'.
49 Lamoreaux, 'The Future of Economic History'; Forsyth and Loy-Wilson, 'New Materialism', 170; Richard White, 'Inventing Australia Revisited', in *Creating Australia: Changing Australian History*, ed. W Hudson and G Bolton (Sydney: Allen & Unwin, 1997), 12–22.
50 Curthoys, 'Labour History'.

in its ability to reveal identities and power.[51] At the same time, cultural historians' discourse and linguistic methods were distinct from the functionalist use of primary source language in work on, say, the history of economic policy.[52] In the US, business history provided an opportunity for common ground between economic and cultural historians at this time, with scholars such as Kenneth Lipartito and others moving away from the 'structuralist–functionalist' Chandlerian revolution and towards understanding cultural practices, systems of meaning and entrepreneurial decision-making.[53] However, in Australia, the small group of business historians were still firmly embedded in Chandlerian work for much of the 1990s and 2000s (see below).

Cultural historians did not deride or dismiss economic history, they simply ignored it. They were not only examining disparate events, actors and processes, but were using different methods to do so. The cultural turn beleaguered social and labour historians as well, with the latter mourning their own 'death' in much the same way that economic historians did at the time.[54] However, social and labour history fared considerably better within the history discipline, as some made inroads with cultural history by converting their work on material matters to interest in communities, identities and language.[55] As Tom Mackay has found for the 2000s, the Australian history curriculum, contents of key journals and the Australian Historical Association prizes all came to represent cultural history, 'excepting perhaps the presence of a few social and labour histories'.[56] There was the occasional piece of economic history published in relevant history journals (see below), but they were far from mainstream. Articles were generally isolated, absent of comment, special issues or further

---

51   Forsyth and Loy-Wilson, 'New Materialism'.
52   For example, Greg Whitwell, *The Treasury Line* (Sydney: Allen & Unwin, 1986).
53   Lamoreaux, 'The Future of Economic History'; Monica Keneley, 'Reflections on the Business History Tradition: Where Has It Come from and Where Is It Going To?', *Australian Economic History Review* 60, no. 3 (2020): 282–300, doi.org/10.1111/aehr.12206; William H Becker, 'Managerial Culture and the American Political Economy', *Business and Economic History* 25, no. 1 (1996): 1–7; Kenneth Lipartito, 'Culture and the Practice of Business History', *Business and Economic History* 24, no. 2 (1995): 1–41.
54   Verity Burgmann, 'The Strange Death of Labour History', in *Bede Nairn and Labor History*, Labor History Essays 3, ed. Bob Carr et al. (Leichhardt: Pluto Press in association with the NSW Branch of the Australian Labor Party, 1991), 72–74; Raelene Frances and Bruce Scates, 'Is Labour History Dead?', *Australian Historical Studies* 25, no. 100 (1993): 470–81, doi.org/10.1080/10314619308595930.
55   Curthoys, 'Labour History'.
56   Mackay, 'Cultural Abundance, Economic Scarcity', 88.

contributions. This compared to work on gender, Indigenous, migration and sexuality histories, which were rightly treated to collective and sustained comment in key history journals.

The disconnect between economic and cultural history thus occurred on multiple fronts: cultural historians actively ignored economic matters and came to favour very different methods and sources. Economic historians, for their part, dismissed cultural approaches and ignored the opportunities they had to develop common ground. The field put lots of its eggs in the economics basket, spending the better part of four decades developing close intellectual and professional relationships with that discipline. They were thus extremely vulnerable to the institutional and intellectual changes in economics, and lacked a basis on which to bargain with other groups. The Dawkins-era reforms were, in part, a catalyst that exposed existing vulnerabilities in the way Australian economic history was organised.

Leadership

Compounding the field's institutional and intellectual challenges was conservatism and a lack of collective action from the field's leaders. Retirements, or 'natural attrition', was a key avenue through which the ranks of Australian economic historians declined. Colin Forster retired from the ANU Faculties in 1991, with other longstanding members of the department retiring gradually over the remainder of the decade. John McCarty retired in 1996, and died two years later in 1998.[57] Stephen Salsbury at the University of Sydney died the same year.[58] Malcolm Falkus was head of the economic history department at UNE until it was folded into economics in 1998. He promptly retired in 2000, on the day he turned 60 and apparently to the surprise of his colleagues.[59] Some of these positions were filled, with Ville hired to the ANU Faculties to replace Forster. On faculty instructions, Ville attempted to hire a God Professor, though the search failed and eventually the money was used to hire two junior scholars instead (Pierre van der Eng and Grant Fleming).[60] Andrew 'Andy' Seltzer completed his PhD in North America, and was appointed to the economic history department at the University of Melbourne in

---

57 Anthony E Dingle, 'John William McCarty, 1931–1998', in *1999 Annual Report* (Canberra: Academy of the Social Sciences in Australia, 1999).
58 'Obituary: Salsbury, Prof. Stephen Matthew', *Sydney Morning Herald*, 5 March 1998.
59 Matthew Cawood, 'Malcolm Falkus Obituary', *Pulse News*, 1 March 2018, blog.une.edu.au/pulsenews/2018/03/01/malcolm-falkus-obituary/ (site discontinued).
60 Ville interview.

1994.[61] Most of the chairs were never replaced, as departments were in the process of being absorbed into economics, and new hires were made into that discipline rather than specifically to an economic history position.

Some moved out of traditional academic research roles to different industries or overseas. Boris Schedvin, by all reports a warrior for economic history at faculty meetings, accepted a position as deputy vice chancellor at Melbourne in 1991. Nicholas was brought in as his replacement shortly after. Wray Vamplew took a position as pro-vice chancellor at Flinders in the early 1990s, before moving back to the UK in 1993.[62] From the late 1980s, Shergold, Withers, Pincus, Maddock and Diane Sydenham left the sector for high-profile positions in banking and the government.[63] Oxley had a very 'troubled career' in Australia. After several short-term contracts at Melbourne, and fellowships on ARC grants, Oxley and Meredith decided to move to the UK where Oxley took up a post in economic and social history at Oxford in 2007.[64]

Arguably the biggest change was at ANU. In April 1991, Noel Butlin passed away in Canberra from complications associated with long-term melanoma and leukaemia.[65] He worked almost until the day he passed, leaving two posthumous works to be completed by his son Matthew Butlin, an economist and economic historian in his own right. Matthew has recalled the process of publishing his father's final works as 'sad but [...] rewarding'.[66] For *Economics and the Dreamtime*, the work was largely completed, with Butlin ordering that 'no word be changed', though he allowed Matthew some rope to complete the subsequent volume, *Forming a Colonial Economy*.[67] Matthew has remembered that in the time before Noel died, they had a number of conversations about the shape of these

---

61 Seltzer completed his Master of Science and PhD at the University of Illinois at Urbana-Champaign.
62 Vamplew correspondence, 19 October 2019; Wray Vamplew, 'Count Me In: Reflections on a Career as a Sports Historian', *Sport in Society* 19, no. 3 (2016): 297–312, doi.org/10.1080/17430437.2015.1056573.
63 Shergold; Withers; Pincus; Maddock; Keneley interviews.
64 Oxley/Meredith interview.
65 Matthew Butlin correspondence, 5 July 2021; Graeme Snooks, '"In My Beginning Is My End": The Life and Work of Noel George Butlin, 1921–1991', *Australian Economic History Review* 31, no. 2 (1991): 3–27, doi.org/10.1111/aehr.312001.
66 Matthew Butlin interview.
67 Noel G Butlin, *Economics and the Dreamtime: A Hypothetical History* (Melbourne: Cambridge University Press, 1993), x, doi.org/10.1017/CBO9780511552311; Noel G Butlin, *Forming a Colonial Economy, Australia 1810–1850* (Melbourne: Cambridge University Press, 1994), doi.org/10.1017/CBO9780511552328.

two books.⁶⁸ The preface and acknowledgments of *Dreamtime* read as urgent – Noel seemed aware that his time was almost up, and he aimed to finish what he started in the 1950s by providing a complete account of the continent's economic development. *Dreamtime* extended the analysis of his 1983 work on the Indigenous population, *Our Original Aggression*, on the assumption that with a revised understanding of the pre-invasion population, it followed that 'we had been the inheritors of enormous Aboriginal effort, most of which was adapted and discarded and their society destroyed'.⁶⁹

Butlin outlined the arrival and settlement of Aboriginal people, the structuring of their economy, the intrusion of Europeans and the ways that Aboriginal resources were absorbed. His approach was 'speculative and counterfactual' rather than definitive, proposing avenues for further research rather than the final word.⁷⁰ He incorporated demographic and scientific research regarding the migration of Aboriginal people and the decline of the population following European invasion. His analysis of the nature of the Aboriginal economy is based on a simple production function model, with dynamic elements given through the division of labour, intergenerational transfers, structural change and technological change. The nature of the written record for the period of analysis meant Butlin was forced to give up most of his adherence to official sources, instead contributing through the application of orthodox economic ideas to the nature and change of the Aboriginal population.

Butlin's *Forming a Colonial Economy* was a sparsely populated manuscript, but connected his interest in the Aboriginal economy with his early contribution on Australia's economic history of the latter half of the nineteenth century. Building on the work he had done throughout the 1980s to expand his national accounting estimates back to 1788, Butlin examined the economic history of the Australian colonies up to 1840, focusing on the interdependence between imperial Britain and colonial Australia, and the procedure through which a rich Western economy had arisen in an unlikely place.⁷¹ His major conclusion was that the national income of the colonial economy only reached the level of the pre-invasion

---

68 These conversations were memorialised in a series of recorded tapes, but Matthew has commented that he (understandably enough) never went back to listen to them. See Matthew Butlin interview.
69 Butlin, *Dreamtime*, viii; Noel G Butlin, *Our Original Aggression* (Sydney: George Allen & Unwin, 1983).
70 Butlin, *Dreamtime*, 9.
71 Noel G Butlin, 'Contours of the Australian Economy 1788–1860', *Australian Economic History Review* 26, no. 2 (1986), doi.org/10.1111/aehr.262002; Noel G Butlin and William Angus Sinclair,

Indigenous population by 1850. The approach was familiar: he presented aggregate quantitative material with a narrative organised around the factors of production – from Britain came money and people, which set about exploiting Australia's natural capabilities. His estimates (really, 'guestimates') of the size of the Indigenous and early colonial economies were bold, as was his ability to reconstruct detailed economic relationships on the basis of sparse records. It was a fitting coda to an innovative life.

Noel was one of the most creative scholars of his generation. Although known for his very mainstream national income accounting method, his body of work demonstrates remarkable disciplinary breadth. Butlin was also very skilled at accessing and retaining resources for the field, and his ability to secure the Coghlan Chair of economic history is testament to his audacity and resourcefulness. Rod Maddock has recalled that, in the 1970s, Noel convinced ANU to invest the money he earned as a consultant on the Botany Bay Project. The project, sponsored by the Australian Academies of Science, Social Sciences and the Humanities, and in conjunction with both Commonwealth and State governments, aimed to understand Sydney's large oceanic port, and the resulting concentration of industry and population.[72] Although political conflict and curtailed resources led to disappointing outcomes, the money Butlin earned for leading the project was substantial.[73] At a time of stagflation, where government bonds were earning 15 per cent, Butlin's initial investment was soon earning a small fortune once inflation fell.[74] The Coghlan Chair was appointed before Noel died, somewhere between 1988 and 1990. Pamela Statham, an economic historian at the University of Western

---

'Australian Gross Domestic Product 1788–1860: Estimates, Sources and Methods', *Australian Economic History Review* 26, no. 2 (1986): 126–47, doi.org/10.1111/aehr.262003; Butlin, *Forming a Colonial Economy*.

72   Snooks, 'In My Beginning Is My End'. See Noel G Butlin, ed. *The Impact of Port Botany* (Canberra: Consultative Committee of the Academy of Social Sciences in Australia, Australian Academy of Humanities and Australian Academy of Science in association with Australian National University Press, 1976); Noel G Butlin, ed., *Sydney's Environmental Amenity, 1970–1975: A Study of the System of Waste Management and Pollution Control* (Canberra: Consultative Committee of the Academy of Social Sciences in Australia, Australian Academy of Humanities and Australian Academy of Science in association with Australian National University Press, 1976); Noel G Butlin, ed., *Factory Waste Potential in Sydney* (Canberra: Consultative Committee of the Academy of Social Sciences in Australia, Australian Academy of Humanities and Australian Academy of Science in association with Australian National University Press, 1977).

73   Hugh Stretton, 'The Botany Bay Project: Historians and the Study of Cities', *Australian Historical Studies* 19, no. 76 (1981): 430–39, doi.org/10.1080/10314618108595648.

74   Maddock interview.

Australia, has recalled that during an 18-month secondment in the RSSS in the late 1980s, she and the other committee member David Pope were encouraged to support the appointment of Graeme Snooks.[75]

Snooks had a long history of expanding Butlin's work. His contribution to understanding Western Australia's long-run economic growth, for example, built regional variation into Butlin's 'numbers' (Chapter 3). Similarly, his discussion with the political economy group in the 1970s defended Butlin's orthodox contribution against heterodox criticism (Chapter 4). In 1994 came his magnus opus – *Portrait of the Family within the Total Economy*. The work had begun while Snooks was at Flinders in the early 1980s, when Maddock invited him to contribute a conference paper on unpaid work.[76] Like Butlin before him, the mammoth task of assembling and interpreting the relevant quantitative data was assisted with the resources and funding of the RSSS's Coghlan Chair.[77] Snooks included household production in Australia's national accounts since 1788, proposing a three-sector model comprising the private and public market sectors, and the household sector. He argued that households had outstripped both public and private market sectors in their contribution to national income.

In theme – including the household sector and its interaction with the market economy – Snooks's work departed quite dramatically from standard economic theory. However, despite his criticism of orthodox economic practice, the work was based on a very orthodox view of human behaviour. In Snooks's work, the 'economic man' seeks to maximise material utility, and the economy is an aggregation of these individual, utility-maximising agents. Snooks's approach was also mainstream with regards to Australian economic history. The work rested on the reconstruction of national accounts from a range of official government sources, and the use of these new data to reinterpret Australia's economic past. Snooks advocated for studying one country at a time rather than a comparative approach, and was in favour of understanding 'real-world processes' inductively rather than testing economic theory.[78] Even reviews

---

75 Statham interview.
76 Maddock interview; Graeme Snooks, *Portrait of the Family within the Total Economy: A Study in Longrun Dynamics, Australia 1788–1990* (Cambridge: Cambridge University Press, 1994), xiv–xv.
77 Snooks, *Portrait of the Family*, xv.
78 Snooks, *Portrait of the Family*, 5–10.

of Snooks's method were similar to those of Butlin's 'numbers' 30 years prior – colleagues argued that his work was innovative, but drew quite a long bow with regards to the quantitative assumptions.[79]

Snooks's work provided important quantitative infrastructure and continuity of orthodox writings, but squandered opportunities to engage with flourishing work in parent disciplines. Regarding economists, the goalposts had shifted away from orthodox techniques, particularly the focus on business cycles and national income accounting, and towards understanding neoclassical micro-foundations and the use of advanced mathematical techniques. Snooks's orthodox approach was no longer at the forefront of economics research, as Butlin's had been in the 1950s. The focus on 'production' and flattening the category of 'households' across Australia was also disconnected from cultural historians' work on families and identity, and the use of official quantitative data was at odds with cultural historians' use of memory, visual and discursive sources to understand the way women and men constructed households and families at different points in time.[80] The conservative and binary conception of gender was also distinctive from feminist histories of women and work; indeed Snooks never referred to this literature.[81] He advanced a biologically essentialist view of gender roles, assuming primary household workers were female, and that women only had 'comparative advantage' in part-time market work combined with household production.[82] This was critiqued by feminist economic historians, including Katrina Alford, who argued:

---

[79] Ralph Shlomowitz, 'Review: Snooks, *Portrait of the Family within the Total Economy*', *Economic History Review* 48, no. 4 (1995): 849, doi.org/10.2307/2598167; Jane Humphries, 'Review: Snooks, *Portrait of the Family Within the Total Economy*', *Economic Journal* 106, no. 1 (1996): 733, doi.org/10.2307/2235593.

[80] Some examples include Alison Mackinnon and Penny Gregory, '"A Study Corner in the Kitchen": Australian Graduate Women Negotiate Family, Nation and Work in the 1950s and Early 1960s', *Australian Historical Studies* 37, no. 127 (2006): 63–80, doi.org/10.1080/10314610608601204; Miriam Dixson, *The Real Matilda: Woman and Identity in Australia, 1788 to 1975* (Sydney: UNSW Press, 1999.

[81] Katrina Alford, *Production or Reproduction? An Economic History of Women in Australia, 1788–1850* (Melbourne: Oxford University Press, 1984); Beverley Kingston, *My Wife, My Daughter, and Poor Mary Ann: Women and Work in Australia* (Melbourne: Thomas Nelson, 1975); Mark Peel, 'Making a Place: Women in the "Workers' City"', *Australian Historical Studies* 26, no. 102 (1994): 19–38, doi.org/10.1080/10314619408595948.

[82] Snooks, *Portrait of the Family*, 81.

Having signalled an intention to embark on a potentially pathbreaking and original journey through economic history, Snooks proceeds to cancel his ticket, as he regresses back to the narrow by-ways of orthodox economics. The considerable potential of this work is not realised as the author resorts to orthodox economic theory on matters to do with the primacy of men, markets and morals in economic history, in Australia and elsewhere.[83]

Snooks's intellectual conservatism, with regards to frontier research in both economics and history, was true of other prominent members of the field in the 1990s. The field was dominated by straight, white, men, particularly at leadership levels, contributing to a reluctance to advance women and other minorities not only as practitioners, but also as subjects for study. Women's work in economic history had been constrained by similar forces to more general employment in academia and the public service, with fewer women qualified at the tertiary level, they were paid unequal salaries and forced to give up work upon marriage until the 1960s.[84] Some worked as long-term research assistants with, for example, Helen Bridge assisting with primary research for economic historians in the ANU Faculties over the course of 30 years, yet only once being half-credited as an author.[85] Similarly, Ruth Inall and Joyce Fisher enabled some of the field's most celebrated contributions, working with Noel and Syd Butlin, respectively, throughout the 1950s and 1960s, in the preparation of their statistical material.[86] Neither were credited as authors.

---

83   Katrina Alford, 'Review: Snooks, *Portrait of the Family within the Total Economy*', *Labour History* 67, no. 1 (1994): 171, doi.org/10.2307/27509290.
84   Anne Summers, *Damned Whores and God's Police* (Sydney: NewSouth, 2016 [first ed. 1975]); Anne Summers, *The Misogyny Factor* (Sydney: NewSouth, 2013); Ray Over and Beryl McKenzie, 'Career Prospects for Women in Australian Universities', *Journal of Tertiary Education Administration* 7, no. 1 (1985): 61–71, doi.org/10.1080/0157603850070105.
85   Ville interview. See Colin Forster and Graham SL Tucker (with Helen Bridge), *Economic Opportunity and White American Fertility Ratios 1800–1860*, Yale Series in Economic History (New Haven: Yale University Press, 1972).
86   For Inall, see acknowledgments in Noel G Butlin, *Private Capital Formation in Australia: Estimates 1861–1900*. Social Science Monographs 5 (Canberra: The Australian National University, 1955); Noel G Butlin, 'Colonial Socialism in Australia', in *The State and Economic Growth: Papers of a Conference Held on October 11–13, 1956 under the Auspices of the Committee on Economic Growth*, ed. HGJ Aitken (New York: Social Science Research Council, 1959), 26–78; Noel G Butlin, *Australian Domestic Product, Investment and Foreign Borrowing 1861–1938/9* (London: Cambridge University Press, 1962); Noel G Butlin, *Investment in Australian Economic Development, 1861–1900* (London: Cambridge University Press, 1964), doi.org/10.1017/CBO9781316530160. For Fisher, see Syd J Butlin, *Foundations of the Australian Monetary System 1788–1851* (Melbourne: Melbourne University Press, 1953); and Syd J Butlin, *Australia and New Zealand Bank: The Bank of Australasia and the Union Bank of Australia Limited, 1828–1951* (London: Longmans, 1961).

Women's increased participation in tertiary education and the paid workforce since the 1970s was slow to change the composition of academia. Men were advantaged by having been qualified for tenured positions in the 1960s and early 1970s, at the time of the sector's expansion, with women qualifying in greater numbers once the job market had contracted from 1980.[87] In addition to the unequal intake of women at the entry level, due to conscious and unconscious bias, women were also much less likely to be appointed to leadership positions.[88] As such, while there have been several female Australian economic historians since the 1960s, there was rarely more than one woman in a department, and they were never in leadership roles such as department chair or editors of major collaborative work. Helen Hughes, for example, completed her DPhil at the London School of Economics in 1954, with the monograph from this work published in 1964 as *The Australian Iron and Steel Industry* (see Chapter 3). At a time when her male contemporaries, with far less published work, were awarded chairs, Hughes was appointed to several short-term lectureships, including as a research fellow in the ANU Research School of Pacific Studies in the mid-1960s. She left the academy for a successful career at The World Bank, before returning to the ANU Research School of Pacific Studies as a professor in 1983.[89] While Hughes was certainly a fellow traveller of economic history, she experienced greater career mobility as member of the economics discipline, compared to female economic historians.[90] Several of the women interviewed recalled, diplomatically, 'different' treatment to their male colleagues,[91] with Alford detailing the 'misogyny and sexism' she experienced in Melbourne's commerce and economics faculty from the mid-1970s to the 1990s.[92]

Intellectual tendrils of the field's gender bias can be found throughout the 1980s, 1990s and 2000s. Work in the field rarely addressed gender directly, the exceptions being research on the labour market that was 'culpable of obscuring and distorting the history of women's labour in Australia'.[93] In *Convict Workers*, women were seen as administratively separate from

---

87   Over and McKenzie, 'Career Prospects'.
88   Summers, *The Misogyny Factor*.
89   Damien Murphy, 'Champion of Social Justice', *Sydney Morning Herald*, 12 June 2013, www.smh.com.au/national/champion-of-social-justice-20130620-2oldc.html.
90   See a discussion of Hughes's integration with Butlin's orthodox school in Chapter 3.
91   Hutchinson; Oxley/Meredith interviews.
92   Alford interview.
93   Katrina Alford, 'Colonial Women's Employment as Seen by Nineteenth-Century Statisticians and Twentieth-Century Economic Historians', *Labour History*, no. 51 (1986): 1–10, 10, doi.org/10.2307/27508793.

the rest of the convict labour market, with Oxley examining several thousand female convict indents that were excluded from the rest of the book.[94] The field's preoccupation with the orthodox school, particularly the reliance on the statistics of Coghlan and other colonial statisticians, institutionalised gender differences by classifying public, market forms of work as 'economic', and domestic work as 'non-economic'.[95] Snooks, of course, examined women in his work on households, but did so in the 'orthodox' manner that saw them as 'other' to market production. Other research on the labour market from the orthodox school adjusted downward Coghlan's already biased statistics to seriously undervalue the role of female workers.[96]

This gender binary was redressed, in part, by contributions to Australian feminist economic history. In the 1984 book based on her University of Melbourne DPhil, Alford challenged the implicit assumption, by the majority of (male) economic historians, that Australia's economic past was entirely occupied by men. She reappraised the field's 'infuriating' discount of the value of women's work by examining labour usually submerged within the household.[97] The resulting book, published a decade before Snooks' work on households, challenged the binary view of women's economic contribution, and highlighted the importance of understanding women in Australia's economy.[98] Oxley also challenged the idea that women were a hinderance to Australia's economic past, inspired by a stint Alford had on staff at UNSW in the mid-1980s, and the growth of women's history in general.[99] For her honours and doctoral projects, Oxley examined the human capital of Australia's female convicts, arguing

---

94 Oxley/Meredith; Dyster interviews.
95 Desley Deacon, 'Political Arithmetic: The Nineteenth-Century Australian Census and the Construction of the Dependent Woman', *Signs: Journal of Women in Culture and Society* 11, no. 1 (1985): 27–47, doi.org/10.1086/494198.
96 Ian W McLean, 'Rural Output, Inputs and Mechanisation in Victoria 1870–1910' (PhD thesis, The Australian National University, 1971); Ian W McLean, SF Molloy and P Lockett, 'The Rural Workforce in Australia 1871–1911', *Australian Economic History Review* 22, no. 2 (1982): 172–81, doi.org/10.1111/aehr.222004; Noel G Butlin and John A Dowie, 'Estimates of Australian Work Force and Employment, 1861–1961', *Australian Economic History Review* 9, no. 2 (1969): 138–55, doi.org/10.1111/aehr.92003; Anthony M Endres, *Australian Workforce Aggregates 1828–1901: Estimates from Colonial Censuses* (Canberra: The Australian National University, 1984).
97 Alford, *Production or Reproduction?*; Alford interview.
98 Alford interview.
99 Oxley/Meredith interview.

that, contrary to popular perception, women were not transported for prostitution, but theft – they were young and healthy and possessed useful and transferable skills for the colony.[100]

In method, Alford and Oxley were largely congruent with the mainstream economic history field. Both were trained in economic history departments – Alford supervised by Alan Beever at the University of Melbourne, and Oxley by Barrie Dyster at UNSW – and reflected this training in their work. Oxley adopted a cliometric procedure similar to others in the 'Convict Workers' project, and Alford demonstrated her familiarity with the Melbourne community by using the sources and techniques of both the orthodox school and the history discipline.[101] However, they diverged substantially from the mainstream field in terms of subject. Both were influenced from the growth of women's history at the time, particularly the emphasis on 'gender as a dynamic in societies'.[102] This aligned with the interest of many contemporary historians in gender and identity. Methodologically, Alford's criticism of orthodox statistics and her own reconstruction of the value of women's work also aligned with the post-structural elements of the cultural turn that interrogated the assumptions and bias behind seemingly 'objective' quantitative material.[103] Alford and Oxley's works were substantial innovations for Australian economic history, and provided concrete links with the history discipline. However, intellectual conservatism from the field's leaders, and their exclusion of women from leadership structures, meant this approach was unfortunately not carried forward in a substantial way.

The lack of large collaborative work in the 1990s and 2000s was, similarly, the result of conservatism and problems defining the field's collective vision.[104] There were efforts towards a Cambridge University Press volume on economic history in the 1990s, with leaders agreeing it would

---

100 Oxley/Meredith interview. Deborah Oxley, 'Female Convicts', in *Convict Workers: Reinterpreting Australia's Past*, ed. Stephen Nicholas (Sydney: Cambridge University Press, 1988), 85–97, doi.org/10.1017/CBO9781139084840.008; Deborah Oxley, *Convict Maids: The Forced Migration of Women to Australia* (Cambridge: Cambridge University Press, 1996); Deborah Oxley, 'Packing Her (Economic) Bags: Convict Women Workers', *Australian Historical Studies* 26, no. 102 (1994): 57–76, doi.org/10.1080/10314619408595950. This work was based on Oxley's UNSW PhD thesis: Deborah Oxley, 'Convict Maids' (PhD thesis, University of New South Wales, 1991).
101 Alford, *Production or Reproduction?* See Chapter 4.
102 Oxley/Meredith interview.
103 See Desley Deacon's use of a similar frame: Deacon, 'Political Arithmetic'.
104 Frost interview; Stephen Morgan and Martin Shanahan, 'The Supply of Economic History in Australasia: The *Australian Economic History Review* at 50', *Australian Economic History Review* 50, no. 3 (2010): 217–39, doi.org/10.1111/j.1467-8446.2010.00303.x.

be a fitting festschrift to Noel's legacy. Bob Jackson and Graeme Snooks worked together, with Jackson editing chapters, and Snooks (through the RSSS economic history program) providing funding. It was not a happy project. Initial drafts of chapters, across two volumes, were presented at the 6th ANU RSSS economic history colloquium in July 1993. Ville has remembered a lack of commitment to the project, with the introduction of the Dawkins reforms reducing the number of scholars and creating anxiety for those who remained.[105] Frost has similarly reflected that 'I thought (and I don't mind this being quoted), I thought "jeez [sic], we've got no hope"'.[106]

A volume such as the authors were trying to achieve was very vulnerable, simply by being so interconnected. Hutchinson has recalled that one of the main roadblocks, for her, was the lack of distinction between chapters, with her work on twentieth century technological progress dependent on chapters on land, capital and so on. When those authors failed to produce the work, she found it difficult to proceed.[107] Ville has similarly argued that edited work such as this can be a house of cards, and that even for the Cambridge volume that did get published (see Chapter 6), even if two or three people didn't write their chapters, 'it probably would have stuffed up the whole volume'.[108]

All but four of the chapters were never completed. At the time, Ville was editor of the *Australian Economic History Review*, and published the completed chapters for a special issue on the nineteenth century. Bob Jackson wrote an overview, Ville the paper on enterprise, Frost on urbanisation and ANU Faculties economic historian H. M. 'Mac' Boot on government.[109] Although most of Jackson's overview was a typically erudite synthesis of the state of knowledge on Australia's colonial economic history, there were occasional glimpses into his loss at the failed project. In a footnote, he commented that:

---

105 Ville interview.
106 Frost interview.
107 Hutchinson interview.
108 Ville interview.
109 Simon Ville, 'Business Development in Colonial Australia', *Australian Economic History Review* 38, no. 1 (1998): 16–41, doi.org/10.1111/1467-8446.00023; Lionel Frost, 'The Contribution of the Urban Sector to Australian Economic Development before 1914', *Australian Economic History Review* 38, no. 1 (1998): 42–73, doi.org/10.1111/1467-8446.00024; HM Boot, 'Government and the Colonial Economies', *Australian Economic History Review* 38, no. 1 (1998): 74–101, doi.org/10.1111/1467-8446.00025.

> I wish to thank those contributors who battled through to deliver revised drafts on time: had more of your fellows done the same the two volumes of the Cambridge economic history would now be in the press.[110]

The fortunes of the Cambridge volume in the 1990s was a symptom of Australian economic history in the doldrums, rather than the cause. Butlin's presence was particularly strong, and papers were deliberately situated in the orthodox school. From what survived on the record from this project, the approach was very familiar: the 'colonial experience' was centred on a production function that involved resources flowing outwards, people, technology and money flowing in, all of which contributed to a range of subsidiary activities that were often located in cities.[111] Jackson's introduction, and Frost and Boot's contributions, built their narratives around aggregated quantitative material, with supplementary qualitative or archival sources. Frost examined the prominence of the urban centres for Australia's economic growth, incorporating contemporary contributions from social and urban historians on both the size and density of major cities. Boot's work on government addressed Noel Butlin's 'colonial socialism' thesis, sticking closely to the orthodox *Government and Capitalism* interpretation on the benefit of public capital assets, the favourable environment for private decision-makers, but the overall mixed record of government intervention in the economy. Ville's article was different, and in line with the reappraisal of Australian business history (see below), moving beyond the Keynesian production function to elaborate the micro-foundations necessary to understand the nature of transacting and business organisation. While this work was congruent with the field's existing character (and the volume's festschrift intentions), it did not engage with the substantial intellectual changes occurring in either economics or history at the time.

Adaptation and survival

The uncertainty of the Dawkins reforms exposed and enhanced anxieties about the future of Australian economic history. Identity and leadership challenges left the field with little basis on which to bargain with parent

---

110 Robert V Jackson, 'The Colonial Economies: An Introduction', *Australian Economic History Review* 38, no. 1 (1998): 1–15, 14, doi.org/10.1111/1467-8446.00022.
111 Jackson, 'Colonial Economies'.

disciplines, or the collective action needed to defend against the necessities of neoliberal universities. No one could seem to agree if a future for economic history in Australia was possible, let alone what it could look like. However, economic history survived this crisis, in part, by leaning into the reasons for the crisis itself – the transition towards a neoliberal university model forced professional broadening. Just as separate departments and other disciplinary structures encouraged members to look inwards in the post–World War II decades, removing these 'protections' forced them to look outwards. The group was smaller, but they were innovative and flexible. They had substantial agency in their professional future, and made concerted efforts to mitigate the field's vulnerability.

Living with the neighbours[112]

Survival required members to expand their professional and intellectual relationships. Post-closure, most scholars were integrated into economics or business groups and, combined with the prevalent logic of economic history as a social science, most worked to secure the field's future within this paradigm. Economic historians actively established their legitimacy in economics or business schools, by adapting teaching, broadening collaborators, hiring or training new members, and concealing historical work in contemporary teaching and research.

Economics

Most members found a home in economics groups. Economic historians at the ANU RSSS, La Trobe, Monash, UNSW and UNE were unilaterally placed in economics, an easy choice considering most economic history departments were already within economics groups, as well as the close intellectual and professional relationships between the two. At Monash, John McCarty was 'increasingly fretful' about what to do with the department – whether to *stay* with economics or *go* to history. While Tony Dingle and colleague Geoffrey Spenceley were keen to go to the history group, the historians were under their own budgetary pressures and so the group was eventually folded into economics.[113] In some cases members were given an ultimatum, with Lloyd remembering that at UNE, the options were for economic history to merge with economics,

---

112 Peter Mathias, 'Living with the Neighbours: The Role of Economic History', in *The Study of Economic History*, ed. NB Harte (London: Frank Cass, 1971), 367–83.
113 Dingle/Davison interview, emphasis mine.

or for the whole group to be axed.¹¹⁴ In other instances, individuals were given a choice, with some members of the ANU Faculties department opting to integrate with economics.¹¹⁵ By the time the department at the University of Sydney closed in 2003, the three remaining members went their separate ways, with Hutchinson the only one to move to economics.

These scholars joined many of their colleagues as single members or small clusters of economic historians in large economics groups. For example, at the universities of Western Australia and Queensland, economic historians had been hired within economics groups since the 1950s. Reg Appleyard, Pamela Statham, Melville 'Mel' Davies and Ian H. Vanden Driesen formed a cluster of a size to rival the ANU RSSS department. At Queensland, A. G. 'George' Kenwood and A. L. 'Alan' Lougheed had worked at the interface between economic history and economics since the early 1960s.¹¹⁶ La Trobe's economic history department was remarkably short-lived, and for most of the postwar decades economic historians had worked in economics. Ian McLean actively preferred to work as part of an economics group at the University of Adelaide, and Pincus similarly cultivated a much closer relationship with economics throughout his career. Even before the Flinders department was closed, in 1990 Pincus accepted a position as the professor and head of economics at the University of Adelaide, and throughout the 1990s and 2000s he transitioned to working primarily on contemporary economics research. As of his interview in 2015, Pincus commented that he 'hadn't done any economic history for a long time'.¹¹⁷ Other members of the same milieu – the Canberran (self-described) *economic* historians Glenn Withers and Rod Maddock – also moved into the economics discipline from the late 1980s. Both accepted positions at La Trobe's economics group from the late 1980s, and chose to stay there during the brief window where there was a separate department of economic history. When the time came for economic history at La Trobe to close, Maddock was the Chair of Economics, and was very supportive of the group's integration back into economics.¹¹⁸

---

114 Lloyd interview.
115 Ville; Cornish interviews.
116 See Albert George Kenwood and Alan Leslie Lougheed, *Growth of the International Economy, 1820–1960* (London: Routledge, 1971); Alan George Kenwood and Alan Leslie Lougheed, *Economics at the University of Queensland, 1912–1997* (Brisbane: University of Queensland, 1997).
117 Pincus interview.
118 Maddock; Withers interviews.

There were several new members hired or trained within economics departments, though this was a coincidence rather than any concerted effort to promote economic history. As Martin Shanahan reflected of the 1990s, 'if you're applying for the job […] you just didn't mention history, you were a macro-economist or a micro-economist'.[119] New members were hired as economists, but were able to incorporate some historical work into their teaching and research. Richard Pomfret, for example, arrived as professor of economics at the University of Adelaide in 1992. He maintained his research on contemporary trade and development, as well as collaborating with economic historians on historical research on trade and economics.[120] Also at the University of Adelaide, John K. Wilson completed his DPhil in economics in 2004, before a career in economics at the University of South Australia. At Monash, Gary Magee was hired to the economics group after a brief stint in the ANU RSSS economic history department in the late 1990s. Tim Hatton was appointed directly to the ANU Faculties' School of Economics in 2004, a comfortable move, as he had 'always been in economics departments'.[121] Edwyna Harris completed her PhD under the supervision of Merrett and Seltzer in the then Department of Management in the early 2000s, and was hired to the Monash economics group.[122] Several other prominent contributions to economic historical writing at this time were written from the perspective of the economics discipline.[123]

---

119 Shanahan interview.
120 Richard Pomfret, 'Trade Policy in Canada and Australia in the Twentieth Century', *Australian Economic History Review* 40, no. 2 (2000): 114–26, doi.org/10.1111/1467-8446.00061; John K Wilson and Richard Pomfret, 'Government Subsidies for Professional Team Sports in Australia', *Australian Economic Review* 42, no. 3 (2009): 264–75, doi.org/10.1111/j.1467-8462.2009.00536.x; Richard Pomfret, 'Expanding the Division of Labour: Trade Costs and Supply Chains in the Global Economy', *Australian Economic History Review* 54, no. 3 (2014): 220–41, doi.org/10.1111/aehr.12047; Richard Pomfret, 'Is Regionalism an Increasing Feature of the World Economy?', *World Economy* 30, no. 6 (2007): 923–47, doi.org/10.1111/j.1467-9701.2007.01038.x.
121 Hatton interview.
122 Edwyna Harris, 'Treading Water: An Analysis of Institutions and Natural Resource Sustainability, the Case of the Murray River' (PhD thesis, University of Melbourne, 2002).
123 Some examples of these scholars' work in Australian economic history include David Greasley and Jakob B Madsen, 'Curse and Boon: Natural Resources and Long-Run Growth in Currently Rich Economies', *Economic Record* 86, no. 274 (2010): 311–28, doi.org/10.1111/j.1475-4932.2009.00617.x; William Coleman, 'Is It Possible That an Independent Central Bank Is Impossible? The Case of the Australian Notes Issue Board, 1920–1924', *Journal of Money, Credit and Banking* 33, no. 3 (2001): 729–48, doi.org/10.2307/2673891; Rod Tyers and William Coleman, 'Beyond Brigden: Australia's Inter-War Manufacturing Tariffs, Real Wages and Economic Size', *Economic Record* 84, no. 264 (2008): 50–67, doi.org/10.1111/j.1475-4932.2008.00446.x; Sean Turnell, 'F. L. McDougall: Eminence Grise of Australian Economic Diplomacy', *Australian Economic History Review* 40, no. 1 (2000): 51–70, doi.org/10.1111/1467-8446.00055; Joe Isaac, 'The Economic Consequences of Harvester', *Australian Economic History Review* 48, no. 3 (2008): 280–300, doi.org/10.1111/j.1467-8446.2008.00242.x; Jon

Scholars made concerted efforts to establish their legitimacy in this discipline. As economic history was generally considered marginal or less scientific within economics, members had to make themselves 'useful' by teaching contemporary economics courses.[124] Shanahan, for example, has remembered that those who hired him at the South Australian Institute of Technology were 'not interested at all in my economic history interests. They were just interested in whether I could teach economics'.[125] Frost has also recalled the marginal place of economic history teaching at La Trobe, with Head of Department Rod Maddock advising that he would be vulnerable if all he taught was economic history. While Frost was initially 'horrified' by Maddock suggesting he teach first-year micro-economics, he was later grateful for the strategic advice.[126] Maddock has confirmed this, arguing that within La Trobe's economics department in the 1990s, there was space for economic history research, but scholars had to teach into the so-called '*core* economics curriculum'.[127] In exceptional cases, economic history units were maintained. For example, after accepting the Chair of Economics at the University of Wollongong in 2000, Ville used his position to leverage a required economic history course within the economics major.[128] Jeff Borland, a member of the economics department at the University of Melbourne, took responsibility for the required economic history subject when the economic history department rebranded as a business history group (see below). There were thus different fortunes for teaching and research in Australian economic history, with the near-absence of the subject in the curriculum, as Thornton notes, yet the continuation of research in the field.[129]

Members were also increasingly pressured to adhere to the norms of the economics discipline in their research. This was partly through choice of outlet, with economic historians publishing in key economics journals

---

C Altman, Nicholas Biddle and Boyd H Hunter, 'A Historical Perspective on Indigenous Socioeconomic Outcomes in Australia, 1971–2001', *Australian Economic History Review* 45, no. 3 (2005): 273–95, doi.org/10.1111/j.1467-8446.2005.00139.x; Jon C Altman, Nicholas Biddle and Boyd H Hunter, 'Prospects for "Closing the Gap" in Socioeconomic Outcomes for Indigenous Australians?', *Australian Economic History Review* 49, no. 3 (2009): 225–51, doi.org/10.1111/j.1467-8446.2009.00264.x.

124 Statham; Keneley interviews.
125 Shanahan interview.
126 Frost interview.
127 Maddock interview, emphasis mine.
128 Ville interview.
129 Thornton, 'Economics Curriculum'.

such as *Economic Record*.[130] There were also intellectual changes, with a greater number of contributions to the *Australian Economic History Review* applying contemporary neoclassical theories and advanced mathematical modelling to historical or long-run data. The share of papers in the *Review* containing regressions increased steadily from around 8 per cent in the mid-2000s, to just over 30 per cent a decade later.[131] In particular, orthodox interest in business cycles was brought into core international economics literature through endogenous growth theory. Popular from the 1980s, this framework is neoclassical in its specification, analysing economic growth through micro-foundations such as technology, innovation and human capital. Wilson and Shanahan, both then at the University of South Australia, assessed the role of lobbying and institutions – in their case tariff protection – in colonial Victoria, transforming orthodox-style aggregate data with a regression method to conclude that protection did little to support industrial development in Victoria in the 1870s and 1880s.[132] Economist Jakob Madsen and Edinburgh economic historian David Greasley assessed natural resource extraction and the resource curse hypothesis against frontier research in endogenous growth theory.[133] Harris's work on property rights for irrigation in northern Victoria also examined resource extraction through micro-foundations such as institutions, game theory and incentive structures.[134] Others, often using regression methods, assessed the role of education and technology

---

130 See, for example, Greasley and Madsen, 'Curse and Boon'; Peter Siminski and Simon Ville, 'I Was Only Nineteen, 45 Years Ago: What Can We Learn from Australia's Conscription Lotteries?', *Economic Record* 88, no. 282 (2012): 351–71, doi.org/10.1111/j.1475-4932.2012.00827.x; Rajabrata Banerjee, 'Population Growth and Endogenous Technological Change: Australian Economic Growth in the Long Run', *Economic Record* 88, no. 281 (2012): 214–28, doi.org/10.1111/j.1475-4932.2011.00784.x; Rajabrata Banerjee and John K Wilson, 'Roles of Education in Productivity Growth in Australia, 1860–1939', *Economic Record* 92, no. 296 (2016): 47–66, doi.org/10.1111/1475-4932.12226.
131 Andrew J Seltzer, 'Publication Trends and Future Challenges for the *Australian Economic History Review*: A Bibliometric Analysis', *Australian Economic History Review* 58, no. 2 (2018): 112–33, doi.org/10.1111/aehr.12143.
132 John K Wilson and Martin P Shanahan, 'Did Good Institutions Produce Good Tariffs? Evidence from Tariff Protection in Colonial Victoria', *Australian Economic History Review* 52, no. 2 (2012): 128–47, doi.org/10.1111/j.1467-8446.2012.00346.x.
133 Greasley and Madsen, 'Curse and Boon'.
134 Harris, 'Treading Water'; Lee J Alston, Edwyna Harris and Bernardo Mueller, 'The Development of Property Rights on Frontiers: Endowments, Norms, and Politics', *Journal of Economic History* 72, no. 3 (2012): 741–70, doi.org/10.1017/S0022050712000356; Edwyna Harris, 'The Impact of Institutional Path Dependence on Water Market Efficiency in Victoria, Australia', *Water Resources Management* 25, no. 15 (2011): 4069–80, doi.org/10.1007/s11269-011-9884-0; Edwyna Harris, 'Institutional Change and Economic Growth: The Evolution of Water Rights in Victoria, Australia 1850–1886', *Economic Papers* 26, no. 2 (2007): 118–27, doi.org/10.1111/j.1759-3441.2007.tb01011.x; Edwyna Harris, 'Development and Damage: Water and Landscape Evolution in Victoria, Australia', *Landscape Research* 31, no. 2 (2006): 169–81, doi.org/10.1080/01426390600638687.

on Australia's long-run economic growth.[135] Work on anthropometric history used a cliometric toolkit to address the human capital dimensions of Australia's long-run growth. This followed earlier interest, particularly from those at UNSW, on slavery (see Chapter 4), with scholars examining historical wellbeing through various heights and weights records.[136]

Collaboration was used to integrate with the core economics discipline. It allowed 'subcontracting' for those not trained in the technical skills needed for acceptance by increasingly narrow economics journals, while leveraging economic historians' abilities in assessing context and sources.[137] Compared to collaboration throughout the 1970s and 1980s, which often occurred within the field, and more specifically within each department (see Chapter 4), partnerships between economic historians and economists were common throughout the 1990s and 2000s. For example, Ville has recalled that he mitigated his 'sense of vulnerability' in economics at the University of Wollongong by collaborating with those with complementary quantitative and mathematical skills.[138] Ville's work with micro-economist Peter Siminski on wellbeing and conscription lotteries was published in *Economic Record*, which was, given the discipline's narrowing, an unlikely event in the absence of Siminski's regression expertise.[139]

---

135 Banerjee, 'Population Growth'; Banerjee and Wilson, 'Roles of Education'; Gary B Magee, 'The Face of Invention: Skills, Experience, and the Commitment to Patenting in Nineteenth-Century Victoria', *Australian Economic History Review* 38, no. 3 (1998): 232–57, doi.org/10.1111/1467-8446.00032; Gary Bryan Magee, 'Technological Development and Foreign Patenting: Evidence from 19th-Century Australia', *Explorations in Economic History* 36, no. 4 (1999): 344–59, doi.org/10.1006/exeh.1999.0721.
136 Greg Whitwell and Stephen Nicholas, 'Weight and Welfare of Australians, 1890–1940', *Australian Economic History Review* 41, no. 2 (2001): 159–75, doi.org/10.1111/1467-8446.00080; Christine de Souza and Stephen Nicholas, 'Height, Health, and Economic Growth in Australia, 1860–1940', in *Health and Welfare During Industrialization*, ed. Richard H Steckel and Roderick H Floud (Chicago: University of Chicago Press, 1997), 379–422; Stephen Nicholas, Robert Gregory and Sue Kimberley, 'The Welfare of Indigenous and White Australians 1890–1955', in *The Biological Standard of Living in Comparative Perspective*, ed. J Baten and J Komlos (Stuttgart: Franz Steiner Verlag, 1998), 35–54; Kris Inwood et al., 'Growing Incomes, Growing People in Nineteenth-Century Tasmania', *Australian Economic History Review* 55, no. 2 (2015): 187–211, doi.org/10.1111/aehr.12071; Robert V Jackson and Mark Thomas, 'Height, Weight, and Wellbeing: Sydney Schoolchildren in the Early Twentieth Century', *Australian Economic History Review* 35, no. 2 (1995): 39–65, doi.org/10.1111/aehr.352003; Ralph Shlomowitz, 'Did the Mean Height of Australian-Born Men Decline in the Late Nineteenth Century? A Comment', *Economics and Human Biology* 5, no. 3 (2007): 484–88, doi.org/10.1016/j.ehb.2007.09.002.
137 Frost interview.
138 Ville interview.
139 Siminski and Ville, 'I Was Only Nineteen'. See also Simon Ville and Peter Siminski, 'A Fair and Equitable Method of Recruitment? Conscription by Ballot in the Australian Army During the Vietnam War', *Australian Economic History Review* 51, no. 3 (2011): 277–96, doi.org/10.1111/j.1467-8446.2011.00335.x.

Once the crisis had settled, most mainstream economic historians saw themselves primarily as members of the economics discipline. In 2007, McLean and Shanahan reported on a forum, held at the annual conference that examined the 'big questions' and 'research challenges' facing Australasian economic history. Although the discussion was wide-ranging in terms of potential new research themes – including government policy, the environment and the Indigenous economy – in terms of disciplinary identity they remained firmly within economics. In commenting that 'it is likely that the position of economic history within departments of economics will be the key to its long-term viability', the authors advocated for economic history coursework to be integrated with other areas of the discipline, and to maintain the same level of 'rigour' to other advanced economics subjects.[140] Although they acknowledged the growing presence of business history and integration with the management discipline, this did not form part of their recommendations for 'practical responses to [the field's] challenges'.[141] They also advocated for disciplinary gatekeeping of the field's entrants, arguing that future 'quality' research required advanced skills in economic theory and statistical techniques, alongside 'careful attention to the graduate training of applicants to entry-level positions in economic history when they arise'.[142]

Business history

Some decided to pivot towards business disciplines. Rather than automatically integrating into economics, this represented a more active way for economic historians to 'resist' the institutional changes around them. As a result of the small economic and business history communities in Australia, the boundaries between each specialty were porous, with similar appointment and professional structures, and members happily working in both areas.[143] Business history, in the form of commissioned firm 'biographies', had been written in Australia since the turn of the twentieth century. Postwar expansion of universities prompted greater interest from professional historians in business history, and while they were often still commissioned by companies, storytellers such as Geoffrey Blainey made the genre more accessible (see Chapter 4). Mainstream economic historians such as Syd Butlin and Alan Barnard also contributed to the field

---

140 McLean and Shanahan, 'Australasian Economic History', 313.
141 McLean and Shanahan, 'Australasian Economic History', 312.
142 McLean and Shanahan, 'Australasian Economic History', 308.
143 In interviews, members often conflated the two fields, with Merrett commenting that he 'hasn't given a great deal of thought to the boundaries'. See Merrett interview.

throughout the 1950s and 1960s.[144] Indeed, the orthodox focus on capital investment required an interest in business archives, with Noel Butlin instrumental in obtaining firm records for his private capital estimates (see Chapter 3).[145] The Business Archives Council began publishing *Business Archives and History* from 1961, which was transferred to the Economic History Society of Australia and New Zealand (EHSANZ) and renamed the *Australian Economic History Review* in the late 1960s. Throughout the 1970s and 1980s there were several important contributions to business history, but there was a drop in momentum and work was characterised by a lack of innovation, collaboration and international engagement.[146] The business 'biography' – the lone scholar creating a narrative of a single company's progress – dominated until the 1990s.[147]

Throughout the 1990s and 2000s, Merrett and others initiated a reorientation of Australian business history research. Harvard business historian Alfred D. Chandler, whose work dominated global business history from the 1960s, explored the development of large-scale enterprise through an understanding of organisational capabilities, structure, technology and managerialism.[148] Chandler's research was enormously influential in a variety of disciplines and fields, and he has been credited with increased theoretical specificity for business historical research, and renewed recognition of the value of historical work for management

---

144 See Butlin, *Foundations*; Butlin, *Australia and New Zealand Bank*; Alan Barnard, *The Australian Wool Market, 1840–1900* (Melbourne: Melbourne University Press, 1958); Alan Barnard, *Visions and Profits: Studies in the Business Career of Thomas Sutcliffe Mort* (Melbourne: Melbourne University Press, 1961).
145 The Business Archives Council used these records to form the Labour and Business Archive (now the Noel Butlin Archive Centre) at ANU.
146 For example, Geoffrey Blainey, *Jumping over the Wheel* (Sydney: Allen & Unwin, 1993); E Alan Beever, *The Launceston Bank for Savings, 1835–1970* (Melbourne: Melbourne University Press, 1972); William Gordon Rimmer, *Portrait of a Hospital, the Royal Hobart* (Hobart: Royal Hobart Hospital, 1981); David Roger Hainsworth, *The Sydney Traders: Simeon Lord and His Contemporaries, 1788–1821* (Melbourne: Melbourne University Press, 1981); Reginald T Appleyard and C Boris Schedvin, eds, *Australian Financiers: Biographical Essays* (Melbourne: Macmillan, 1988); Kenneth D Buckley and Kris Klugman, *The History of Burns Philp: The Australian Company in the South Pacific* (Sydney: Burns, Philp & Company Limited, 1981); Tim Hewat, *The Elders Explosion: One Hundred and Fifty Years of Progress from Elder to Elliott* (Sydney: Bay Books, 1988); Peter Richardson, 'The Origins and Development of the Collins House Group, 1915–1951', *Australian Economic History Review* 27, no. 1 (1987): 3–30, doi.org/10.1111/aehr.271001.
147 David T Merrett, 'Business Institutions and Behaviour in Australia: A New Perspective', *Business History* 42, no. 3 (2000): 1–12, doi.org/10.1080/00076790000000264.
148 Particularly Alfred D Chandler, *Strategy and Structure: Chapters in the History of the Industrial Enterprise* (New York: Doubleday, 1966); Alfred D Chandler, *Scale and Scope: The Dynamics of Industrial Competition* (Cambridge, MA: Harvard Business School, 1990); Alfred D Chandler, *The Visible Hand* (Cambridge MA: Harvard University Press, 1993).

research and practice.[149] Chandler's work, and the ensuing debate, was particularly important in business history internationally throughout the 1970s and 1980s; a revolution that had largely passed Australia by.[150]

Prior to collective efforts towards the so-called 'new' business history research, several scholars individually worked within the Chandlerian revolution. Merrett's research on the corporate strategy and organisational structure of the Australia and New Zealand Bank was directly influenced by Chandler, through colleagues at Monash who gave him a copy of *Strategy and Structure* to read one day at morning tea.[151] Ville's work on British shipping firm Michael Henley and Sons engaged with macro-economic questions on the history of the maritime trade, as well as exploring the development of business practice within the firm.[152] He then turned his attention to Australia's stock and station agents, applying the Chandlerian concept of the multidivisional corporation to argue that these were complex organisations run by competent, modern, professional businesspeople.[153] At ANU, Ville hired Grant Fleming in the early 1990s, and they worked together on 'new' business history topics.[154] Stephen Nicholas, similarly, had a background in the topic, and supervised Diane Hutchinson's DPhil in business history in the early 1980s.[155] Hutchinson's work in business history focused on technology, organisational structure and entrepreneurship, primarily in manufacturing firms.[156]

---

149 Richard Whittington, 'Alfred Chandler, Founder of Strategy: Lost Tradition and Renewed Inspiration', *Business History Review* 82, no. 2 (2011): 267–77, doi.org/10.1017/S0007680500062760; Merrett, 'Business Institutions'; Keneley, 'Reflections'.
150 Merrett, 'Business Institutions'; Keneley, 'Reflections'.
151 Merrett interview; David T Merrett, *ANZ Bank: An Official History* (Sydney: Allen & Unwin, 1985). Lionel Frost also commented that Merrett had been interested in business history for a good while before he started at Monash in the 1980s. See Frost interview.
152 Ville interview; Simon P Ville, *English Shipowning During the Industrial Revolution: Michael Henley and Son, London Shipowners, 1770–1830* (Manchester: Manchester University Press, 1987).
153 Primarily, Simon Ville, *The Rural Entrepreneurs: A History of the Stock and Station Agent Industry in Australia and New Zealand* (Cambridge: Cambridge University Press, 2000).
154 For example, Simon Ville and Grant Fleming, 'Financial Intermediaries and the Design of Loan Contracts within the Australasian Pastoral Sector before the Second World War', *Financial History Review* 7, no. 2 (2000): 201–18, doi.org/10.1017/S0968565000000111; Grant Fleming, 'Social Norms, Economic Behaviour, and the Law: A Theoretical Introduction', *Australian Economic History Review* 39, no. 3 (1999): 163–71, doi.org/10.1111/1467-8446.00047.
155 Hutchinson; Nicholas interviews.
156 Diane Hutchinson, 'Australian Manufacturing Business: Entrepreneurship or Missed Opportunities?', *Australian Economic History Review* 41, no. 2 (2001): 103–34, doi.org/10.1111/1467-8446.00078; Diane Hutchinson, 'The Transformation of Boral: From Dependent, Specialist Bitumen Refiner to Major Building Products Manufacturer', *Business History* 42, no. 3 (2000): 109–32, doi.org/10.1080/00076790000000269; Diane Hutchinson and Stephen Nicholas, 'Modelling the Growth Strategies of British Firms', *Business History* 29, no. 4 (1987): 46–64, doi.org/10.1080/00076798700000080.

The Dawkins reforms created opportunities to further develop this interest in new business history. The move towards a user-pays system – particularly the deregulation of postgraduate course fees – encouraged the growth of business disciplines like management, finance and human resources.[157] The work of Chandler and others had established the usefulness of business history for contemporary theory and practice, and the forced relocation of Australia's economic and business historians created opportunities to engage with business disciplines in both teaching and research.[158] For example, throughout the 1990s Ville and Gordon Boyce taught international business at ANU and the Queensland University of Technology, respectively, and included a fair amount of historical material in their textbook, *The Development of Modern Business*.[159]

Facing possible obscurity within economics, the University of Melbourne economic history department pivoted towards business education. Schedvin left the group in 1991 for the deputy vice chancellor role, and Nicholas was hired as his replacement. Nicholas noticed an opportunity to contribute to business education: the Melbourne Business School provided postgraduate instruction, including an Masters of Business Administration (MBA), and there was a separate economics and business faculty that had student demand for business education yet no dedicated management department.[160] Members of the economic history group – including Merrett, Whitwell and Nicholas – were predisposed towards business history and, as Whitwell argued, 'a very loose approach to the nature and purpose of the discipline'.[161] As such, they decided to rebrand the department and establish a new Masters of International Business to attract students.

The group established their credibility in international business in a similar way to those who moved to economics: by hiring and training new staff, broadening the research agenda and collaborating with relevant colleagues. PhD students supervised by members of the department worked on contemporary and historical business topics with, for example, Andre

---

157 Claire EF Wright and Hannah Forsyth, 'Managerial Capitalism and White-Collar Professions: Social Mobility in Australia's Corporate Elite', *Labour History* 121, no. 1 (2021): 99–127, doi.org/10.3828/jlh.2021.20.
158 Keneley, 'Reflections'.
159 Ville interview. Gordon Boyce and Simon Ville, *The Development of Modern Business* (London: Palgrave Macmillan, 2002), doi.org/10.1007/978-1-137-12008-3.
160 Nicholas interview.
161 Whitwell, 'Future Directions'.

Sammartino examining human resources practices and the labour market in Victorian railways.[162] Elizabeth Maitland's thesis reflected the group's transition to contemporary international business research, examining Australian multinationals in Asian 'transition' economies.[163] New hires in 1994 and 1995 – Stephen Morgan, Howard Dick and Andy Seltzer – targeted international business and labour economics, and members upskilled in these areas by using a historical perspective to contribute to contemporary business outlets.[164] Business history also became part of their research agenda, with members publishing contemporary articles in addition to their historical work.[165] They developed new connections in teaching and research, working with Melbourne colleagues in international business and micro-economics, as well as prominent overseas scholars.[166] The key to the sell was the name. They called the new group 'business development and corporate history', and, as Nicholas has argued, 'the great advantage of that [was] that no one actually knew what it meant, but it sounded quite good [laughter]'.[167]

---

162 Andre Sammartino, 'Human Research Management Practices and Labour Market Structures in the Victorian Railways, 1864–1921' (PhD thesis, University of Melbourne, 2002).

163 Elizabeth Maitland, 'Contract and Expansion: Sovereignty, Transitional Economies and Australian Mines' (PhD thesis, University of Melbourne, 1998).

164 David T Merrett, 'The Internationalization of Australian Banks', *Journal of International Financial Markets, Institutions and Money* 12, no. 4–5 (2002): 377–97, doi.org/10.1016/S1042-4431(02)00020-3; David T Merrett, 'Australia's Emergent Multinationals: The Legacy of Having a Natural-Resource Intensive, Small, and Closed Economy as Home', *International Studies of Management & Organization* 32, no. 1 (2002): 109–35, doi.org/10.1080/00208825.2002.110436 55; Andrew Seltzer and David Merrett, 'Personnel Policies at the Union Bank of Australia: Evidence from the 1888–1900 Entry Cohorts', *Journal of Labor Economics* 18, no. 4 (2000): 573–613, doi.org/10.1086/209970; David T Merrett, 'Some Lessons from the History of Australian Banking', *Economic Papers* 25, Suppl. S1 (2006): 52–60, doi.org/10.1111/j.1759-3441.2006.tb00415.x; Simon Ville and David Merrett, 'A Time Series for Business Profitability in Twentieth-Century Australia', *Australian Economic Review* 39, no. 3 (2006): 330–39, doi.org/10.1111/j.1467-8462.2006.00423.x.

165 Some examples include Elizabeth Maitland and Andre Sammartino, 'Flexible Footprints: Reconfiguring MNCs for New Value Opportunities', *California Management Review* 36, no. 4 (2012): 92–117, doi.org/10.1525/cmr.2012.54.2.92; Elizabeth Maitland and Stephen Nicholas, 'Modeling Multinationals from Small, Open Economies', *International Studies of Management and Organization* 32, no. 1 (2002): 3–15, doi.org/10.1080/00208825.2002.11043653; André Sammartino, Janine L O'Flynn and Stephen J Nicholas, 'The Employer Perspective of Indigenous (Un)Employment', *Economic Papers* 22, no. 4 (2003): 45–60, doi.org/10.1111/j.1759-3441.2003.tb01133.x; Elizabeth Maitland, Elizabeth L Rose and Stephen Nicholas, 'How Firms Grow: Clustering as a Dynamic Model of Internationalization', *Journal of International Business Studies* 36, no. 4 (2005): 435–51, oi.org/10.1057/palgrave.jibs.8400140; Ben Jensen and Andrew Seltzer, 'Neighbourhood and Family Effects in Educational Progress', *Australian Economic Review* 33, no. 1 (2000): 17–31, doi.org/10.1111/1467-8462.00133.

166 Nicholas interview; Seltzer correspondence, 2 June 2021.

167 Nicholas interview.

The gamble initially paid off, with Nicholas happily reporting a 20–25 per cent increase in student numbers in 1997.[168] However, a short time later, the group was merged with others to form a Department of Management. The same result (a merger) as economic history departments elsewhere prompts the question as to whether they should have bothered. It was, arguably, good work to do, as it kept the group together. A cohesive team was a much better 'safeguard against marginalisation' than individuals, and they were able to maintain their collaborative relationships in both international business and more traditional economic history topics.[169] The relative youth of the management discipline meant it had a broader set of acceptable approaches compared to the narrowing of the economics discipline at the time. The Melbourne group aligned with a more diverse approach to the subject, and the work they had done to establish credibility gave them bargaining power in a new and expanding department. An active, if unorthodox, move was preferable to them than none at all.

As a result of these intellectual and administrative changes, Melbourne became the focus of a 'new' Australian business history that actively engaged with contemporary, international theory and practice. In 2000, Merrett edited a special issue of *Business History*, consolidating new work on the subject.[170] In the introduction, he made his manifesto for the field clear – it was to be comparative, and it was to be Chandlerian. He argued that, in the 1970s and 1980s, work on the subject had 'increasingly diverged from international best practice', lamenting that Chandler's work had barely made waves across the Pacific.[171] This became a symbol of what was lacking in Australian business history, that 'bereft of the conceptual advances that were raising business history to new levels of sophistication abroad, Australian work no longer excited the interest of

---

168 Nicholas, 'The Future of Economic History'.
169 Nicholas, 'The Future of Economic History', 274.
170 Simon Ville and David T Merrett, 'The Development of Large Scale Enterprise in Australia, 1910–64', *Business History* 42, no. 3 (2000): 13–46, doi.org/10.1080/00076790000000265; David T Merrett and Andrew Seltzer, 'Work in the Financial Services Industry and Worker Monitoring: A Study of the Union Bank of Australia in the 1920s', *Business History* 42, no. 3 (2000): 133–52, doi.org/10.1080/00076790000000270; Hutchinson, 'Transformation of Boral'; Helen Fountain, 'Technology Acquisition, Firm Capability and Sustainable Competitive Advantage: A Case Study of Australian Glass Manufacturers Ltd, 1915–39', *Business History* 42, no. 3 (2000): 89–108, doi.org/10.1080/00076790000000268; Grant Fleming, 'Collusion and Price Wars in the Australian Coal Industry During the Late Nineteenth Century', *Business History* 42, no. 3 (2000): 47–70, doi.org/10.1080/00076790000000266; Peter Burn, 'Opportunism and Long-Term Contracting: Transactions in Broken Hill Zinc Concentrates in the 1930s', *Business History* 42, no. 3 (2000): 71–88, doi.org/10.1080/00076790000000267.
171 Merrett, 'Business Institutions', 3.

academic peers'.[172] Applying a Chandlerian framework to unexplored Australian topics, Merrett and Ville traced the evolution of large-scale enterprises in Australia from World War I until the mid-1960s. This was later expanded to encompass the twentieth century in their monograph with Grant Fleming, *The Big End of Town*.[173] Other contributions were smaller-scale studies of firms or industries that drew on modern theories of firm behaviour.[174] Chandler and the new institutional economics were front-and-centre, as was the comparative context.

The expansion of business history was evident in the field's structures. Grants from the ARC provided resources to conduct large-scale projects on the history of big business, profitability and cartels. Business historians – including Whitwell, Fleming, van der Eng and Ville – edited the *Australian Economic History Review* between 1996 and 2003, and the journal published work on insurance firms, the professions, advertising and consumer culture, and multinational expansion.[175] Compared to the friction between economic and labour historians in the 1970s, contact between business and industrial relations history was also fruitful. Many labour historians were absorbed into business schools by the 2000s, and were thus similarly motivated to connect with business disciplines such as human resources.[176] The *Review* provided a platform for some of these conversations, including work by key business historians such as Malcolm Abbott and Andre Sammartino, labour historians Charles Fahey and Erik

---

172 Merrett, 'Business Institutions', 3.
173 Grant A Fleming, David T Merrett and Simon Ville, *The Big End of Town: Big Business and Corporate Leadership in Twentieth-Century Australia* (Melbourne: Cambridge University Press, 2004), doi.org/10.1017/CBO9780511481567.
174 Hutchinson, 'Transformation of Boral'; Fountain, 'Technology Acquisition'; Fleming, 'Collusion'; Burn, 'Opportunism'.
175 Garry D Carnegie, 'The Development of Accounting Regulation, Education, and Literature in Australia, 1788–2005', *Australian Economic History Review* 49, no. 3 (2009): 276–301, doi.org/10.1111/j.1467-8446.2009.00266.x; Gordon Boyce, 'A Professional Association as Network and Communicating Node: The Pharmaceutical Society of Australasia, 1857–1918', *Australian Economic History Review* 39, no. 3 (1999): 258–83, doi.org/10.1111/1467-8446.00052; Robert Crawford, 'Emptor Australis: The Australian Consumer in Early Twentieth Century Advertising Literature', *Australian Economic History Review* 45, no. 3 (2005): 221–43, doi.org/10.1111/j.1467-8446.2005.00137.x; Helen Fountain, 'Managing Multinational Expansion and Related Diversification: The Case of Australian Consolidated Industries Ltd, 1939–72', *Australian Economic History Review* 42, no. 2 (2002): 160–82, doi.org/10.1111/1467-8446.t01-1-00028; Monica Keneley, 'The Origins of Formal Collusion in Australian Fire Insurance 1870–1920', *Australian Economic History Review* 42, no. 1 (2002): 54–76, doi.org/10.1111/1467-8446.t01-1-00022; Monica Keneley and Tom McDonald, 'The Nature and Development of the General Insurance Industry in Australia to 1973', *Australian Economic History Review* 47, no. 3 (2007): 278–99, doi.org/10.1111/j.1467-8446.2007.00212.x.
176 Frank Bongiorno, 'Australian Labour History: Contexts, Trends and Influences', *Labour History* 100, no. 1 (2011): 1–19, doi.org/10.5263/labourhistory.100.0001.

Eklund, and business scholars Charles Livingstone and Peter Sheldon.[177] The agenda of this era was also set by several pieces that reflected on trends in business history, including accounting history, the history of management, theoretical work on firms and entrepreneurs, and insights from prominent business history archives.[178] In 2007, McLean and Shanahan reported that members of the conference forum emphasised business history as the 'the principal "area" towards which a refocus was being advocated', and Glenn Withers has commented that it was 'how economic history survive[d]'.[179]

History

As opposed to members' directed efforts to secure their future within economics and business schools, economic historians did not deliberately make themselves useful to the history discipline. The 1990s and 2000s was a hostile time to engage with most historians, with the cultural turn making it difficult to find common ground. There was also very little institutional imperative to 'convince' cultural historians of the value of economic matters, with most economic historians merging with economics or business schools throughout the 1990s.[180] As such, work with the history discipline was done to improve the vibrancy of the research

---

177 Charles Fahey and André Sammartino, 'Work and Wages at a Melbourne Factory, the Guest Biscuit Works 1870–1921', *Australian Economic History Review* 53, no. 1 (2013): 22–46, 22, doi.org/10.1111/aehr.12003; Charles Livingstone, 'Dealing with Class: Orthodox Public Discourse and Australian Trade Unionism', *Australian Economic History Review* 43, no. 1 (2003): 66–82, doi.org/10.1111/aehr.12003; Erik Eklund, 'Managers, Workers, and Industrial Welfarism: Management Strategies at ER&S and the Sulphide Corporation, 1895–1929', *Australian Economic History Review* 37, no. 2 (1997): 137–57, doi.org/10.1111/aehr.372004; Peter Sheldon, 'State-Level Basic Wages in Australia During the Depression, 1929–35: Institutions and Politics over Markets', *Australian Economic History Review* 47, no. 3 (2007): 249–77, doi.org/10.1111/j.1467-8446.2007.00211.x.

178 Garry D Carnegie and Brad N Potter, 'Accounting History in Australia: A Survey of Published Works, 1975–99', *Australian Economic History Review* 40, no. 3 (2000): 287–313, doi.org/10.1111/1467-8446.00069; Paul L Robertson, 'The Future of Management: Does Business History Have Anything to Tell Us?', *Australian Economic History Review* 43, no. 1 (2003): 1–21, doi.org/10.1111/1467-8446.t01-1-00038; Jane Ellen et al., 'Making Archival Choices for Business History', *Australian Economic History Review* 44, no. 2 (2004): 185–96, doi.org/10.1111/j.1467-8446.2004.00116.x; Paul L Robertson and Gianmario Verona, 'Post-Chandlerian Firms: Technological Change and Firm Boundaries', *Australian Economic History Review* 46, no. 1 (2006): 70–94, doi.org/10.1111/j.1467-8446.2006.00152.x; Stephen L Morgan, 'Australian Immigration Archives as Sources for Business and Economic History', *Australian Economic History Review* 46, no. 3 (2006): 268–82, doi.org/10.1111/j.1467-8446.2006.00181.x; James Reveley, 'Using Autobiographies in Business History: A Narratological Analysis of Jules Joubert's *Shavings and Scrapes*', *Australian Economic History Review* 50, no. 3 (2010): 284–305, doi.org/10.1111/j.1467-8446.2010.00306.x.

179 McLean and Shanahan, 'Australasian Economic History', 306; Withers interview.

180 Robert Aldrich at the University of Sydney, and Robin Haines and Ralph Shlomowitz at Flinders, are the exceptions.

program, rather than to shield against institutional change or establish legitimacy for teaching. Connections were largely on economic historians' turf, and terms, with the *Australian Economic History Review* acting as a communicating infrastructure to bring together a range of perspectives servicing existing synergies with urban, social and environmental history.

Urban history continued as a key theme in Australian economic history, incorporating both the existing emphasis on industrialisation and urban planning, and the more recent interest in 'maintain[ing] living standards while not destroying its environment'.[181] In 2009, Frost and urban historian Seamus O'Hanlon co-edited a special issue of the *Australian Economic History Review* on 'New Essays in Urban History'. Contributors included members of Monash's former economic history group – including Frost and Dingle – as well as several historians.[182] The editors attempted to update the work McCarty and Schedvin had initiated 40 years prior, informing broader environmental and policy discussions by discerning lessons across time and place.[183] Dingle's contribution examined the decline of manufacturing in Melbourne using fairly standard orthodox methods. There were some gestures to recent advances in cultural history,[184] however, the focus was on urban planning, the environment (as structure) and regional economies rather than a poststructuralist scope. Methodologically, contributors were largely informed by their background in social sciences, incorporating aggregated quantitative evidence rather than discourse.

Work on resources and pollution in urban history aligned with recent advances in environmental history. The study of interactions between human societies and the extreme Australian environment is, of course,

---

181   Lionel Frost and Seamus O'Hanlon, 'Urban History and the Future of Australian Cities', *Australian Economic History Review* 49, no. 1 (2009): 1–18, 15, doi.org/10.1111/j.1467-8446.2008.00246.x.
182   Frost and Hanlon, 'Urban History'; Peter Spearritt, 'The 200 km City: Brisbane, the Gold Coast, and Sunshine Coast', *Australian Economic History Review* 49, no. 1 (2009): 87–106, doi.org/10.1111/j.1467-8446.2009.00251.x; Andrew May, 'Ideas from Australian Cities: Relocating Urban and Suburban History', *Australian Economic History Review* 49, no. 1 (2009): 70–86, doi.org/10.1111/j.1467-8446.2009.00250.x; Jenny Gregory, 'Development Pressures and Heritage in the Perth Central Business District, 1950–90', *Australian Economic History Review* 49, no. 1 (2009): 34–51, doi.org/10.1111/j.1467-8446.2008.00248.x; Tony Dingle and Seamus O'Hanlon, 'From Manufacturing Zone to Lifestyle Precinct: Economic Restructuring and Social Change in Inner Melbourne, 1971–2001', *Australian Economic History Review* 49, no. 1 (2009): 52–69, doi.org/10.1111/j.1467-8446.2009.00249.x; Nancy Cushing, 'Australia's Smoke City: Air Pollution in Newcastle', *Australian Economic History Review* 49, no. 1 (2009): 19–33, doi.org/10.1111/j.1467-8446.2008.00247.x.
183   Frost and Hanlon, 'Urban History'.
184   Cushing, 'Australia's Smoke City'; Spearritt, 'The 200 km City'.

a major component of any history of the continent. In the 1990s, rising concern with human climatic impacts translated to interest in environmental history. This incorporated the insights of the cultural turn to understand the way the environment shaped identities and lived experiences, and the specificity of living not simply in 'Australia', but in her myriad different zones. The synergies between these new environmental histories and the cultural turn meant the field gradually became a core component of the history discipline throughout the 1990s and 2000s.[185]

Economic historians, on the other hand, had an interest in the environment drawn from the work of economics on resource extraction and externalities. Work by Harris, Madsen and Greasley (above) was demonstrative of an economics perspective for understanding environmental history. In 2008, the EHSANZ selected 'Responses to Environmental Change' as the conference theme, exploring the 'economic responses that past episodes of climate changes triggered' in periods of pollution, deforestation, drought, flood and disease.[186] The conference was followed in 2010 by a special issue, co-edited by ANU economic historian Pierre van der Eng, on climate and the economy in several international contexts. The editors of the 2010 issue aimed to inform the '*economics* of environmental change', and contributions were organised around the principles of resource extraction: rent-seeking by lobbying groups, and the efficiency or otherwise of environmental protections.[187] Similarly, Deakin economic and business historian Monica Keneley examined land use, rent-seeking and the success of the closer settlement program in the Western District of Victoria.[188] Also in the *Review*, research on Queensland's dugong and turtle fisheries included a range of qualitative and oral history sources, though used them to understand the economic imperative of the trade

---

185 Libby Robin and Mike Smith, 'Australian Environmental History: Ten Years On', *Environment and History* 14, no. 2 (2008): 135–43, doi.org/10.3197/096734008X303692; Libby Robin and Tom Griffiths, 'Environmental History in Australasia', *Environment and History* 10, no. 4 (2004): 439–74, doi.org/10.3197/0967340042772667; Richard White, 'From Wilderness to Hybrid Landscapes: The Cultural Turn in Environmental History', *Historian* 66, no. 3 (2004): 557–64, doi.org/10.1111/j.1540-6563.2004.00089.x.
186 'Announcements', *Australian Economic History Review* 47, no. 3 (2007): 335.
187 Jean-Pascal Bassino and Pierre van der Eng, 'Responses of Economic Systems to Environmental Change: Past Experiences', *Australian Economic History Review* 50, no. 1 (2010): 1–5, doi.org/10.1111/j.1467-8446.2009.00268.x. Emphasis mine.
188 Monica Keneley, 'Closer Settlement in the Western District of Victoria: A Case Study in Australian Land Use Policy, 1898–1914', *Journal of Historical Geography* 28, no. 3 (2002): 363–79, doi.org/10.1006/jhge.2002.0458.

rather than addressing identities and lived experiences.[189] While this expanded focus on the environment aligned with growing interest from historians on similar issues, at this time it was in service of an economics-based agenda, rather than the cultural–environmental approach from historians.

Mining history also provided space for engagement with the history discipline, with an emphasis on trade, capital investment and employment integrating with some historians' interest in labour, industrial relations, geography, technology and the environment. There was some professional alignment with the core of the history discipline on these matters, with the Australian Historical Association (AHA) organising their 2001 conference in Kalgoorlie on the history of mining. The EHSANZ partnered with the AHA, organising their conference to be held at the same time, and encouraging cross-submission of papers and joint membership fees.[190] A special issue on the history of mining in the Asia-Pacific followed in the *Review* in 2005, with another specifically on gold in 2010. While key members of the field – Boyce, Frost and Dingle – edited these volumes, other contributors were members of the history, geography or sociology disciplines in Australia and elsewhere. In the 2010 issue, the authors aimed to integrate 'histories of migration, trade, colonisation, and environmental history to identify endogenous factors that […] generated sustained economic growth'. Contributions in both issues focused on industry, firm and capital structure, the creation of markets, and aspects of endogenous growth such as innovation and technology. Scholars used a range of qualitative and quantitative sources familiar to economic, social and labour historians, and although some examined individual experiences it was within the framework of understanding production, class and work, rather than identity.[191] These contributions broadened

---

189 Ben Daley, Peter Griggs and Helene Marsh, 'Exploiting Marine Wildlife in Queensland: The Commercial Dugong and Marine Turtle Fisheries, 1847–1969', *Australian Economic History Review* 48, no. 3 (2008): 227–65, doi.org/10.1111/j.1467-8446.2008.00240.x.

190 Christopher Lloyd, 'Editorial Notes', *Australian Economic History Review* 42, no. 1 (2002): 91, doi.org/10.1111/1467-8446.t01-1-00024.

191 Keir Reeves, Lionel Frost and Charles Fahey, 'Integrating the Historiography of the Nineteenth-Century Gold Rushes', *Australian Economic History Review* 50, no. 2 (2010): 111–128, 111, doi.org/10.1111/j.1467-8446.2010.00296.x. See also Gordon Boyce and Jeremy Mouat, 'Introduction: Mining History In Context', *Australian Economic History Review* 45, no. 2 (2005): 115–18, doi.org/10.1111/j.1467-8446.2005.00130.x; Barry McGowan, 'The Economics and Organisation of Chinese Mining in Colonial Australia', *Australian Economic History Review* 45, no. 2 (2005): 119–38, doi.org/10.1111/j.1467-8446.2005.00131.x; Diane Menghetti, 'Invention and Innovation in the Australian Non-Ferrous Mining Industry: Whose Technology?', *Australian Economic History Review* 45, no. 2 (2005): 204–19, doi.org/10.1111/j.1467-8446.2005.00135.x; John Hillman,

economic history's collaborators and thematic emphasis, though they did so in a way that aligned with mainstream economic history work while doing little to integrate with the majority of the history discipline.

Looking to the world

In addition to expanding the field's disciplinary focus, members also connected to global conversations. In the 1980s and 1990s, the field was divided between those who worked on overseas research topics and published in international outlets, and those who published in the *Review* on Australian economic history (see Chapter 4). In addition to internal advocacy for international engagement, particularly from those in Canberra and Adelaide,[192] the introduction of neoliberal university policy incentivised internationalisation of the research program. University managers, rankings and the ARC encouraged overseas conference presentations, international collaborations and contributions to global or regional journals (see Chapter 6). These incentives enabled international travel, particularly to conferences in the European and North American metropoles. Strikingly, attendance at the World Economic History Congress (WEHC), organised by the International Economic History Association (IEHA), went from a rare occurrence to reasonably ubiquitous, with attendance commented on in the *Australian Economic History Review* throughout the 2000s, and the society changing the dates and location of their annual conference to suit the WEHC schedule. The EHSANZ also engaged with the IEHA by having a representative on their council, and (unsuccessfully) bidding to hold the WEHC in Australia in 2006.[193]

These institutional incentives reinforced existing connections to the US. Ian McLean was an important conduit to North America, commenting that from the mid-1980s, he embedded himself in the more 'exciting' US community of economic historians.[194] During the 1990s and 2000s, McLean spent the equivalent of 10 full academic years on secondments,

---

'Australian Capital And South-East Asian Tin Mining, 1906–40', *Australian Economic History Review* 45, no. 2 (2005): 161–85, doi.org/10.1111/j.1467-8446.2005.00133.x; Charles Fahey, 'Peopling the Victorian Goldfields: From Boom to Bust, 1851–1901', *Australian Economic History Review* 50, no. 2 (2010): 148–61, doi.org/10.1111/j.1467-8446.2010.00298.x; Geoffrey Blainey, 'The Momentous Gold Rushes', *Australian Economic History Review* 50, no. 2 (2010): 209–16, doi.org/10.1111/j.1467-8446.2010.00302.x.
192 Pincus and Snooks, 'Editorial Reflections'; McLean; Gregory interviews.
193 A bid that was ultimately won by Helsinki. Shanahan; Lloyd interviews.
194 McLean interview.

visiting fellowships and professorships at Harvard, Yale, the University of California – Berkeley, and Stanford, focusing on comparative economic histories of Australia and the US.[195] In outlining recommendations for the field's future, McLean and Shanahan advocated for the group to be guided by 'developments in the US universities over the last four decades or so'.[196] They argued that conducting research at the field's frontier, at a 'quality', 'international standard', involved the close relationship with the economics discipline that characterised the field in the US. In 2003 the EHSANZ established the annual Noel Butlin lecture, inviting prominent international scholars to the conference, with their lecture then published in the *Australian Economic History Review*.[197] Much like the visiting scholars program at ANU in the 1980s, this was a key connection between the field's professional structures and prominent scholars overseas, while also being particularly directed towards those in the US.[198]

Despite the prominence of North American connections for some, others were able to combine a broader set of local, global and comparative perspectives. The professional response to broader internationalisation started in the 1990s with *Review* editors Pincus and Snooks pivoting the journal towards an Asia-Pacific focus by welcoming 'articles on other regions, provided that they are of a more general kind'.[199] They promoted greater international readership, appointing international scholars to the editorial committee, and encouraging others to referee, review books and

---

195 Kris Mitchener and Ian W McLean, 'The Productivity of US States since 1880', *Journal of Economic Growth* 8, no. 1 (2003): 73–114, doi.org/10.1023/A:1022812917582; Kris James Mitchener and Ian W McLean, 'U.S. Regional Growth and Convergence, 1880–1980', *Journal of Economic History* 59, no. 4 (1999): 1016–42, doi.org/10.1017/S0022050700024128; Ian W McLean, 'Consumer Prices and Expenditure Patterns in Australia 1850–1914', *Australian Economic History Review* 39, no. 1 (1999): 1–28, doi.org/10.1111/1467-8446.00036; Ian W McLean, 'Recovery from Depression: Australia in an Argentine Mirror 1895–1913', *Australian Economic History Review* 46, no. 3 (2006): 215–41, doi.org/10.1111/j.1467-8446.2006.00179.x; Ian W McLean, 'Australian Economic Growth in Historical Perspective', *Economic Record* 80, no. 250 (2004): 330–45, doi.org/10.1111/j.1475-4932.2004.00192.x.
196 McLean and Shanahan, 'Australasian Economic History', 308. They invoked Douglas Irwin's Butlin Lecture in the same year, in which he commented on the lessons the antipodes could learn from economic history in North America.
197 Revised versions of the lecture have then been published in the *Australian Economic History Review*.
198 Jeffrey Williamson, Douglas Irwin and Barry Eichengreen gave early Butlin Lectures. Jeffrey G Williamson, 'The Inaugural Noel Butlin Lecture: World Factor Migrations and Demographic Transitions', *Australian Economic History Review* 44, no. 2 (2004): 118–41, doi.org/10.1111/j.1467-8446.2004.00113.x; Barry Eichengreen, 'It May Be Our Currency, But It's Your Problem', *Australian Economic History Review* 51, no. 3 (2011): 245–53, doi.org/10.1111/j.1467-8446.2011.00334.x; Douglas A Irwin, 'The Third Noel Butlin Lecture: Australian Exceptionalism Revisited', *Australian Economic History Review* 47, no. 3 (2007): 217–37, doi.org/10.1111/j.1467-8446.2007.00209.x.
199 Pincus and Snooks, 'Editorial Reflections', 6.

submit articles. At the same time, ANU Economic History of Southeast Asia Project (ECHOSEA) began as a five-year 'strategic initiative' within the Research School of Pacific Studies. After an initial workshop in 1989, scoping papers were published in a special issue of the *Australian Economic History Review* in 1991, under the editorship of Pincus and Snooks.[200] Full-time academic positions on the project, short-term fellowships, workshops and a visiting scholars program enabled joint work, including a book series edited by Graeme Snooks, A. J. S. 'Tony' Reid and Anne Booth at ANU, and Malcolm Falkus at UNE.[201] This was a key collaborative space for those in Australia who worked on Southeast Asian economic history.

The next major changes came in 1997, when Whitwell, as editor of the *Review*, negotiated to publish the journal through major international publisher Blackwell. This utilised Blackwell's global marketing service, and provided the infrastructure for electronic distribution.[202] In the 2000s, Pierre van der Eng and Stephen Morgan both served as co-editors, contributing their specialties in Asian economic history. Membership of the editorial board at this time expanded to include colleagues in Japan and Korea alongside those in Europe and North America. In 2005, the annual conference was renamed the Asia-Pacific Economic and Business History (APEBH) conference, which, alongside changing the journal's subtitle, signalled the society's desire to orient towards regional connections.[203] Ville has recalled that this first 'Asia-Pacific' conference was successful, attracting scholars from Japan, Taiwan and China.[204] Prominent Japanese economic historian Kaoru Sugihara gave the Butlin Lecture in 2006, and a few years later the EHSANZ worked with Sugihara and colleagues Takeshi Yuzawa and Osama Saito to hold the conference outside of

---

200 Eric Lionel Jones, 'A Framework for the History of Economic Growth in Southeast Asia', *Australian Economic History Review* 31, no. 1 (1991): 5–19, doi.org/10.1111/aehr.311002; Anne Booth, 'The Economic Development of Southeast Asia: 1870–1985', *Australian Economic History Review* 31, no. 1 (1991): 20–52, doi.org/10.1111/aehr.311003; Malcolm Falkus, 'The Economic History of Thailand', *Australian Economic History Review* 31, no. 1 (1991): 53–71, doi.org/10.1111/aehr.311004; Irene Nørlund, 'The French Empire, the Colonial State in Vietnam and Economic Policy: 1885–1940', *Australian Economic History Review* 31, no. 1 (1991): 72–89, doi.org/10.1111/aehr.311005; PJ Drake, 'Southeast Asian Monies and the Problem of a Common Measure, with Particular Reference to the Nineteenth Century', *Australian Economic History Review* 31, no. 1 (1991): 90–96, doi.org/10.1111/aehr.311006.
201 Pierre van der Eng was initially appointed as a postdoctoral fellow in the ECHOSEA group prior to his position in the Faculties economic history department. See van der Eng correspondence, 3 June 2021.
202 Whitwell, 'Future Directions'.
203 Subtitle: 'An Asia-Pacific Journal of Economic, Business and Social History'.
204 Ville interview.

Australasia for the first time.²⁰⁵ As the society executive put it, they hoped it would be a 'further step towards association of economic historians in the Asia-Pacific region'.²⁰⁶

These initiatives were effective in internationalising the journal's research. The share of the journal's research with an Australian focus declined from 79 per cent in the 1980s to 48 per cent in the 2000s.²⁰⁷ At the same time, the share of work on New Zealand almost doubled, while Europe and North America remained stable. Pages on Asian topics increased dramatically, from 1 per cent in the 1980s to almost 20 per cent in the 2000s. Comparative research in the *Review* increased fourfold across the 1990s and 2000s, and there was a growing diversity of affiliations, including scholars from Singapore, Spain, Japan, Denmark and Canada. In the 2000s, 55 per cent of authors had an Australian university affiliation, with 37 per cent based in the metropole or other former settler colonies like New Zealand and Canada. The remaining 9 per cent were based at institutions in Asia.²⁰⁸ Many contributors were attracted to the publication through international branding and marketing strategies, as well as special issues on comparative or Asia-Pacific economic history. Frost has argued that 'strengthening links with Asia' has been crucial for the journal's survival; that if it 'remained an Australian economic history journal, it would have died long ago'.²⁰⁹

The field's outward-looking behaviour, ability to engage with international professional structures and pressure to publish work of global interest led to some collective efforts to understand Australia as part of global varieties of capitalism. Lloyd's work throughout his career emphasised 'heterodox' economic history, particularly the field's status as the intersection of the social sciences.²¹⁰ In 2002, Lloyd edited a special issue of the *Australian Economic History Review* on institutions, policy and

---

205 The 2009 conference was held at Gakushuin University in Tokyo, and the 2013 conference was held at Seoul National University in South Korea. See 'Announcements', *Australian Economic History Review* 48, no. 2 (2008); 'Announcements', *Australian Economic History Review* 52, no. 2 (2012).
206 'Announcements', *Australian Economic History Review* 48, no. 2 (2008): 206.
207 Morgan and Shanahan, 'Supply of Economic History', 227.
208 With thanks to Martin Shanahan and Andy Seltzer for the provision of this data.
209 Frost interview.
210 For example, Lloyd, 'Core of Social Science?'; Christopher Lloyd, 'Australian Capitalism since 1992: A New Regime of Accumulation?', *Journal of Australian Political Economy*, no. 61 (2008): 30–55.

economic change.²¹¹ In the same year, at the IEHA meeting in Buenos Aires, Lloyd and others began discussing a major collaborative effort to compare the economic histories of various settler colonies. A workshop in Sydney in 2005 brought the group together, as did papers presented at the WEHC conference in Helsinki in 2006.²¹² The resulting monograph included Australian economic historians Lloyd, David Meredith, Martin Shanahan, John Wilson and Bernard Attard, and New Zealand economic historian Jim McAloon. Other contributors represented Uruguay, the UK, Sweden, Switzerland, Finland, Spain, France, the US, Canada, South Africa and Israel.

The settler economy framing allowed comparative research that drew links based on socio-political context, natural resources and location. Chapters by those specialised in Australasia set their analysis within a comparative context with, for example, Meredith outlining the high labour requirements for settler economies in Latin America, South Africa, Australia and New Zealand, and examining the various patterns of labour coercion in these areas.²¹³ Shanahan and Wilson compared wages, labour hours and occupations, between countries and over time, finding substantial differences in the nature and timing of changes to each labour market.²¹⁴ Attard examined Wakefeldian flows of capital in the nineteenth century, particularly its role for facilitating settlement and encouraging rural industries. McAloon compared twentieth-century economic policy in Australia and New Zealand, particularly elements of its convergence encouraged by similar industry structures and settler colonial contexts.²¹⁵ Other chapters on immigration, international trade and economic growth embedded Australian research within the settler economy context. The book's broad comparative and disciplinary scope nodded to Denoon's earlier socio-economic and political analysis of settler capitalism, with the editors adopting his ability to 'transcend the explanatorily distorting

---

211 Christopher Lloyd, 'Introduction', *Australian Economic History Review* 42, no. 3 (2002): 235–37, doi.org/10.1111/1467-8446.t01-1-00033.
212 Christopher Lloyd, Jacob Metzer and Richard Sutch, *Settler Economies in World History* (Leiden: Brill, 2013).
213 David Meredith, 'Coerced Labor in Southern Hemisphere Settler Economies', in Lloyd et al., *Settler Economies in World History*, 315–44.
214 Martin P Shanahan and John K Wilson, 'Labor Market Outcomes in Settler Economies between 1870 and 1913: Accounting for the Differences in Labor Hours and Occupations', in Lloyd et al., *Settler Economies in World History*, 345–68.
215 Jim McAloon, 'The State and Economic Policy in Twentieth Century Australia and New Zealand: Escaping the Staples Trap?', in Lloyd et al., *Settler Economies in World History*, 521–43.

boundaries between branches of the social sciences'.[216] Contributors drew on orthodox and other official quantitative statistics, though interpreted this material with a mix of mainstream and heterodox approaches. For example, Shanahan and Wilson's work on labour markets drew on a neoclassical specification of factor prices, institutions and productivity, while also incorporating the approach of US social scientist Louis Hartz's 'fragments' thesis. Rather than the 'isolation' of Australian economic history,[217] through this project and the work of the journal, the field embedded itself in key global economic history conversations.

Conclusions

This chapter was almost called 'the wilderness'. Many have seen Australian economic history as largely passive at this time; as unfortunately caught in the crossfire of neoliberal universities and the neglect of parent disciplines. The contribution here is to examine the active role Australia's economic historians played in shaping their own destiny. While they certainly had to negotiate a very uncertain external situation, in both positive and negative ways scholars had some responsibility for the nature of their teaching and research, the progression of mergers, and the manner in which they engaged with parent disciplines. Whether they were defending their patch, mounting an offensive operation or attempting covert tactics, economic historians were creative and innovative in their attempts to survive the field's crisis in the 1990s and 2000s. This period was undoubtedly traumatic, but it forced scholars to broaden their professional horizons, and expand the field's limits to demonstrate its value in a very hostile environment.

Much like the interwar period, the era of 'resistance' has generally been underrated. Indeed, if one sees disciplinary growth as the gold standard, it is understandable to see this period as a failure. However, this chapter demonstrates that interdisciplinary fields require different measures of success as compared with disciplines. For any discipline, the loss of departments, dispersal of personnel and decline of students would be catastrophic. For this interdisciplinary field, on the other hand, as hard as

---

216 Christopher Lloyd and Jacob Metzer, 'Settler Colonization and Societies in World History: Patterns and Concepts', in Lloyd et al., *Settler Economies in World History*, 1–34, 28.
217 Donald Denoon, 'The Isolation of Australian History', *Australian Historical Studies* 22, no. 87 (1986): 252–60, doi.org/10.1080/10314618608595747.

this period was, it encouraged broad, outward-looking behaviour that was necessary to negotiate interdisciplinary relationships. This chapter also demonstrates the value of different types of communicating infrastructures. While disciplines do best with dense connections, strong collaborations and intellectual consistency, interdisciplinary fields have value when they have porous communicating infrastructures that are able to bring together a range of different scholars. Rather than the death of economic history, the period of resistance created opportunities for members to re-establish the field as a meeting place for broad, cross-disciplinary inquiry.

6

Renaissance

In October 2014, the *Cambridge Economic History of Australia* was finally published. Almost a generation on, the production function approach was abandoned, as were the old editors. Many of the contributors were the same, and they were determined to make this one work. The volume was a success, sparking conversation in international academic circles, and making its way into media and parliament discussions. It was, incidentally, also the first major project in Australian economic history that I ever worked on. I was a research assistant for Simon Ville, and was charged with sorting out the final touches, and coordinating between the authors, editors and publishers. It all seemed terribly exciting – I remember the day the advanced copy of the *Cambridge* arrived and sitting with Simon in his office, as he marvelled at the look and feel of the book. He was very proud of it, and so was I. It was a remarkable apprenticeship in Australian economic history.

The authors made a definitive statement on the progress and contribution of Australian economic history. I'm sure many hoped it was the start of a new golden era, similar to Noel Butlin publishing 'the words' and 'the numbers'.[1] Some may have seen it as the final death rattle of a field that had been on life support for a while. As it turns out, the *Cambridge* was part of a global and specifically Australian revival in interest in economic historical matters. Recent reflections in the US have argued that 'historians are examining the economy again' and that economic history 'should be

---

1   'The words' and 'the numbers' refer to Butlin's seminal works, respectively: Noel G Butlin, *Australian Domestic Product, Investment and Foreign Borrowing 1861–1938/9* (London: Cambridge University Press, 1962) and Noel G Butlin, *Investment in Australian Economic Development, 1861–1900* (London: Cambridge University Press, 1964), xiv, doi.org/10.1017/CBO9781316530160.

at the heart of economics instruction'.[2] In Australia, there have been calls to support a 'new materialism', with capitalism re-emerging as a 'pervasive framework for understanding a world in momentous flux'.[3] This chapter contributes to these reflections by systematically examining the progress of the so-called revival in Australia, particularly connections between the field and its parent disciplines, fragmentation away from mainstream professional structures and the impact of a still very hostile higher education sector. The assessment is cautiously optimistic: while there are promising signs of the field's renaissance, it is faced with substantial uncertainties.

The revival

Although the institutional space afforded to Australian economic historians declined in the 1990s and 2000s, outward-looking behaviour meant members had greater capacity to take advantage of favourable external conditions in the early 2010s. At the start of the new millennium, public and policy attention was drawn to globalisation, inequality and debt, and the influence of multinational corporations.[4] Within economics, 'new' forms of micro-economics utilised a range of qualitative, quantitative and historical evidence to understand inequality, wellbeing and happiness. Endogenous growth theory focused on the role of technology, human capital and innovation for long-run economic development.[5] Greater interest in institutions, particularly the effects of political, legal and social structures, aligned with historical and long-run data.[6] The Great

---

2   Kenneth Lipartito, 'Reassembling the Economic: New Departures in Historical Materialism', *American Historical Review* 121, no. 1 (2016): 101–39, 101, doi.org/10.1093/ahr/121.1.101; M Pettis, 'How Has the Crisis Changed the Teaching of Economics?', *The Economist*, 17 September 2010.
3   Hannah Forsyth and Sophie Loy-Wilson, 'Seeking a New Materialism in Australian History', *Australian Historical Studies* 48, no. 1 (2017): 169–88, doi.org/10.1080/1031461X.2017.1298635; Ben Huf and Glenda Sluga, '"New" Histories of (Australian) Capitalism', *Australian Historical Studies* 50, no. 4 (2019): 405–17, doi.org/10.1080/1031461X.2019.1663773.
4   Simon Ville and Claire EF Wright, 'Neither a Discipline nor a Colony: Renaissance and Re-Imagination in Economic History', *Australian Historical Studies* 48, no. 2 (2017): 152–68, doi.org/10.1080/1031461X.2017.1279197; Sven Beckert et al., 'Interchange: The History of Capitalism', *Journal of American History* 101, no. 2 (2014): 503–36, doi.org/10.1093/jahist/jau357.
5   Paul M Romer, 'The Origins of Endogenous Growth', *Journal of Economic Perspectives* 8, no. 1 (1994): 3–22, doi.org/10.1257/jep.8.1.3; Iñaki Iriarte-Goñi, 'Spanish Economic History: Lights and Shadows in a Process of Convergence', in *Routledge Handbook of Global Economic History*, ed. Francesco Boldizzoni and Pat Hudson (London: Routledge, 2015), 160–74, doi.org/10.4324/9781315734736.
6   Work has been inspired by DC North, *Institutions, Institutional Change and Economic Performance* (Cambridge: Cambridge University Press, 1990), doi.org/10.1017/CBO9780511808678. More recently, Acemoglu and Robinson's work on comparative economic history has been particularly influential. See Daron Acemoglu and James A Robinson, *Why Nations Fail: The Origins of Power, Prosperity, and Poverty* (New York: Crown, 2012).

Divergence debate has been a site to bring together economists and economic historians, examining different rates of development between Europe and Asia, and a range of other polities, over the last 300 years.[7] Work has incorporated familiar economic determinants such as capital formation, natural resources and the role of the State, as well as institutions in the form of comparative legal systems and general propensities for entrepreneurship.[8] Historians, on the other hand, have been motivated to integrate the insights of the cultural turn with the material forces of money, production and distribution. The history of capitalism movement emerged in the US as a 'meeting place' for disparate fields to understand the contingency of capitalism across time and place.[9]

These intellectual trends were crystallised by the Global Financial Crisis (GFC) of 2007–08, which triggered an increase in understanding the development and impact of economic systems. The recession was particularly important for the growth of the history of capitalism movement in the US, with students flocking to undergraduate and postgraduate instruction in the subject.[10] As Elizabeth Shermer has recalled:

> rarely did I find a student who mentioned the Great Depression, Social Security (or Medicare), or unions before 2008. Now, half the class wants to know about the 1930s and the New Deal.[11]

---

7   Kenneth Pomeranz, *The Great Divergence: Europe, China and the Making of the Modern World Economy* (Princeton: Princeton University Press, 2000), doi.org/10.1515/9781400823499; Ian Morris, *Why the West Rules – for Now: The Patterns of History and What They Reveal About the Future* (London: Profile books, 2010); Jeffrey G Williamson, *Trade and Poverty: When the Third World Fell Behind* (Cambridge, MA: MIT Press, 2011), doi.org/10.7551/mitpress/9780262015158.001.0001; Prasannan Parthasarathi, *Why Europe Grew Rich and Asia Did Not: Global Economic Divergence, 1600–1850* (Cambridge: Cambridge University Press, 2011), doi.org/10.1017/CBO9780511993398; Jean-Laurent Rosenthal and Roy Bin Wong, *Before and Beyond Divergence* (New Haven: Harvard University Press, 2011); Gareth Austin and Kaoru Sugihara, eds, *Labour-Intensive Industrialization in Global History* (New York: Routledge, 2014), doi.org/10.4324/9780203067611; Christopher Lloyd, Jacob Metzer and Richard Sutch, *Settler Economies in World History* (Leiden: Brill, 2013). See Ville's review of this literature: Simon Ville, 'Divergence and Convergence: New and Shifting Paradigms in Comparative Economic History', *Australian Economic History Review* 55, no. 1 (2015): 80–94, doi.org/10.1111/aehr.12059.
8   Ville, 'Divergence and Convergence'.
9   Beckert et al., 'Interchange', 506.
10   Ville and Wright, 'Neither a Discipline nor a Colony'; Naomi Lamoreaux, 'The Future of Economic History Must Be Interdisciplinary', *Journal of Economic History* 75, no. 4 (2015): 1251–57; Beckert et al., 'Interchange', 530. See also Jennifer Schuessler, 'In History Departments, It's Up With Capitalism', *New York Times*, 6 April 2013.
11   Beckert et al., 'Interchange', 530.

Economists were, embarrassingly, surprised by the GFC, with US economist Tyler Cowan noting that it was the 'people schooled in economic history who came to terms with the crisis most readily'.[12] With the aim of contextualising contemporary challenges and guiding policy responses, the Great Depression received much greater attention, and economists became preoccupied by 'warning signs' of long-run instability. Harvard economists Carmen Reinhart and Kenneth Rogoff's ironically titled *This Time is Different* identified common patterns of financial crises across the world over nearly a millennium.[13] It became a *New York Times* bestseller.

The economic history field globally responded to these trends, advocating for research more inclusive of both parent disciplines. Most of the chapters in the 2015 *Routledge Handbook of Global Economic History* advocated for cooperation between different disciplinary traditions as a safeguard against marginalisation.[14] In North America, economic historians such as Naomi Lamoreaux similarly argued for economic history to 'transcend the breakdown of the field's original interdisciplinary structure and its transformation into a sub-field of economics'.[15] Barry Eichengreen agreed, encouraging an integrated approach to contextualising contemporary economic challenges.[16] Even in the UK and Europe, where there has been less division of those who examine economic historical phenomena, scholars have called for broader interdisciplinary conversations. British scholar Stephen Broadberry argued that the field should 'embrace economic historians from diverse backgrounds and celebrate that diversity'.[17] Francesco Boldizzoni, from his vantage in Northern Italy, provided a more critical analysis, lamenting economic history's identity crisis at the hands of the North American 'cliometric threat', and calling for the field's renewed interdisciplinary engagement.[18]

---

12 Pettis, 'Teaching of Economics'.
13 Carmen M Reinhart and Kenneth S Rogoff, *This Time Is Different: Eight Centuries of Financial Folly* (Princeton: Princeton University Press, 2009), doi.org/10.1515/9781400831722.
14 Boldizzoni and Hudson, *Global Economic History*.
15 Lamoreaux, 'Future of Economic History'.
16 Barry Eichengreen, 'Economic History and Economic Policy', *Journal of Economic History* 72, no. 2 (2012): 289–307, doi.org/10.1017/S0022050712000034.
17 Geoffrey Jones, Marco HD van Leeuwen and Stephen Broadberry, 'The Future of Economic, Business and Social History', *Scandinavian Economic History Review* 60, no. 3 (2012): 225–53, doi.org/10.1080/03585522.2012.727766.
18 Francesco Boldizzoni, *The Poverty of Clio: Resurrecting Economic History* (Princeton: Princeton University Press, 2011), doi.org/10.23943/princeton/9780691144009.001.0001.

These international conversations have influenced Australian academia. Economists have acknowledged the importance of understanding long-run determinants of economic development, particularly for the GFC, and historians have emphasised material matters for historical work.[19] Interest in the Great Depression, inequality, globalisation and multinationals contributed to a steady increase in the number of articles and authors publishing economic historical work in both *Economic Record* and *Australian Historical Studies*, from the 2000s and 2010s, respectively. In the *Record*, subjects like business cycles, international trade, the Great Divergence, inequality and wellbeing, as well as the connection between the Great Depression and the GFC, have comprised this 'new' interest in economic history.[20] In *Australian Historical Studies*, articles have examined consumption behaviour, business history, finance and the economic aspects of race, migration and labour, as well as special issues on big data, the 'new materialism' and Australian histories of capitalism.[21] Much of this new research *on* economic history has been written by those who would not consider themselves primarily 'economic historians'.

---

19   Steve Keen, 'Predicting the "Global Financial Crisis": Post-Keynesian Macroeconomics', *Economic Record* 89, no. 285 (2013): 228–54, doi.org/10.1111/1475-4932.12016; Peter Docherty, 'The Role of Economic History and the History of Economic Thought in Macroeconomics and Finance Courses after the Global Financial Crisis', *Australasian Journal of Economics Education* 11, no. 2 (2014): 1–24; Forsyth and Loy-Wilson, 'New Materialism'.

20   For example: Lee E Ohanian, 'Understanding Economic Crises: The Great Depression and the 2008 Recession', *Economic Record* 86, Suppl. S1 (2010): 2–6, doi.org/10.1111/j.1475-4932.2010.00667.x; Noel Gaston and Gulasekaran Rajaguru, 'The Long-Run Determinants of Australian Income Inequality', *Economic Record* 85, no. 270 (2009): 260–75, doi.org/10.1111/j.1475-4932.2009.00539.x; Anthony B Atkinson and Andrew Leigh, 'The Distribution of Top Incomes in Australia', *Economic Record* 83, no. 262 (2007): 247–61, doi.org/10.1111/j.1475-4932.2007.00412.x; Anthony B Atkinson and Andrew Leigh, 'The Distribution of Top Incomes in Five Anglo-Saxon Countries over the Long Run', *Economic Record* 89, Suppl. S1 (2013): 31–47, doi.org/10.1111/1475-4932.12004; Paul Frijters and Robert Gregory, 'From Golden Age to Golden Age: Australia's "Great Leap Forward"?', *Economic Record* 82, no. 257 (2006): 207–24, doi.org/10.1111/j.1475-4932.2006.00316.x.

21   Alister Bowen, 'The Merchants: Chinese Social Organisation in Colonial Australia', *Australian Historical Studies* 42, no. 1 (2011): 25–44, doi.org/10.1080/1031461X.2010.542766; Julie McIntyre, 'Adam Smith and Faith in the Transformative Qualities of Wine in Colonial New South Wales', *Australian Historical Studies* 42, no. 2 (2011): 194–211, doi.org/10.1080/1031461X.2011.560611; Sophie Loy-Wilson, 'Rural Geographies and Chinese Empires: Chinese Shopkeepers and Shop-Life in Australia', *Australian Historical Studies* 45, no. 3 (2014): 407–24, doi.org/10.1080/1031461X.2014.948020; Jo Hawkins, 'Anzac for Sale: Consumer Culture, Regulation and the Shaping of a Legend, 1915–21', *Australian Historical Studies* 46, no. 1 (2015): 7–26, doi.org/10.1080/1031461X.2014.994539; Hamish Maxwell-Stewart, 'The State, Convicts and Longitudinal Analysis', *Australian Historical Studies* 47, no. 3 (2016): 414–29, doi.org/10.1080/1031461X.2016.1203963; Kris Inwood and J Andrew Ross, 'Big Data and the Military: First World War Personnel Records in Australia, Britain, Canada, New Zealand and British Africa', *Australian Historical Studies* 47, no. 3 (2016): 430–42, doi.org/10.1080/1031461X.2016.1205639; Melissa Bellanta, 'Business Fashion: Masculinity, Class and Dress in 1870s Australia', *Australian Historical Studies* 48, no. 2 (2017): 189–212, doi.org/10.1080/1031461X.2017.1300178.

Within Australian economic history, new interest from parent disciplines and the public sparked new major undertakings. Barrie Dyster and David Meredith published a new edition of *Australia in the Global Economy* in 2012.[22] The first edition, pitched at undergraduate students, was published 1990, and synthesised consensus opinion on Australian economic history in relation to key touchstones of the international economy – trade, capital flows and immigration.[23] The macroeconomics framework and the use of aggregated quantitative material was familiar to most undergraduate economics students. They argued that connection to the international economy contributed to Australia's economic growth primarily through demand for exports, and the supply of capital and labour, with public policy shaping the nature of this integration.[24] The new edition was prompted by interest from contemporary economists and policymakers in understanding the past. In 2010, while Dyster was at the University of New South Wales, his colleague, economist Tim Harcourt, mentioned that Wayne Swan (then the federal treasurer) was to deliver an address to leading businessmen, and that Swan had asked Harcourt for academic work from which to draw detail. In parliament, Swan said something to the effect that Dyster and Meredith were the experts in the way the economy has evolved, which prompted 'every chairman of the board and every CEO […] to get a copy of this book'.[25] Dyster and Meredith received some encouragement ('harassment') from Cambridge University Press to update the volume, with the authors maintaining the same framework but revising the quantitative material and focusing on economic reform, globalisation and the GFC.[26]

Ian McLean's *Why Australia Prospered* complements Dyster and Meredith, and was the most influential book in Australian economic history penned by a single author since the early 1990s. With echoes of Coghlan's 'progress', McLean focused on 'prosperity'– in this case income per capita. He examined the way Australia became rich by the middle of the nineteenth century and maintained this status for the next 150 years. The periodisation is familiar – it was organised into the first

---

22   Barrie Dyster and David Meredith, *Australia in the Global Economy: Continuity and Change* (Cambridge: Cambridge University Press, 2012).
23   Dyster; Oxley/Meredith interviews. Unless otherwise specified, interviews cited are those conducted by the author: see Appendix for details.
24   Barrie Dyster and David Meredith, *Australia in the International Economy in the Twentieth Century* (Melbourne: Cambridge University Press, 1990).
25   Dyster interview.
26   Dyster and Meredith, *Australia in the Global Economy*.

60 years of convict and settler experience; the 'Butlin era', including the gold rush and the long boom of the nineteenth century; the external shocks of two depressions and two world wars up to 1945; and then the (mostly) unfaltering boom of the remaining 70 years. McLean argued that Australia's prosperity owed to capitalising on natural resources ('luck') through a good policy setting and a decent capitalist environment.[27]

As with other major works at the time, *Why Australia Prospered* was an economists' economic history. The historical approach aimed to understand how the 'roots of prosperity are embedded in the past', contributing to growing interest in historical approaches from development economists.[28] Weaving analysis and narrative, endogenous growth theory was central to McLean's framework, through an interest in natural resource endowments, institutional quality, government policy and cultural attributes. McLean was aware of geographic, political, social, cultural and environmental elements, though in a similar way to the Great Divergence literature, these served as the structural background rather than aspects to be interrogated. McLean kept one eye on California, with the 'especially appropriate' origins of the book 'in an office affording a breathtaking view across San Francisco Bay and through the Golden Gate to the Pacific beyond'. Observing Australian experience from the outside, in relation to other settler colonies such as Canada, Argentina, New Zealand and the West Coast of the US, was crucial for McLean's perspective, as it 'heightens one's perceptions of what seems noteworthy or unusual'.[29] His method was also largely orthodox, with no interest in statistically testing relationships between variables, but incorporating counterfactual speculation as to why Australia did better or worse than elsewhere. McLean's work was like sinking into a warm bath for most mainstream Australian economic historians. Reviewers were very comfortable with his approach, with Withers particularly praising it as the 'best overview of Australian economic history that has been published to date'.[30]

---

27   Ian W McLean, *Why Australia Prospered: The Shifting Sources of Economic Growth* (Princeton: Princeton University Press, 2013), doi.org/10.23943/princeton/9780691154671.001.0001.
28   McLean, *Why Australian Prospered*, 1–3.
29   McLean, *Why Australia Prospered*, xiii. See Chapters 4 and 5 for a discussion of McLean's integration with US economic history.
30   Glenn Withers, 'Review: Mclean, *Why Australia Prospered*', *Economic Record* 90, no. 290 (2014): 400–1, doi.org/10.1111/1475-4932.12143; Tim Hatton, 'Review: Mclean, *Why Australian Prospered*', *Australian Economic History Review* 53, no. 2 (2013): 210–14, doi.org/10.1111/aehr.12011; Simon Ville, 'Review: Mclean, *Why Australian Prospered*', *American Historical Review* 118, no. 4 (2013): 1170–71, doi.org/10.1093/ahr/118.4.1170.

Simon Ville and Glenn Withers's edited *Cambridge Economic History of Australia* was similar in audience, speaking to economists and policymakers interested in Australia's long-run economic development.[31] Ironically, the book emerged from the history discipline. Ville and Lionel Frost both contributed chapters to the *Cambridge History of Australia*, published in 2013 and edited by historians Alison Bashford and Stuart Macintyre.[32] At some point, Macintyre pulled Ville aside and asked if it would be possible to get an economic history volume going. Macintyre contacted the Cambridge publishers, Ville enlisted Glenn Withers, and they were away. Unfortunately, despite the clear interest from historians in the subject at the time, members of this discipline were not represented. In addition to self-described members of the field, academic and professional economists made up the contributors. This was deliberate, with Ville recalling that:

> we also needed some economists that were interested in economic history because there just weren't enough economic historians who could write in this space.[33]

The *Cambridge* had a strong economic policy imperative. Withers spent time as a policymaker throughout the 1990s and 2000s, and he recruited members of the Canberra–Adelaide group of economic historians – such as Michael Keating, Rod Maddock and Jonathan Pincus – who had since moved on to policy work (see Chapters 3 and 4). Matthew Butlin also participated, fulfilling the family legacy by compiling the statistical appendix, and providing his perspective as a macro-economic policy official. Withers has argued that his motivation for editing the book came from his time as a policymaker:

> Particularly, I was convinced from all that practical work that we are at a key stage of Australian development [...] I insisted, I think, upon [...] *engaged* economic history. I wanted not just the scholarly economic history without reference to how [it] could be used to interpret current policy formation and evolution.[34]

---

31   Simon Ville and Glenn Withers, eds, *The Cambridge Economic History of Australia* (Melbourne: Cambridge University Press, 2015), doi.org/10.1017/CHO9781107445222.
32   Alison Bashford and Stuart Macintyre, eds, *The Cambridge History of Australia* (Melbourne: Cambridge University Press, 2013), doi.org/10.1017/CHO9781107445758.
33   Ville interview.
34   Withers interview.

Figure 5: Participants at the second workshop for the *Cambridge Economic History of Australia*, Trinity College, University of Melbourne, February 2013

Back row (l–r): Lionel Frost, Diane Hutchinson, William Coleman, Jonathan Pincus, Rod Maddock, Chris Lloyd, Simon Ville, Glenn Withers, Nicholas Biddle, Boyd Hunter.

Front row (l–r): Andy Seltzer, David Meredith, Deborah Oxley, Monica Keneley, Edwyna Harris, David Merrett, Tim Hatton, Michael Keating, David Greasley.

Source: Supplied by Simon Ville.

Contributors met on two major occasions. The new Australian National University (ANU) Centre for Economic History hosted a workshop in July 2012 to scope chapters. Ville's role in leading the 'unruly' group of people was acknowledged, with work starting out as 'almost a reunion' of those who had lost touch through the period of resistance.[35] The second workshop was held at Trinity College at the University of Melbourne in February 2013, in a building with no air conditioning, at the height of summer. Frost has likened the 'bloody hot' weather outside to the intense discussions inside, with critical but constructive feedback from authors.[36] My role came later, in the latter part of 2013 and throughout 2014, and I was similarly struck by their sense of joint endeavour.

---

35 Hatton; Keneley; Frost; Hutchinson interviews.
36 Frost interview.

The volume was mainstream in its interpretation and approach, summarising consensus opinion on various topics in Australian economic history. The importance of natural resources and migrant human capital, the uneasy partnership between governments and the economy, the dominance of big business and Australia's strong connection to flows of international trade and capital were valuable summaries, although not terribly radical interpretations. The most noticeable intellectual broadening was two chapters on Indigenous economic history that built on work throughout the 2000s to re-examine Butlin's estimates of the pre-invasion population, contributions of Indigenous enterprises and Indigenous socio-economic outcomes over time.[37] The approach was also orthodox, underpinned by a comprehensive statistical appendix that was used to inductively build a narrative of Australia's economic development. As with McLean's work, cliometrics was sometimes in the background, with the results of recent deductive work reported on, but not actively conducted in any of the chapters.[38] While the editors argued that 'varying disciplinary backgrounds are a source of creative tension among contributors', as with other major contributions at the time the spectrum of approaches extended from economic history to the economics

---

37   Boyd H Hunter, 'The Aboriginal Legacy', in Ville and Withers, *The Cambridge Economic History of Australia*, 73–96, doi.org/10.1017/CHO9781107445222.008; Jon C Altman and Nicholas Biddle, 'Refiguring Indigenous Economies: A 21st-Century Perspective', in Ville and Withers, *The Cambridge Economic History of Australia*, 530–54, doi.org/10.1017/CHO9781107445222.032. These built on the following literature: Ian Keen, ed., *Indigenous Participation in Australian Economies: Historical and Anthropological Perspectives* (Canberra: ANU E Press, 2010), doi.org/10.22459/IPAE.12.2010; Natasha Fijn et al., eds, *Indigenous Participation in Australian Economies II: Historical Engagements and Current Enterprises* (Canberra: ANU E Press, 2012), doi.org/10.22459/IPAE.07.2012. See also Tony Smith, 'Indigenous Accumulation in the Kimberley During the Early Years of "Self-Determination", 1968–1975', *Australian Economic History Review* 42, no. 1 (2002): 1–33, doi.org/10.1111/1467-8446.t01-1-00020; Tony Smith, 'Welfare, Enterprise, and Aboriginal Community: The Case of the Western Australian Kimberley Region, 1968–96', *Australian Economic History Review* 46, no. 3 (2006): 242–67, doi.org/10.1111/j.1467-8446.2006.00180.x; Jon C Altman, Nicholas Biddle and Boyd H Hunter, 'A Historical Perspective on Indigenous Socioeconomic Outcomes in Australia, 1971–2001', *Australian Economic History Review* 45, no. 3 (2005): 273–95, doi.org/10.1111/j.1467-8446.2005.00139.x; Jon C Altman, Nicholas Biddle and Boyd H Hunter, 'Prospects for "Closing the Gap" in Socioeconomic Outcomes for Indigenous Australians?', *Australian Economic History Review* 49, no. 3 (2009): 225–51, doi.org/10.1111/j.1467-8446.2009.00264.x; Boyd H Hunter and John Carmody, 'Estimating the Aboriginal Population in Early Colonial Australia: The Role of Chickenpox Reconsidered', *Australian Economic History Review* 55, no. 2 (2015): 112–38, doi.org/10.1111/aehr.12068.
38   Tim Hatton has argued that authors were given the task of reflecting on the relevant literature, and capturing the essence of quantitative–deductive results, but that chapters were not supposed to be technical. Hatton interview.

discipline, but not to history.[39] This body of 'new' work in Australian economic history was thus not really new at all, but reasserted the field's orthodox intellectual position, and its contribution to economics.

Persistent challenges

Fragmentation

Economic history, all of a sudden, became trendy again, with a rush of new work, public and policy interest in the subject, and renewed engagement from parent disciplines. However, in Australia, the field's intellectual and professional structures remained conservative, speaking primarily to economists through an orthodox frame. This has resulted in new research clusters bypassing mainstream professional structures and fragmenting of the field's efforts.

In Australia, the 'new histories of capitalism' has provided a focus for work on economic history topics from Australian historians. Adding an Australian voice to the intellectual movement of the same name that emerged in the US in the early 2000s, historians have examined the contingency of Australia's capitalist experience in an international and comparative frame. The seeds for this movement were found in the neglect of economic matters from cultural historians, as it left out capitalism as 'too totalising, too deterministic, too Euro-centric, and blind to gender, race and contingency'.[40] Australian scholars trained in cultural history methods acknowledged that disregard for economic forces left a gap in understanding, and were motivated to understand the historical path dependencies of a system that had come under increasing scrutiny.[41] They also positioned themselves against mainstream economic history, arguing that this 'traditional' approach saw capitalism as a background structure rather than interrogating its change over time.[42] Members have

---

39 Simon Ville and Glenn Withers, 'Introduction: Connecting Past, Present and Future', in Ville and Withers, *The Cambridge Economic History of Australia*, 1–10, 7, doi.org/10.1017/CHO978 1107445222.002.
40 Huf and Sluga, '"New" Histories of (Australian) Capitalism', 408. See also Chapter 5.
41 Forsyth and Loy-Wilson, 'New Materialism'; Ben Huf et al., 'Capitalism in Australia: New Histories for a Reimagined Future', *Thesis Eleven* 160, no. 1 (2020): 95–120, doi.org/10.1177/07255 13620949028.
42 Huf and Sluga, '"New" Histories of (Australian) Capitalism'; Forsyth and Loy-Wilson, 'New Materialism'; Huf et al., 'Capitalism in Australia'.

used their training in cultural history to provide new perspectives on traditional economic history topics. For example, Hannah Forsyth has provided a cultural scrutiny of balance sheets and accreditation standards to examine the moral and economic role of professionals in Broken Hill.[43] Yves Rees's work on interwar Australian economists – a very traditional topic in mainstream economic history – offered a new perspective by 'dissecting [the] constitutive discourses' that established economist's expert status and reputation.[44] Ben Huf has similarly examined the discourse of economic knowledge in colonial Australia to understand the way 'the economy' was established as a separate category to be understood and controlled through policy.[45] These contributions have been embedded within several collaborative projects on the 'new histories of Australian capitalism', with scholars primarily operating within the history discipline's professional structures, but collaborating with economic historians, political economists, labour and social historians, and geographers.[46]

Prompted, in part, by the integration of many labour historians with human resources and management groups, the Academic Association of Historians in Australian and New Zealand Business Schools (AAHANZBS) launched in 2009 as an initiative of the University of Sydney's Business and Labour History group. Much like mainstream economic and business historians, members of this group engaged in their own process of negotiation following the Dawkins reforms, expanding their collaborations, ideas and teaching to secure their position in business faculties.[47] Work on firm and industry structure, and the history of work, technology and education have used a range of qualitative and quantitative source data, and various social, business and institutional theories. For example, Greg Patmore and Nikola Balnave utilised a combination of aggregated quantitative data and detailed case studies to examine the complex global history of cooperative business, including in Australia. They assessed the various

---

43 Forsyth Hannah, 'Class, Professional Work, and the History of Capitalism in Broken Hill, C. 1880–1910', *Labor: Studies in Working-Class History of the Americas* 15, no. 2 (2018): 21–47, doi.org/10.1215/15476715-4353680.
44 Huf and Sluga, '"New" Histories of (Australian) Capitalism', 412; Yves Rees, 'From Socialists to Technocrats: The Depoliticisation of Australian Economics', *Australian Historical Studies: New Histories of Capitalism* 50, no. 4 (2019): 463–82, doi.org/10.1080/1031461X.2019.1628787.
45 Ben Huf, 'Making Things Economic: Theory and Government in New South Wales, 1788–1863' (PhD thesis, The Australian National University, 2018).
46 See Huf and Sluga, '"New" Histories of (Australian) Capitalism'; Huf et al., 'Capitalism in Australia'.
47 Frank Bongiorno, 'Australian Labour History: Contexts, Trends and Influences', *Labour History* 100, no. 1 (2011): 1–19, doi.org/10.5263/labourhistory.100.0001.

forms of cooperative firms against other modes of business organisation, particularly large-scale industrial firms and multinationals, arguing that cooperatives emerged due to the failure of the neoliberal market economy in marginalising substantial groups, particularly the working class.[48] The group has an annual conference and regular events, and is heavily involved in the journal *Labour History*. Despite intellectual alignment, the separation between the Business and Labour History group and the Economic History Society of Australia and New Zealand (EHSANZ) appears to be irreconcilable, with members of each telling me that it was the 'others' who refused to cooperate when the former group was established in the 2000s. Also regrettable is the separation between the Business and Labour History group and the historians of capitalism, with members aligned on the critique of capitalism as a theme, though adopting disparate methods.

The OzClio group provides a conduit to the economics discipline. The group is linked to the ANU Centre for Economic History, which came to life in 2012 as a revival of the University's postwar role in the field. The centre has a porous presence institutionally, providing a website, newsletter and events, with members maintaining their roles in their faculties and departments. As Tim Hatton has argued, it is an identifiable place where scholars in Australia and overseas can be assured of a cluster of relevant researchers.[49] The OzClio group has been supported by the appointment of new cliometricians to ANU and elsewhere, and members run an annual workshop to 'mobilise the new generation, if you like, of economic historians'.[50] Adhering to US 'clio rules', papers are distributed beforehand, with authors providing very short presentations before contributions by 'discussants'. The familiar intellectual features of cliometrics – mathematical modelling, quantitative testing and the use of neoclassical theory focusing on micro-foundations of economic growth – unite members' work, and their scope is global through research on Europe, Asia, Africa and the

---

48 Greg Patmore and Nikola Balnave, *A Global History of Co-operative Business* (London: Routledge, 2018), doi.org/10.4324/9781315638164. See also Nikola Balnave and Greg Patmore, 'The Labour Movement and Co-Operatives', *Labour History*, no. 112 (2017): 7–24; Nikola Balnave and Greg Patmore, 'The Outsider Consumer Co-Operative: Lessons from the Community Co-Operative Store (Nuriootpa), 1944–2010', *Business History* 57, no. 8 (2015): 1133–54, doi.org/10.1080/00076791.2015.1015998; Nikola Balnave and Greg Patmore, 'Rochdale Consumer Co-Operatives in Australia: Decline and Survival', *Business History* 54, no. 6 (2012): 986–1003, doi.org/10.1080/00076791.2012.706899.
49 Hatton interview.
50 Hatton interview.

US.⁵¹ For example, Melbourne economic historian Laura Panza and US scholar Jeffrey Williamson quantitatively assessed Australia's economic growth through micro-economic labour market data, arguing that rapid economic growth from the 1820s to the 1870s was not associated with rising inequality.⁵² Similarly, John Tang's work on Japanese and American industrialisation incorporated aspects of endogenous growth theory by examining the slow adoption but quick catch-up in use of new technologies in large Japanese firms.⁵³

There is relatively strong top-level integration between OzClio and EHSANZ, with the ANU centre formally partnered with the society, and some collaboration and cross-attendance between groups. This reflects the existing intellectual character of Australian economic history, with cliometrics a mainstream feature of the field since the 1980s, and increasingly present in the *Australian Economic History Review* since the 2000s (see Chapter 5). However, similar to the other groups, OzClio was established for a particular purpose, one that does not necessarily align with the broader approach of the EHSANZ. As such, many members, particularly those who identify as economists, participate solely in OzClio.

The current fragmentation away from mainstream professional structures is understandable. Each of these newer groups began as an 'intellectual movement' – as something new and distinctive from the 'establishment'.⁵⁴ Butlin did so with Shann and Fitzpatrick; Snooks did the same with Butlin; Nicholas did so with the convict literature; and Merrett and Ville with

---

51   Some examples include John P Tang, 'The Engine and the Reaper: Industrialization and Mortality in Late Nineteenth Century Japan', *Journal of Health Economics* 56 (2017): 145–62, doi.org/10.1016/j.jhealeco.2017.09.004; John P Tang, 'A Tale of Two SICs: Japanese and American Industrialisation in Historical Perspective', *Australian Economic History Review* 56, no. 2 (2016): 174–97, doi.org/10.1111/aehr.12097; Laura Panza, Simon Ville and David Merrett, 'The Drivers of Firm Longevity: Age, Size, Profitability and Survivorship of Australian Corporations, 1901–1930', *Business History* (2017): 157–77, doi.org/10.1080/00076791.2017.1293041; Laura Panza and Jeffrey G Williamson, 'Australian Squatters, Convicts, and Capitalists: Dividing up a Fast-Growing Frontier Pie, 1821–71', *Economic History Review* 72, no. 2 (2019): 568–94, doi.org/10.1111/ehr.12739; Laura Panza, 'De-Industrialization and Re-Industrialization in the Middle East: Reflections on the Cotton Industry in Egypt and in the Izmir Region', *Economic History Review* 67, no. 1 (2014): 146–69, doi.org/10.1111/1468-0289.12019; Martine Mariotti, 'Estimating the Substitutability of African and White Workers in South African Manufacturing, 1950–1985', *Economic History of Developing Regions* 27, no. 2 (2012): 47–60, doi.org/10.1080/20780389.2012.745664; Jakob B Madsen, James B Ang and Rajabrata Banerjee, 'Four Centuries of British Economic Growth: The Roles of Technology and Population', *Journal of Economic Growth* 15, no. 4 (2010): 263–90, doi.org/10.1007/s10887-010-9057-7.
52   Panza and Williamson, 'Australian Squatters'.
53   Tang, 'A Tale of Two SICs'.
54   Scott Frickel and Neil Gross, 'A General Theory of Scientific/Intellectual Movements', *American Sociological Review* 70, no. 2 (2005): 204–32, doi.org/10.1177/000312240507000202.

traditional business history. It's the circle of life. Intellectual conservatism from mainstream economic historians, particularly integration with economics and business disciplines throughout the period of resistance, and adherence to the orthodox approach in recent collective efforts, has likely promoted an image of the society that is incongruous with various intellectual movements that have sought to 'shake up' the field's dominant thematic, ideological and methodological traditions. Demographically, the society is also relatively conservative, with leaders aligning with a profile that may appear exclusionary to members of the humanities, younger scholars, women and those from non-white ethnic backgrounds. The *Australian Economic History Review* has recently had its first female editor, Edwyna Harris, and although very welcome, it is the exception rather than the rule. Although I have never felt excluded in the EHSANZ, I can understand how the demographic structure could appear to those from the considerably more diverse OzClio and history of capitalism groups.

The relationship of the movement to the establishment also depends on relative institutional power. In some cases, intellectual movements are 'inducted' into the mainstream community by scholars convincing others of the new approach in order to secure appointments and funding.[55] This occurred with the postwar cliometrics movement in the US, and with antipodean cliometrics in the 1980s (see Chapter 4). The key question is, who are the newer groups trying to convince? The loss of identity for Australian economic history over the last few decades has meant that it no longer carries the institutional bargaining power that it once did. There are no longer departments with God Professors in charge of hiring and firing, and the field's leadership is unable to offer protections for newer scholars who manage to convince them of the validity of a new approach. Members of these intellectual movements then have to look for larger 'establishments' to which they can direct their efforts. Historians of capitalism have embedded themselves primarily within history: AAHANZBS within business disciplines and OzClio in economics groups. Ironically, these are the same parent disciplines through which mainstream economic historians are also seeking protection. The mainstream economic group is thus simultaneously perceived as the 'establishment' in terms of approach and profile, yet is competing with these other groups for institutional space.

---

55   Frickel and Gross, 'Scientific/Intellectual Movements'.

The global, neoliberal university

Marginalisation of Australian economic history has generally been blamed on the closure of departments. This has been the most obvious symbol of change, and members of the field cite this as the main change in the field's fortunes. While previous chapters have demonstrated that separate departments are not necessary, and indeed can be counterproductive, for an interdisciplinary field, their establishment and subsequent closure were both the result of a higher education system that fundamentally misunderstands interdisciplinary research. As an extension of this, recent advocacy of interdisciplinary knowledge by Australian governments and universities has been met with the escalation of policies that reinforce disciplines.[56] Universities since the Dawkins reforms have been funded through a combination of student income and research funding. Domestic students attract fees paid by the federal government, with individuals repaying subsidised tuition costs in the form of the Higher Education Contribution Scheme, or HECS. International students pay full tuition costs upfront directly to the university. University income from students is thus tied to consumer demand, which is in turn determined by the requirements of external stakeholders (the labour market for professions), as well as the reputation of the university. Research income, on the other hand, is distributed through a centralised government agency, the Australian Research Council (ARC). Funding depends on external stakeholders ('national benefit'), as well as the reputation of scholars and the university environment. These various accountabilities largely reinforce disciplinary modes of learning and research.

Professional enclosure

Tertiary education is designed to prepare students for their working life and, in the Scottish model that dominates Australian universities, student demand is determined by the types of jobs that people are likely to do.[57] The Dawkins reforms were geared towards increasing Australia's capacity in professional work, with business disciplines, as well as

---

56 Peter Woelert and Victoria Millar, 'The "Paradox of Interdisciplinarity" in Australian Research Governance', *Higher Education* 66, no. 6 (2013): 755–67, doi.org/10.1007/s10734-013-9634-8.

57 John C Smart, Kenneth A Feldman and Corinna A Ethington, *Academic Disciplines: Holland's Theory and the Study of College Students and Faculty* (Nashville: Vanderbilt University Press, 2000); John Gascoigne, 'The Cultural Origins of Australian Universities', *Journal of Australian Studies* 20, no. 50–51 (1996): 18–27, doi.org/10.1080/14443059609387275; Hermann Röhrs, 'The Classical Idea of the University', in *Tradition and Reform of the University Under an International Perspective*, ed. Hermann Röhrs and Gerhard Hess (Verlag: Peter Lang, 1987), 13–27.

nursing, teaching, engineering and law, expanding substantially. Growth professions have responded to the expansion of their ranks by enclosing territory through new professional associations and accreditation.[58] This has incentivised universities to adhere to specific coursework guidelines in order to attract students and then admit them to each profession.[59] Professional enclosure is bad for most interdisciplinary fields, with standardised training and qualifications used to ensure members have comparable knowledge and skills. While standardisation works well with disciplinary instruction, it operates in contention with broad, flexible interdisciplinary knowledge. Professional instruction often occurs 'in house', with students disincentivised to take courses in other disciplines or fields (see Chapter 5).

While 'real-world' experience is ostensibly valued by relevant stakeholders, neither the professions, new professionals nor universities have incentives to incorporate interdisciplinary curricula. Working with enclosed professions is nothing new for Australian economic history. Expansion of 'new' business disciplines in the 1990s removed compulsory economic history subjects during the resistance. Similarly, the enclosure of economics postgraduate research constrained the potential for PhD supervision in historical subjects (see Chapter 5). Even though professionals in business and economics need a range of skills in the workforce, the situation has only deteriorated recently. Many have noted the increasingly narrow instruction within business and economics degrees – dictated partly by accreditation – and the pressure this has put on economic history teaching.[60] Keneley has argued that the 'curriculum has narrowed so much that there is no scope for anything outside'.[61] Tim Hatton has, similarly, noted restrictions on the economic history graduate program at ANU have been 'a great shame'.[62]

---

58 Andrew Abbott, *The System of Professions: An Essay on the Division of Expert Labor* (Chicago: University of Chicago Press, 2014).
59 Victoria Millar, 'Interdisciplinary Curriculum Reform in the Changing University', *Teaching in Higher Education* 21, no. 4 (2016): 471–83, doi.org/10.1080/13562517.2016.1155549; Woelert and Millar, 'Paradox of Interdisciplinarity'.
60 Oxley/Meredith; Withers interviews.
61 Keneley interview.
62 Hatton interview.

Rankings

University rankings structure both student demand and research income. Through a general lack of trust in seemingly 'inefficient' and 'esoteric' academic work, the Dawkins reforms introduced formal measurement systems to evaluate performance (see Chapter 5). In 1993, the Australian Bureau of Statistics released the Australian Standard Research Classification, which designates various Field of Research (FoR) codes. Although FoR classifications have expanded over time, there are still no categories that adequately capture interdisciplinary research. The government then ranks relative research 'quality' through their 'objective' 'Excellence in Research for Australia' (ERA) assessment procedure.[63] Various performance indicators – research income, quantity of publications and citations – are applied across activities within the same 4- or 6-digit FoR codes, to determine the rank of that particular group or university regardless of the relative institutional or intellectual context. The procedure assumes that outputs and citations are proxies of peer-assessed quality.[64] Compared to research assessment overseas, there is little use of expert peer review in Australia for ERA, and no scope for those assessed to contextualise the material in the report. While ERA rankings have no explicit, direct control over universities, they modify university behaviour through reputation.[65] A university's place in ERA rankings can drive ARC and other funding, and can influence student decision-making. Universities are thus cognisant of the evaluation exercise, and seek to maximise their place in the hierarchy.[66]

To conform to ERA criteria, academics are appointed and promoted based on publishing in what are seen as the 'right' places.[67] If you are hired to an economics group, you are expected to have a suitable record of publications in that discipline. This presents challenges to those who occupy the interdisciplinary space, as they are often hired to a range of groups, each with their own set of rules regarding publication outlets.

---

63 ERA started life as the Federal Liberal Howard Government's 'Research Quality Framework', which was transformed into ERA under the Labor Rudd Government.
64 Peter Woelert and Lyn Yates, 'Too Little and Too Much Trust: Performance Measurement in Australian Higher Education', *Critical Studies in Education* 56, no. 2 (2015): 175–89, doi.org/10.1080/17508487.2014.943776.
65 Jen Tsen Kwok, *Impact of ERA Research Assessment on University Behaviour and their Staff* (Melbourne: NTEU National Policy and Research Unit, 2013).
66 Raewyn Connell, *The Good University: What Universities Actually Do and Why It's Time for Radical Change* (London: Zed Books Ltd., 2019).
67 Woelert and Millar, 'Paradox of Interdisciplinarity'.

If you are lucky, parent disciplines simply disagree on what specific journals you should target; if you are unlucky they disagree on the fundamentals of what you should be writing. Economic history is unlucky: economics and business disciplines emphasise journal articles, while in history scholarly monographs are of prime importance. Each discipline has their own rankings of suitable outlets. For business and economics, the Australian Business Dean's Council (ABDC) list is taken seriously. For historians, global databases like SCImago are used to rank journal quality.[68] As with ERA assessment, most journal rankings are based on relative citation rates. ABDC, for example, is informed by 'globally recognised [...] journal ranking lists, appropriate and select citation metrics and, if required, expert peer review'.[69] Citations take first place in this procedure, with qualitative assessment by experts the exception rather than the rule.

Citation analysis is a limited method for determining quality. Data collection is challenging, with citations determined by online repositories that are often unreliable with regards to government reports or books. Citations are limited in their ability to reveal article quality, offering no insight into perceptions of the piece – indeed an article may have a high rate of citation through disagreement.[70] Citations also reflect social realities and cronyism, with authors tending to disproportionately cite their friends and colleagues.[71] Bias is also found through the Matthew Effect, where prominent scholars are cited with relative frequency, simply because they are seen to be important.[72] Citations systemically reinforce

---

68 Connell, *The Good University*.
69 See the 2018 ABDC methodology review: abdc.edu.au/research/abdc-journal-list/2018-journal-quality-list-methodology-review/.
70 Loet Leydesdorff and Olga Amsterdamska, 'Dimensions of Citation Analysis', *Science, Technology, and Human Values* 15, no. 3 (1990): 305–35, doi.org/10.1177/016224399001500303; MH MacRoberts and Barbara R MacRoberts, 'Problems of Citation Analysis', *Scientometrics* 36, no. 3 (1996): 435–44, doi.org/10.1007/BF02129604; TJ Phelan, 'A Compendium of Issues for Citation Analysis', *Scientometrics* 45, no. 1 (1999): 117–36, doi.org/10.1007/BF02458472; Chris Alen Sula, 'Visualizing Social Connections in the Humanities: Beyond Bibliometrics', *Bulletin of the American Society for Information Science and Technology* 38, no. 4 (2012): 31–35, doi.org/10.1002/bult.2012.1720380409.
71 SE Cozzens, 'Taking the Measure of Science: A Review of Citation Theories', *Newsletter of the International Society for the Sociology of Knowledge* 7, no. 1 (1981): 16–21; D Crane, *Invisible Colleges: Diffusion of Knowledge in Scientific Communities* (Chicago: University of Chicago Press, 1972); G Nigel Gilbert, 'Referencing as Persuasion', *Social Studies of Science* 7, no. 1 (1977): 113–22, doi.org/10.1177/030631277700700112; Neha Gondal, 'The Local and Global Structure of Knowledge Production in an Emergent Research field: An Exponential Random Graph Analysis', *Social Networks* 33, no. 1 (2011): 20–30, doi.org/10.1016/j.socnet.2010.09.001.
72 Robert K Merton, 'The Matthew Effect in Science', *Science* 159, no. 3810 (1968): 56–63, doi.org/10.1126/science.159.3810.56.

the power of disciplines, with disciplinary tribes characterised by common ideas, approaches and jargon, making it easier for scholars to assimilate and thus cite relevant material.[73] The enclosure of disciplines also reinforces social networks, with a greater role for cronyism and the Matthew Effect. Journal rankings, ERA and, ultimately, university hiring decisions are thus based on indicators that structurally disadvantage interdisciplinary knowledge.

Rankings are a major ongoing challenge for Australian economic historians. Scholars in business and economics schools (which is a lot of them) are evaluated based on the norms of those disciplines. The ABDC list is very influential, with department or faculty management demanding their staff send material to A*- or A-ranked journals. As with all interdisciplinary outlets, the ABDC ranks historical journals such as the *Australian Economic History Review* relatively poorly. This creates problems for the flow of new material, despite the importance of the journal for understanding Australia. Keneley, for example, has commented that her research in the *Review* and other economic and business history outlets do not 'count for anything – so I get no recognition in my workload for the research I do [...] The ERA has a lot to answer for, it has basically killed scholarly inquiry; forced people into silos'.[74] Similarly, when I asked Frost what he would like to do today to improve the fortunes of Australian economic history, without hesitation he argued that he would 'get everyone to rip up the ABDC journal ranking lists'.[75]

With the marginalisation of interdisciplinary journals, in order to succeed scholars need to publish in disciplinary journals. They face barriers here as well. Journal editors function as gatekeepers for disciplinary tribes by controlling the flow and direction of legitimised work.[76] By virtue of it conforming to the group's norms, journals publish a higher proportion of disciplinary work, and lower proportions that challenge orthodoxy or integrate different perspectives. It takes quite a bit to convince disciplinary journal editors of the value of an interdisciplinary piece. Even then,

---

73 Rafols et al., 'How Journal Rankings Can Suppress Interdisciplinary Research: A Comparison between Innovation Studies and Business and Management', *Research Policy* 41, no. 7 (2012): 1262–82, doi.org/10.1016/j.respol.2012.03.015.
74 Keneley interview.
75 Frost interview.
76 Collyer et al., *Knowledge and Global Power: Making New Sciences in the South* (Johannesburg: Wits University Press, 2019); Raewyn Connell, *Southern Theory: The Global Dynamics of Knowledge in Social Science* (Crows Nest: Allen & Unwin, 2007).

it may still be rejected if the editors believe it might be uninteresting to the members of the tribe, or if they struggle to find referees with suitable expertise.[77]

Compounding these disciplinary issues is intellectual imperialism. Book publishers are strongly ranked on imperial lines, with Oxbridge or Ivy League imprints at the top of the hierarchy. Journal rankings follow similar trends, with UK or US outlets ranked much higher than comparable journals in the antipodes. In the ABDC rankings, just as economic and business history research is structurally disadvantaged, so too are Australian journals.[78] The *Australian Economic History Review* is ranked lower than counterparts in the UK, US or Europe. Again, the assessment is based on faulty logic: rankings are drawn from citation rates, and citations are higher for metropole journals in part because the market for readers is so much larger. Citations also reflect unconscious bias, with imperial knowledge structures conditioning us to look to the metropole for legitimate scholarship.[79] Neither of these factors have much to do with quality. Just as they are resistant to interdisciplinary work, overseas journals are rarely inclined to publish Australian research, with editors of US or UK journals often rejecting Australian scholarship unless it is comparative, or strongly demonstrates something they deem as valuable to their region.

University ranking systems are thoroughly cooked. Comparing work produced in different knowledge domains enforces a flat system of assessment guided by seemingly objective quantitative measures of 'quality'. However, the fundamental assumption is flawed – citations are not objective: they reflect disciplinary, social and colonial structures of privilege. Governments and universities claim they want interdisciplinary research that is of national benefit, and yet the work that achieves this is structurally disadvantaged by the university system.

The ARC

Australia has a relatively sparse funding landscape. Since the Dawkins reforms, the government has progressively increased the proportion of research funds allocated competitively through the ARC, with Australia

---

77 Ehud Shapiro, 'Correcting the Bias against Interdisciplinary Research', *eLife* 3, no. 1 (2014): 1–3, doi.org/10.7554/eLife.02576; Collyer et al., *Knowledge and Global Power*.
78 Collyer et al., *Knowledge and Global Power*; Connell, *Southern Theory*.
79 Connell, *The Good University*; Connell, *Southern Theory*.

also faced with comparatively lower levels of philanthropic or industry funding compared to other OECD nations.[80] As funding directly increases the research budget and influences ERA assessments, as well as the success of future funding applications, universities take the ARC very seriously when designing hiring, promotion or incentive procedures.

The ARC makes a concerted effort to encourage interdisciplinary knowledge. Funding was important for sustaining economic history projects during the period of resistance (see Chapter 5), and has enabled broader interdisciplinary engagement more recently, including work on environmental histories of water, convicts and anthropometric history, histories of multinationals and histories of capitalism. The application process appears to support projects that span the interdisciplinary space, and there is the opportunity to list multiple relevant FoR codes. Contrasting with ERA, applicants are able to contextualise their research outputs relative to the norms of the disciplines they work in. Innovation and national benefit are major criteria for assessment, and the practical, flexible and innovative insights of interdisciplinary knowledge are ostensibly taken seriously. This has been beneficial for interdisciplinary scholars, as universities have tried to increase their funding success through various internal seeding schemes. University research fellowships are common at the early career stage, and aim to support those who would be good candidates for future ARC funding. These fellowships are assessed in a similar way to the ARC, which provides space for interdisciplinary scholars to penetrate normally siloed hiring processes. Many universities also now distribute seed funding for interdisciplinary projects, under the expectation that ARC applications will follow.[81]

Nevertheless, some of the ARC's assessment criteria reinforces disciplines. Internationally, the success rate for interdisciplinary applications to similar research funding agencies is lower than for single-discipline applications.[82] In Australia, similar patterns have been reported, with lower success for applications that involve diverse knowledge.[83] Journal rankings, citation rates and ERA scores are still important for evaluating

---

80   The ARC was established in 1988. University medical research is funded separately through the National Health and Medical Research Council (NHMRC).
81   For example, the University of Wollongong has a very active 'Global Challenges' program that funds projects with collaborators from three of the five faculties.
82   Shapiro, 'Interdisciplinary Research'.
83   Lindell Bromham, Russell Dinnage and Xia Hua, 'Interdisciplinary Research Has Consistently Lower Funding Success', *Nature* 534, no. 7609 (2016): 684–87, doi.org/10.1038/nature18315.

the candidate and the research environment. Interdisciplinary research is not captured directly in FoR codes, and so applicants essentially divide their project into its various disciplinary components. For example, in an economic history application, scholars decide whether to pitch the project to a humanities or social sciences audience. If it goes to the humanities panel, most of the assessors will be historians, and if goes to social sciences most of the assessors will be economists. The research will be up against those within that discipline, and although the panel will be cognisant of relative research context, naturally a panel of humanities assessors will view the approach very differently to their colleagues in social sciences. Rather than evaluated holistically, interdisciplinary applications are still valued based on disciplinary markers of success. Deborah Oxley has acknowledged the strategy necessary to make an interdisciplinary ARC application work, commenting that 'it's very hard to satisfy [assessors], if you are genuinely interdisciplinary', and that the same project, with the same national benefit, will perform very differently based on the panel.[84]

Conclusions

Despite a revival of interest in economic history in recent years, the field faces substantial uncertainties. In very welcome developments, new research has increased the scope for collaboration, teaching and impactful research. However, conservatism from the 'establishment', particularly through the maintenance of an orthodox, economics perspective, has led some to bypass the field's professional structures in favour of their own intellectual movements. Fragmentation of scholars' efforts has been combined with significant challenges with regards to the higher education environment, particularly the escalation of neoliberal policies that have disincentivised interdisciplinary research. This assessment of the field's recent position highlights the distinctive progress of interdisciplinary fields within universities – particularly the need to redesign policies – and the challenges associated with maintaining the field's identity while also negotiating relationships with parent disciplines.

---

84 Oxley/Meredith interview.

7

Epilogue

> I would like to see it flourish, not narrowly as a little branch of economics, but for what it is [...] a big, eclectic agenda.
>
> Deborah Oxley, February 2020[1]

Pessimism is easy, interdisciplinarity is hard. Although it is difficult to do good economic history research in modern Australian universities, by acknowledging the work still to be done, I hope to be constructive. There are several important lessons from this history that can help policymakers and practitioners do better for Australian economic history moving forward, and for the myriad other interdisciplinary fields that change how we see the world. Economic historical work grew from the colonial project, and the need for governments to count, understand and govern the various aspects of the antipodes. In the interwar period, cooperation between governments, universities and the Workers' Educational Association, and porous boundaries between disciplines, allowed broad economic history research to flourish. Post–World War II saw the expansion of universities, with Noel Butlin's ambitious research agenda at The Australian National University (ANU) developing a close-knit community of scholars who understood Australia's development through quantitative data and an inductive, economics-based approach. Parent disciplines were indulgent, as was the higher education sector, and, as a result, the subject bloomed primarily through separate departments established from the 1960s to the 1990s. While this was considered a 'golden age' by some, these departments encouraged inward-looking behaviour, and isolated some

---

1   Oxley/Meredith interview. Unless otherwise specified, interviews cited are those conducted by the author: see Appendix for details.

scholars from parent disciplines. The Dawkins reforms from the late 1980s compounded these vulnerabilities, leading to the closure of departments, dispersal of students and attrition of scholars. However, this period also provided new opportunities, particularly with economics and business schools. Members were thus well-placed to capitalise on the field's revival in recent years.

Negotiating the interdisciplinary space has required Australian economic historians to work within multiple intellectual, professional and institutional domains. Individual scholars have made choices regarding the frameworks, data, research questions and publication outlets they adopt from parent disciplines, and scholarship exists along a spectrum from historians interested in economic matters, to economists with long-run data. The pendulum has shifted several times over the past century, from Sir Timothy Coghlan and Noel Butlin's social science–based national income accounting, to the integrated social, political and economic research of interwar scholars and the Melbourne group, to the dominance of cliometrics, and the recent broad, but somewhat fragmented body of work. As others have reflected, it is difficult to determine a unifying or uniquely 'Australian' approach. A key feature of the field's story is the ongoing debate about the 'best' or 'most appropriate' method for understanding Australia's economic past, with many acknowledging the field's diversity as a key contribution.[2]

Negotiating space has also required economic historians to convince parent disciplines of the validity of their approach. Disciplines can protect interdisciplinary fields by providing funding, a student base and validation of new research. Interdisciplinary fields thus depend on the indulgence of disciplines through key research questions or the skills that are seen as appropriate for professional instruction. This has worked in economic history's favour, with support from both disciplines in the post–World War II decades corresponding with professional space, high student numbers, command over resources and the ability to maintain a dedicated workforce. On the other hand, the retraction of support from both the history and economics disciplines in the 1990s was a very hard lesson in the risks associated with conducting interdisciplinary research and instruction. Economic history's progress has thus been characterised by the uncertainty of having to integrate with, yet work independently

---

[2] Oxley/Meredith interview. See also Lloyd; Ville; Hatton; Alford interviews.

from, multiple knowledge domains. This can make it hard to define appropriate research questions and methodologies, or even know the best way to ensure one's future career prospects. Economic historians have grappled with these questions, identifying the excitement associated with producing new knowledge, as well as the vulnerability they feel from dependence on the prosperity of larger groups.

These risks can be mitigated or exacerbated by the higher education environment, with the progress of Australian economic history demonstrating the interaction between research *place* and research *outcome*. Institutions like universities have been key organising structures for research, and university settings – the physical space, funding structure, students, and hierarchical aspirations – have influenced the research that scholars do. The cross-disciplinary support afforded to Butlin's efforts at ANU in the 1950s, for example, or the Australian Research Council's funding of large economic history projects more recently, have been invaluable for the field's visibility, recognition and bargaining power. On the other hand, neoliberal universities and performance incentives based on disciplinary measures of success have been detrimental to the field's vibrancy, with the attrition of scholars, and substantial decline of the student base.

Departments of economic history presented a different form of existential threat. For a relatively brief period (the 1960s through to the 1990s), many Australian economic historians worked in small departments. This form of organisation was determined externally, through university expansion and the underlying logic of small departmental groups led by a 'God Professor'. While departments did stabilise some professional uncertainties such as the number of students, they discouraged interdisciplinary integration. The isolation and strong ties developed within small departments have been, at times, inappropriate for the broad networks needed to work in the interdisciplinary space. This book demonstrates that departments are not necessary for the field's progress, with some of the most celebrated contributions produced in the absence of economic history departments. On the other hand, less constrained communicating infrastructures such as collaborations, dedicated outreach efforts, and the activities of the *Australian Economic History Review* and the Economic History Society of Australia and New Zealand have made much greater inroads with regards to interdisciplinary integration.

The progress of Australian economic history demonstrates the unique features of interdisciplinary fields. While disciplines are designed to operate through consensus, shared paradigms and agreement on best practice, interdisciplinary research is valuable for integrating and communicating knowledge between disciplines. For university policymakers and administrators, this case emphasises the disconnect between rhetoric promoting interdisciplinary knowledge, and university structures and incentives that reinforce disciplines. For practitioners, this book highlights not only the field's diverse intellectual possibilities, but also advocates for the creation of broad, vibrant cross-disciplinary spaces as the key to ensuring the field's continued value and relevance.

Appendix and data

Departments of economic history in Australia

The following outlines individual appointments within dedicated economic history departments at Australian universities, for the time that department existed. Keep in mind that many members of the field were never employed in a separate department, and many were appointed to a mix of economic history groups, parent disciplines and overseas throughout their career. The data also include short-term postdoctoral or visiting fellowships, if the fellow was included in the department's annual report. It captures the movement, sometimes fleeting, of scholars in and out of economic history groups, but should not be read as the totality of the field or of any individual's career.

Sources: Staff lists contained in the *Commonwealth Universities Yearbook* (CUY, as titled from 1958 onwards). The same publication has been titled *The Yearbook of the Universities of the Commonwealth* (1948–58) and *The Yearbook of the Universities of the Empire* (1914–47). I have utilised copies of the 1970–2008 editions held at the Macquarie University Library, and copies of the 1948–69 editions at the State Library of New South Wales. The CUY compiles information contained in individual university annual reports and yearbooks; these are held online or in university archives.

The Australian National University

What became The Australian National University (ANU) began as two separate institutions. Canberra University College (CUC) was established in 1930 as a branch of the University of Melbourne, and this became the School of General Studies (the 'Faculties'). 'ANU', the research-only arm of the institution, was established in 1946. These research schools then became the Institute of Advanced Studies, which was home to the Research School of Social Sciences (RSSS). The two institutions were amalgamated in 1960, which meant ANU had two departments of economic history – one in the Faculties and another in the RSSS. Herbert Burton was appointed professor of economic history at CUC in 1948, and was responsible for a small separate group from 1957 (this then became the Faculties department). Scholars who formed the RSSS department were drawn from the economics group.

In 1990, a restructure saw the RSSS department converted to the 'economic history program' within the Politics and Economics Division. There was also the Economic History of South East Asia (ECHOSEA) project, which operated as a five-year strategic initiative in the Research School of Pacific Studies (RSPacS) at the same time. By 1998, the economic history program was down to a single staff member, and shortly after Snooks was merged into the economics group. The department in the Faculties existed relatively unchanged until 2000–01, at which point members either went to economics or to business groups.

Table 1: Economic history staff of ANU

Alford, Katrina A.	RSSS	1985–87
Barnard, Alan	RSSS	1962–88
Boot, H. M. 'Mac'	Faculties	1970–2001
Bourke, P. F.	RSSS	1989
Buck, A. R.	Faculties	1988
Burton, Herbert	Faculties	1957–65
Butlin, Noel G.	RSSS	1962–85
Butlin, Sydney J.	RSSS	1972–75
Cain, Neville G.	Faculties; RSSS	1962–67; 1968–89
Cornish, Selwyn H.	Faculties	1968–2001
Coward, D. H.	RSSS	1977–82
Dobbs, S. J.	Faculties	1992–94
Dowie, J. A.	Faculties; RSSS	1965–66; 1969–70
Fleming, Grant	Faculties	1994–96
Forster, Colin	Faculties	1957–91
Gage, John E. S.	Faculties	1969–96
Gerritsen, R.	RSSS	1979–81
Glynn, Sean	Faculties	1966–68

Grove, Richard H.	RSSS	1993–96
Haig, Bryan D.	RSSS	1963–72
Huff, W. G.	RSPacS–ECHOSEA	1991
Hughes, D. L.	Faculties	1989–96
Hutchings, R. F. D.	RSSS	1963–67
Jackson, R. V. 'Bob'	Faculties; RSSS	1969–90; 1992–93
Johnson, P.	RSSS	1991
Joy, C. S.	RSSS	1976
Maddock, Rod	RSSS	1981–84
Magee, Gary	RSSS	1996
Martina, Alan	Faculties	1969–96
McLean, Ian W.	RSSS	1981–82
Pincus, Jonathan J.	RSSS	1972–85
Pope, David H.	RSSS	1991–93
Reid, Anthony J. S.	RSPacS–ECHOSEA	1991–95
Snooks, Graeme D.	RSSS	1990–98
Stevens, F. S.	RSSS	1965–68
Sullivan, E.	Faculties	1993
Troy, Pat N.	RSSS	1967–71
Tsokhas, Kosmas	RSSS	1987–91
Tucker, Graham S. L.	Faculties	1959–78
Tucker, K. A.	RSSS	1973–77
van der Eng, Pierre	RSPacS–ECHOSEA; Faculties	1992–93; 1994–2001
Ville, Simon P.	Faculties	1991–2001
Withers, Glenn A.	RSSS	1983–85

Flinders University

The Department of Economic History at Flinders was established in 1970, with Seymour Broadbridge at the helm. Appointments to the new group were also new to the university, but the group was based within the economics faculty. The department closed in 1992, at which point the remaining members (Ralph Shlomowitz and Robin Haines) went to the history department.

Table 2: Economic history staff of Flinders University

Broadbridge, Seymour A.	1970–71
Deng, Kent G.	1992
Haines, Robin F.	1992
Mein Smith, Philippa L.	1990–91
Pincus, Jonathan J.	1985–90
Richards, Eric S.	1971–74
Shlomowitz, Ralph	1975–92
Sinclair, W. A. 'Gus'	1973–82
Snooks, Graeme D.	1973–88
Vamplew, Wray	1976–92

La Trobe University

The Department of Economic History at La Trobe was established late, and it was very short-lived. Before and after the department, scholars worked in the economics group.

Table 3: Economic history staff of La Trobe University

Anderson, J. L.	1990–92
Frost, Lionel E.	1990–92
Jones, Eric L.	1990–92
White, Colin	1990–92

University of Melbourne

The University of Melbourne economic history department was established in 1947. Before the department, economic historians such as Edgars Dunsdorfs were in commerce and economics groups. Herbert Burton had held joint appointments between the faculties of Arts and Commerce since 1930, and was appointed head of the new economic history department in 1947. The department transformed into 'Business Development and Corporate History' in 1995, and scholars were merged with the Department of Management in 1998.

Table 4: Economic history staff of University of Melbourne

Alford, Katrina A.	1991–94
Ali, C. I.	1981–83
Bain, N.	1960
Beever, E. Alan	1958–88
Blainey, Geoffrey	1959–75
Burton, Herbert	1947
Cairns, James F. 'Jim'	1947–54
Carter, Benita	1977
Chernick, S.	1951–53
Clarkson, L. A.	1958–60
Dick, Howard W.	1995
Dunsdorfs, Edgars	1948–69
Egerton, R. A.	1947–49
Fogarty, John P.	1969–88
Forde, D. G.	1973–74
Forster, Colin	1956
Freeman, Richard D.	1963–72
Hancock, Keith J.	1956
Harper, Marjorie (nee Ronaldson)	1948–56; 1975–89
Hodgart, Allan W.	1971–75
Hutchinson, Diane	1986–89
Killip, J. H.	1958–61; 1989–90
Kolko, G.	1961
Kotono, Takashi	1961–67
La Nauze, John A.	1949–54
Macneil, I. P.	1958–60
Maitland, Elizabeth	1995
Merrett, David T.	1990–95
Middleman, Raoul	1964–74
Mitchell, Anne McK.	1949
Morgan, Stephen L.	1994–95
Nicholas, Stephen J.	1993–95
Oxley, Deborah	1990–93
Parsons, T. G.	1968–69
Rangnekar, D. K.	1958

Remenyi, Joseph	1970-72
Richardson, Peter G. L.	1985-87
Robertson, Paul L.	1976-90
Schedvin, C. Boris	1979-91
Schnierer, F.	1947-48
Seltzer, Andrew	1994-95
Sinclair, W. A. 'Gus'	1951-52; 1957-60
Sydenham, Diane M.	1990-93
Thompson, Allan G.	1961-94
Trace, Keith	1964-66
Tucker, Graham S. L.	1949-58
Vicziany, Antonia M.	1977-79
Whitwell, Greg J.	1982-95
Woodruff, William	1956-66

Monash University

The Monash economic history department was established in 1972. Prior to that, relevant scholars such as Sinclair, Dingle, Merrett and McCarty were appointed to the economics groups in the economics and politics (ECOPS) faculty. The department was closed in 1993, at which point scholars were merged with economics.

Table 5: Economic history staff of Monash University

Dingle, A. E. 'Tony'	1972-93
Gribble, I. A.	1977-78
McCarty, John W.	1972-93
Merrett, David T.	1972-89
Schedvin, C. Boris	1972-79
Spenceley, Geoffrey F. R.	1972-93
Sydenham, Diane M.	1979-82
Trace, Keith	1972-93
Vicziany, Antonia M.	1981-93

University of Sydney

A department was established at the University of Sydney within the economics faculty in 1970. Prior to the department, economic historians worked in the economics faculty in dedicated economic history positions. The economic history department operated until 2003, at which point the remaining three members went their separate ways – Aldrich to history, Hutchinson to economics and Tipton to business.

Table 6: Economic history staff of University of Sydney

Aldcroft, Derek H.	1973–75
Aldrich, Robert	1982–2003
Allen, M.	1991–93
Buckley, Ken D.	1970–86
Drabble, John H.	1974–93
Ginswick, Jules	1970–79
Hall, P. K.	1970–88
Hutchinson, Diane	1989–2003
Jack, Sybil M.	1970–71
Koenig, Linda	1975–76
Rahim, Lily Z.	1996
Salsbury, Stephen M.	1976–98
Schedvin, C. Boris	1970–72
Tipton, F. Ben	1979–2003
Tucker, Barbara	1973–78
Wotherspoon, Garry C.	1974–98

University of New England

The UNE department was established within the newly formed Faculty of Economics in 1965. Prior to that, economic history subjects were taught within the economics group. After the closure of the department in 1998, members were reappointed to economics.

Table 7: Economic history staff of UNE

Abbott, Graham J.	1970–71
Attard, Bernard P.	1992–93
Boot, H. M. 'Mac'	1969

Cage, R. A.	1975-98
Diehl, F. W.	1973-88
Falkus, Malcolm E.	1987-98
Fisher, S. A.	1982
Fitzgerald, Shirley H.	1986
Henning, Graydon R.	1973-98
Kaplan, Gisela T.	1988
Kaur, Amarjit	1990-98
Kitching, B. M.	1987-88
Lai, C.-K.	1992-94
Lloyd, A. Christopher	1975-96; 1986-98
McMichael, Phillip D.	1977-78
Morris-Suzuki, Teresa I. J.	1982-91
Neale, Ron S.	1965-85
Nichol, W.	1982
Purcell, W. R.	1979
van der Kraan, Alfons	1990-98
Whitehead, D. M.	1965-66
Wilkinson, J.	1992

University of New South Wales

The UNSW department was established in 1970–71. Prior to the department, relevant scholars were appointed to a mix of economics and history positions. The department was established within economics following the appointment of Gordon Rimmer to the chair. The department was closed in 1995–96, with the relevant scholars unilaterally folded into the economics group.

Table 8: Economic history staff of UNSW

Ambirajan, Srinivasa	1971-81
Blair, A. L.	1990
Clark, David L.	1971-96
Dunn, A.	1990
Dyster, Barrie D.	1974-96
Hendrischke, B.	1993-94
Inkster, Ian C.	1974-95

Johnson, M. R.	1986-88
Meredith, David	1973-96
Nicholas, Stephen J.	1976-93
Nolan, P. H.	1976-77
Perkins, John A.	1971-96
Pope, David H.	1976-90
Rimmer, W. Gordon	1971-85
Shergold, Peter J.	1972-88
Sigel, Louis T.	1981-89

Oral history interviews

Table 9: Interviews conducted for this text's research

Who	Where	When
Pat Troy	In person, Canberra	February 2015
Bob Gregory	In person, Canberra	February 2015
Selwyn Cornish	In person, Canberra	February 2015
David Merrett	In person, Melbourne	March 2015
Stuart Macintyre	In person, Melbourne	March 2015
Gus Sinclair	In person, Melbourne	March 2015
Geoffrey Blainey	In person, Melbourne	March 2015
Matthew Butlin	In person, Melbourne	March 2015
Alan Hall	In person, Sydney	June 2015
Ian McLean	In person, Adelaide	July 2015
Jonathan Pincus	In person, Adelaide	July 2015
Boris Schedvin	Part 1: In person, Melbourne	July 2015
	Part 2: Virtually	April 2017
Tony Dingle/Graeme Davison	In person, Melbourne	July 2015
Rod Maddock	In person, Melbourne	December 2015
Bob Jackson	In person, Canberra	March 2016
Peter Shergold	In person, Sydney	March 2016
Pamela Statham	Virtually	April 2016
Stephen Nicholas	Part 1: In person, Sydney	April 2016
	Part 2: Virtually	October 2019
Diane Hutchinson	In person, Sydney	April 2016

Who	Where	When
Mac Boot	In person, Canberra	April 2016
Greg Whitwell	Part 1: Virtually	March 2017
	Part 2: Virtually	April 2017
Christopher Lloyd	Virtually	June 2019
Monica Keneley	Virtually	July 2019
Tim Hatton	Virtually	September 2019
Glenn Withers	In person, Canberra	October 2019
Lionel Frost	Virtually	October 2019
Barrie Dyster	In person, Blue Mountains	January 2020
Deborah Oxley/David Meredith	In person, Canberra	February 2020
Simon Ville	In person, Wollongong	May 2020
Martin Shanahan	Virtually	June 2020
Katrina Alford	Virtually	June 2020

Source: Author's summary of research.

Index

Note: page numbers in italics indicate images. A page number followed by an 'n' indicates a reference appearing in a footnote on that page.

AAHANZBS. *see* Academic Association of Historians in Australian and New Zealand Business Schools (AAHANZBS)
Abbott, Graham J., 93
Abbott, Malcolm, 151
ABDC list. *see* Australian Business Dean's Council (ABDC) list
Academic Association of Historians in Australian and New Zealand Business Schools (AAHANZBS), 174–175
accounting, 72, 73, 117, 118
    see also national income accounting
agriculture, 23, 83–84, 97
AHA. *see* Australian Historical Association (AHA)
Aldcroft, Derek, 75
Alford, Katrina, 98, 111, 114, 134, 135
Anderson, Kym, 86
Annales d'histoire économique et sociale (journal), 40
Annales school, 40, 124
ANU. *see* Australian National University (ANU)
ANU Centre for Economic History, 171, 175
ANU Economic History of Southeast Asia Project (ECHOSEA), 158, 192

ANU Institute of Advanced Studies (the 'Institute'), 53–54, 192
ANU Research School of Pacific Studies (RSPacS), 58, 66, 134, 192
ANU Research School of Social Sciences (RSSS), 54–58, 74, 77, 80, 114, 139, 192
ANU School of General Studies (the 'Faculties'), 53–54, 80, 191
APEBH. *see* Asia-Pacific Economic and Business History (APEBH) conference
Appleyard, Reginald ('Reg'), 103–104, 140
ARC. *see* Australian Research Council (ARC)
Archer, William, 23
Arndt, Heinz, 45, 63–64, 92
Asia-Pacific Economic and Business History (APEBH) conference, 158
Atkinson, Meredith, 32–33, 41
    New Social Order, 33, 36–37
Attard, Bernard, 160
Australia
    national character, 64
    relationship with Britain, 40–41, 47–48, 65–66, 76
    relationship with United States, 81–82, 85, 120, 156–157

structural disadvantages in higher
education, 183
study of, 47–48
see also Australian history
Australian Business Dean's Council
(ABDC) list, 181, 182, 183
Australian Commonwealth
Department of Postwar
Reconstruction, 31, 42, 49
see also postwar reconstruction
*Australian Domestic Product,
Investment and Foreign Borrowing
1861–1938/9* ('the numbers'),
46–51
Australian Economic History Review
(journal), 18
communicating infrastructure, 111
contributions to, 84–85, 92, 93,
94, 98
on economic history crisis, 113,
120
editorial board, 151, 158
editorial direction, 101–102, 143
first female editor, 177
international focus, 157–159
publisher, 158
renaming, 146
urban history, 153
Australian Historical Association
(AHA), 155
Australian Historical Studies (journal),
167
Australian history. *see* history
Australian Institute of Political
Science, 30
Australian National University
(ANU), 11, 191–193
Centre for Economic History,
171, 175
Economic History of Southeast
Asia Project (ECHOSEA),
158, 192
impact on economic history, 67,
80–82, 187

Institute of Advanced Studies (the
'Institute'), 53–54, 192
post–World War II growth, 53–62
relationship with University of
Adelaide, 80
Research School of Pacific Studies
(RSPacS), 58, 66, 134, 192
Research School of Social Sciences
(RSSS), 54–58, 74, 77, 80,
114, 139, 192
School of General Studies (the
'Faculties'), 53–54, 80, 191
Australian Research Council (ARC),
116, 119, 151, 178, 183–185,
189
Australian Research Grants
Commission, 52
Australian Society for the Study of
Labour History, 106
Australian Standard Research
Classification, 180

Bailey, John D., 54
Balliol College (Oxford), 29
Balnave, Nikola, 174
Bambrick, Susan, 58, 59
banking, 31, 88
Barnard, Alan, 54, 55, 58, 145
*Government and Capitalism:
Public and Private Choice in
Twentieth Century Australia*,
110–111
The Simple Fleece, 56
Beever, Alan, 50–51, 98, 136
Benham, Frederic, 30, 41
The Prosperity of Australia, 34,
36, 39
Bentick, Brian L., 72
Biddle, Nicholas, *171*
Birch, Alan, 101
Blainey, Geoffrey, 93, 94, 145
A Land Half Won, 94
Peaks of Lyell, 94
The Rush That Never Ended, 94
The Tyranny of Distance, 94

Boehm, Ernst A., 49, 50, 51, 65
Boot, H.M. ('Mac'), 137, 138
Booth, Anne, 158
Borland, Jeff, 142
Botany Bay project, 130
Boulding, Kenneth, 100
Boyce, Gordon, 148
Bridge, Helen, 133
British Colonial Office, 38
British economic history, 65
British education systems, 76
British Empire. *see* imperialism
British Government, 23
Broadberry, Stephen, 166
Broadbridge, Seymour A., 74, 193
Buckley, Kenneth ('Ken'), 106, 107–108
  Essays in the Political Economy of Australian Capitalism, 107
  No Paradise for Workers, 107–108
Bulletin for the Society of Labour History (journal), 106
  see also *Labour History* (journal)
Bulletin of the Business Archives Council of Australia (journal), 101
Burton, Herbert ('Joe'), 29, 54, 94, 192, 194
business
  business history, 145–152, 174–175
  cartels, 151
  studies in, 72, 73, 117, 148–150
  see also public enterprises
Business Archives and History (journal), 101, 146
Business Archives Council, 146
business cycles, 63, 122, 143
Butlin, Matthew, 128–129
Butlin, Noel G., 3, 5, 42, *47,* 82–83, 99
  Australian Domestic Product, Investment and Foreign Borrowing 1861–1938/9 ('the numbers'), 46–51

at Australian National University (ANU), 53, 54–57, 67
Coghlan Chair, 130
colonial socialism, 138
comparison with Sydney Butlin, 90
criticism of, 50–51
death, 128
Economics and the Dreamtime, 128–129
Forming a Colonial Economy, 128, 129–130
frameworks, 49
as God Professor, 57, 58, 61
Government and Capitalism: Public and Private Choice in Twentieth Century Australia, 110–111
impact of, 49–51, 62–64, 66–67
Investment in Australian Economic Development, 1861–1900 ('the words'), 46–51
Our Original Aggression, 129
Recovery from the Depression, 86, 110
reputation, 45–46
Butlin, Sydney James ('Syd'), 5, 28, 75, *89,* 145
  comparison with Noel Butlin, 90
  Foundations of the Australian Monetary System, 88, 90
  influence of, 90–91, 94
  at University of Sydney, 87–88
  war service, 88

Cain, Neville ('Nev'), 58, 84
Cairncross, Alec, 65
Cambridge University, 39, 41, 76
Cambridge University Press
  Cambridge Economic History of Australia, 163, 170–173
  festschrift project, 136–138
Canberra University College (CUC), 53–54, 191

capital formation, 49, 54, 55, 165
capital imports, 34–35
capitalism, 105, 107–108, 110
    as framework, 164
    global varieties, 159
    and government, 85–86
    new histories of capitalism, 165, 173–174, 175, 177
Carter, Michael, 86
Carver, Stanley, 23
Chandler, Alfred D., 146–148
    Strategy and Structure, 147
Churchward, Lloyd G., 72
citations, 181–182, 183
Clark, Colin, 32, 38–39, 62
Clark, Dave, 106, 107, 109–110
class, 108, 125, 155
    class conflict, 27–28, 105, 106, 107–108
cliometrics, 4, 80–86, 123–124, 144, 175–176
Coghlan, Timothy, 2–3, 21–22, *24,* 37–38
    as government statistician, 25, 40
    influence on Butlin, 48–49, 62
    Labour and Industry in Australia, 22, 25, 40
    research papers, 45
Coghlan Chair, 130, 131
Coleman, William, 5, 6, 17, *171*
colonial socialism, 138
Commonwealth Department of Postwar Reconstruction, 31, 42, 49
    see also postwar reconstruction
Commonwealth Scientific and Industrial Research Organisation (CSIRO), 52
Commonwealth statisticians, 31. *see also* government statisticians
Connell, Raewyn, 11
Conrad, Alfred H., 81
Convict Workers: Reinterpreting Australia's Past, 104–105

Convict Workers project, 104–105
Copland, Douglas, 30
Council for Scientific and Industrial Research (CSIR). *see* Commonwealth Scientific and Industrial Research Organisation (CSIRO)
Cowan, Tyler, 166
Craig, Russell, 118
Crawford, John G., 32, 38–39, 41, 62
Crawford, R.M. ('Max'), 31, 94
CSIRO. *see* Commonwealth Scientific and Industrial Research Organisation (CSIRO)
CUC. *see* Canberra University College (CUC)
cultural history, 124–125, 126–127, 132, 152, 173–174

Davies, Melville ('Mel'), 140
Davison, Graeme, 64, 99
    The Rise and Fall of Marvellous Melbourne, 99
Dawkins, John, 115
Dawkins reforms, 115–119, 137, 138, 148, 156, 178, 188
de Meel, H., 48, 54–55
debt, 164
demography, 122, 129
Denoon, Donald, 92, 109
    Settler Capitalism, 108
1890s depression, 48, 51, 65, 72, 97
Dick, Howard, 149
Dingle, Tony, 92, 97, 100, 139, 153
disciplinary knowledge, 13–14
disciplinary norms, 180–183
Dowie, J.A., 58, 60, 83
Duncan, Tim, 77, 99–100
    Australia and Argentina: On Parallel Paths, 100
Dunsdorfs, Edgars, 56, 194
Dyster, Barrie, 73, 104, 118, 119, 136
    Australia in the Global Economy, 168

ECHOSEA. *see* Economic History of Southeast Asia Project (ECHOSEA)
ecology. *see* environmental history
econometrics, 73, 122
economic development, 39–40, 72, 129–130
    Australia, 172
    comparative development, 100–101, 108, 160, 165
economic growth, 59, 61–62, 168
    see also economic development
economic history
    adaptation of discipline, 113–115, 161–162
    in Britain, 65, 76
    challenges to, 113–114, 120
    cliometrics, 4, 80–86, 123–124, 144, 175–176
    clusters, 79–80, 103–105, 173
    collaboration, 7–8, 56, 60–62, 93–94, 120, 144
    comparative research, 159
    conservatism, 173
    defining, 16–17
    disciplinary identity, 120–127, 145
    and economics, 82, 120, 121–124, 127, 139–145
    fragmentation, 111–112, 173–177
    global study, 3–4, 124, 156–161
    growth of, 187–188
    and history, 152–156
    institutional crisis, 115–119
    internationalisation, 156, 160, 175–176
    limitations of, 133
    Nobel Prize, 122
    and other disciplines, 28–31, 37–38, 73, 114, 118, 177, 188
    and policy, 170
    professional divisions, 37–38, 69, 95
    quantitative frameworks, 23–24, 55, 62–63, 65–66
    risks of insularity, 78–79
    as a social science, 30, 122
Economic History Association (United States), 40, 81–82
Economic History of Southeast Asia Project (ECHOSEA), 158, 192
Economic History Review (journal), 39
economic history scholars, 74–78, 127–128
    attrition, 127–128
    Melbourne school, 87, 90–102, 148–150
    mobility, 33–34
    Sydney school, 102–105
    women scholars, 133–136
    see also under individual names throughout index
Economic History Society (Britain), 39
Economic History Society of Australia and New Zealand (EHSANZ), 18, 175
    as communicating infrastructure, 111
    conferences, 154
    ownership of *Australian Economic History Review,* 101, 146
    and OzClio, 176
    publications, 100
economic modelling, 83, 122
Economic Record (journal), 47
    Butlin and Beever disagreement, 50–51
    contributions to, 85, 94, 95, 98
    editorial direction, 122–123, 143
    publication of historical research, 72, 167
economics
    econometrics, 73, 122
    economic growth, 59, 61–62, 168
    see also economic development
    economic modelling, 83, 122

environmental economics,
    154–155
mainstream and radical, 106,
    109–111
political economy, 23, 39,
    105–107, 110, 131
relationship with economic
    history, 82, 120, 121–124,
    127, 139–145
role of the State, 107–108,
    110–111, 165
social indicators in economic
    analysis, 83
students, 165
see also frameworks
Eggleston, Frederic, 32, 34, 42
    State Socialism in Victoria, 32, 37
EHSANZ. *see* Economic History
    Society of Australia and New
    Zealand (EHSANZ)
Eichengreen, Barry, 82, 166
Eklund, Erik, 152
emigration. *see* immigration
Empire. *see* imperialism
Engermann, Stanley, 104
environmental history, 153–155.
    see also resource extraction
ERA. *see* Excellence in Research
    Australia (ERA)
Erickson, Charlotte, 76
*Essays in the Political Economy of
    Australian Capitalism,* 107
ethnicity, 107, 125, 177
    see also Indigenous Australians
Excellence in Research Australia
    (ERA), 180–183, 184

Fahey, Charles, 151
Falkus, Malcolm, 75, 127, 158
Fels, Allan, *96*
feminist economic history, 98,
    132–136
    see also women scholars
fertility, 84

financial crises
    1890s depression, 48, 51, 65, 72,
        97
    Global Financial Crisis, 165–167
    Great Depression, 32, 84, 91,
        165–166, 167
Fisher, Joyce, 133
Fitzpatrick, Brian, 3, 47, 50, 62
    background, 27–28
    The British Empire in Australia, 27
    British Imperialism and Australia,
        27
    history training, 31
    overseas study, 41–42
    research approach, 37, 38
Fleming, Grant, 127, 147
    The Big End of Town, 151
Flinders University, 71, 77, 80–81
    economic history department,
        114, 193–194
Fogarty, John P., 99–100
    *Australia and Argentina:
        On Parallel Paths,* 100
Fogel, Robert, 122
    Time on the Cross, 104
foreign investment, 48
    capital imports, 28, 34–35, 39,
        51, 65, 107
Forster, Colin, 54, 55, 61, 81, 127
Forsyth, Hannah, 174
*Foundations of the Australian Monetary
    System,* 88, 90
frameworks, 61, 82
    Annales school, 40, 124
    capitalism, 164
    Chandlerian revolution, 126,
        146–148, 150–151
    classical school, 36, 38
    cliometrics, 81–82
    Dutch disease, 83
    endogenous growth theory, 143,
        164, 169
    externalities, 154
    and gender, 135–136

Hartz's fragments theory, 161
heterodox schools, 105–111
Keynesian economics, 49, 63–64,
    72, 77, 82, 110
logical positivism, 123
Marxist analysis, 27–28, 37, 106,
    108, 109, 124–125
neoclassical economics, 49, 82,
    110, 124, 132, 143
neoliberalism, 11, 77, 115–119,
    178–180
orthodox school, 46, 52–62,
    64–66, 80–81, 99, 138, 169
post-Keynesianism, 109
poststructuralism, 124–125, 136,
    153
quantitative–historical approach,
    65
resource curse theory, 143
Solow economic growth model,
    83
staples thesis, 92–93
Turner's frontier thesis, 65
Wakefield's theory of systematic
    colonisation, 35–36, 39
see also capitalism; cliometrics;
    orthodox school
Freebairn, John, 86
Frost, Lionel, 137, 138, *171,* 182
    career opportunities, 77
    editorship of *Australian Economic
        History Review,* 153, 159
    at La Trobe, 118, 142
    research focus, 119
    thesis, 97

Gage, John, 81
Gallo, Ezequiel, 100
gender. *see* feminist economic history;
    women scholars
Giblin's Platoon, 31
Ginswick, Jules, 56, 101n132
Global Financial Crisis, 165–167
globalisation, 164, 167

God Professor, 57, 75–77, 78, 189
gold mining, 84
government
    colonial socialism, 138
    public enterprises, 36, 37
    role in the economy, 36–37,
        107–108, 110–111, 165
    state socialism, 37, 138
    taxation, 85
*Government and Capitalism: Public
    and Private Choice in Twentieth
    Century Australia,* 110–111
Government and Capitalism project,
    85–86
government statisticians, 21, 23–25,
    50
    see also Commonwealth
        statisticians
Greasley, David, 143, *171*
Great Depression, 32, 84, 91,
    165–166, 167
Great Divergence debate, 164–165
Gregory, R.G. ('Bob'), 81
    Recovery from the Depression, 86,
        110
Gruen, Fred, 123

Haig, Bryan, 58
Hall, Alan, 51, 66, 74, 90
Hancock, W. Keith, 31, 49–50, 51, 56
    Australia, 37, 38
    war service, 42
Harris, Edwyna, 141, 143, *171,* 177
Hartwell, Max, 64–65
    *The Economic Development of Van
        Dieman's Land,* 64–65
Hartz, Louis, 161
Harvard University, 41, 75, 157
Hatton, Tim, 82, 141, *171,* 175, 179
Hawke, Bob, 115
Hayter, Henry, 23
Heaton, Herbert, 33, 37, 41
    Economic History, 33
    Modern Economic History, 38

HECS. *see* Higher Education Contribution Scheme (HECS)
hierarchy of knowledge, 11–14, 53, 57–58, 183
  overseas legitimacy, 65, 76
higher education
  in Australia, 10–12
  Australian structural disadvantages, 183
  career opportunities, 76–78
  curriculum, 1, 93, 122, 124, 126, 142, 179
  Dawkins reforms, 115–119, 137, 138, 148, 156, 178, 188
  English model, 9–10
  Eurocentrism, 11–12, 41
  expansion, 2, 52–53, 69–74
  funding, 119, 120, 178, 183–184
    see also Australian Research Council (ARC)
  German/Humboldtian model, 9–10, 11, 13, 53
  God Professor, 57, 75–77, 78, 189
  Higher Education Contribution Scheme (HECS), 116, 178
  history, 9–13
  impact of World War II, 42–43
  imperialism in, 41, 65, 76, 183
  intellectual communities, 7–9, 13–14, 17–18, 69–70, 102–105
  intellectual enclaves, 79–80, 178–179
  interdisciplinary research, 1, 7–19
  Murray Report, 71
  neoliberalism, 115–119, 178–180
  Oxbridge model, 9, 10
  postgraduate studies, 52–53, 58–59, 75
  post–World War II growth, 52–53
  privilege structures, 76–77
  professional enclosure, 13–14, 178–179
  rankings, 180–183
  relationship with professions, 9
  role in professions, 71–72
  sandstone universities, 11, 41, 52
  Scottish model, 9, 10, 13, 117, 178
  sexism, 134
  silos, 42, 78–79, 93–94, 182
  specialisation of disciplines, 30
  staff, 71, 74–78
  teaching, 142
  women in, 134–136
Higher Education Contribution Scheme (HECS), 116, 178
Historical Studies (journal), 87, 94, 98
history
  business history, 145–152, 174–175
  colonial era, 22–25, 129–130
  convict labour, 104–105
  cultural history, 124–125, 126–127, 132, 152, 173–174
  environmental history, 153–155
  historiography, 17, 37–38, 49
  immigration, 36
  interwar era, 25–42
  labour history, 64, 105–106, 126, 160
  microhistories, 125
  new histories of capitalism, 165, 173–174, 175, 177
  relationship with economic history, 2–3, 5–7, 29–30, 38, 72–73, 91–92, 94, 124–127, 172, 187–188
  social history, 99, 106, 107, 125
  urban history, 153
  women's history, 95
  see also frameworks
home ownership, 97, 99
household production, 131, 132, 135
Hudson, Pat, 17
Huf, Ben, 17, 22–23

Hughes, Helen, 58, 66, 134
  The Australian Iron and Steel Industry, 134
human capital, 36, 135–136, 144, 164, 172
  see also immigration; labour
Hunter, Boyd, *171*
Hutchinson, Diane, 77, 103, 137, 140, 147, *171*

IDRF. *see* interdisciplinary research field (IDRF)
IEHA. *see* International Economic History Association (IEHA)
immigration, 23, 36, 84–85, 107.
  see also human capital
  Immigration into Eastern Australia, 36, 38
imperialism, 27–28, 37, 40
  in trade relations, 107
Inall, Ruth, 54, 133
Indigenous Australians
  Indigenous economic history, 119, 145, 172
  Indigenous history, 11, 64, 129–130
  Our Original Aggression, 129
industrial development, 61
industrial relations, 73, 151, 155
inequality, 83, 164, 167, 176
inflation, 35, 39
Inkster, Ian, 76
innovation
  in economic development, 155, 164
  in research, 1, 14, 78
Instituto Torcuato di Tella (Buenos Aires), 100
intellectual imperialism. *see* hierarchy of knowledge
intellectual movements, 176–178, 185
interdisciplinary research
  adaptation of, 161–162, 188–189
  advantages of, 1–2, 14–15, 190
  Australian Research Council (ARC), 184–185
  challenges for historians, 12
  challenges to, 93–94, 123, 180–181
  communicating infrastructure, 8, 14, 15–16, 22, 111, 153, 189
  disciplinary gatekeeping, 182–183, 184–185
  frameworks, 15
  identification, 17–18
  impact of Dawkins reforms, 116–119
  impact of departments, 78–79, 114, 118–119, 178, 188–189
  impact of rankings, 180–183
  place of, 16–18
  publication, 101–102
  response to the Global Financial Crisis, 166
interdisciplinary research field (IDRF), 15–16
International Economic History Association (IEHA), 156, 160
international trade, 34–35, 47–48, 65, 107, 108, 168
  see also trade
Investment in Australian Economic Development, 1861–1900 ('the words'), 46–51

Jackson, R.V. ('Bob'), 53, 81, 97, 137–138
  Australian Economic Development, 60
Johnston, Robert, 23
Jones, Eric, 74, 75, 103
Journal of Australian Political Economy, 106
Journal of Economic History, 40

Keating, Michael, 59, 83, *171*
Keneley, Monica, 154–155, *171,* 179, 182

Kenwood, A.G. ('George'), 140
Keynes, John Maynard, 49
Keynesian economics, 49, 63–64, 72, 77, 82, 110
Knibbs, G.H., 23, 34
knowledge hierarchy, 11–14, 53, 57–58, 183
    overseas legitimacy, 65, 76
knowledge production, 7, 11, 16
Kuznets, Simon, 63

La Nauze, John Andrew, 29, 31, 35, 56, 94, 95, 99
La Trobe University, 71, 74, 75, 87, 93
    economic history department, 114, 140, 194
    economics department, 139, 142
labour
    bonded labour, 104–105
    convict labour, 92, 104–105, 107, 134–135
    Convict Workers: Reinterpreting Australia's Past, 104–105, 134–135
    influx of, 65
    labour history, 64, 105–106, 126, 160
    labour markets, 84, 107
    trade union movement, 32, 34
    wages, 104, 107, 160
    women's workforce participation, 95, 98, 132–133, 134–136
    see also human capital; immigration
labour history, 64, 105–106, 126, 160
Labour History (journal), 18, 64, 87, 109, 175
Lamoreaux, Naomi, 166
land settlement, 26, 35–36, 38
    see also squatters
Lawson, Bruce, 72
liberalism, 26, 32, 36

Livingstone, Charles, 152
Lloyd, Chris, 6, 17, 76, 121, 139–140, 159–160, *171*
London School of Economics, 30, 35, 41, 66, 76, 97, 134
Lougheed, A.L. ('Alan'), 140
Lydall, H.F., 49

Macintyre, Stuart, 64
Maddock, Rod, 128, 130, 140, 142, *171*
    at ANU Research School of Social Sciences (RSSS), 77, 81, 82, 85
    The Australian Economy in the Long Run, 86
    Butlin's legacy, 63
Madgwick, Robert, 29
    Immigration into Eastern Australia, 36, 38
Madsen, Jakob, 143
Magee, Gary, 141
Maitland, Elizabeth, 149
manufacturing, 47, 55, 61, 153
Marxist analysis, 27–28, 37, 106, 108, 109, 124–125
Matthew Effect, 181–182
Matthews, Robin, 65
Maxwell-Stewart, Hamish, 119
McAloon, Jim, 160
McCarty, John W., 66, 139
    editorship of *Business Archives and History,* 101
    interdisciplinary approach, 92–93, 94
    at Monash University, 74
    overseas study, 75, 76
    retirement, 127
McCloskey, Dierdre, 82
McFarlane, Bruce, 109
McKinnon, Mary, 82
McLean, Ian, 58, 83, 121, 140, 152
    The Australian Economy in the Long Run, 86

international postings, 77, 82, 156–157
orthodox approach, 59
Why Australia Prospered, 168–169
McMichael, Philip, 106, 108
Settlers and the Agrarian Question, 109
Meredith, David, 5, 6, 76, 128, 160, *171*
Australia in the Global Economy, 168
Convict Workers: Reinterpreting Australia's Past, 104–105
Merrett, David, 76, 90, 97, 100, *171*
The Big End of Town, 151
Meyer, John R., 81
migration. *see* immigration
Millmow, Alex, 123
Mills, R.C., 30, 31, 35–36, 39
mining. *see* resource extraction
Monash University, 71, 87, 93, 97
economic history department, 114, 196
economics department, 139, 141
monetary systems. *see* banking
Morgan, Stephen, 149

National Bureau of Economic Research (United States), 40
national income accounting, 39, 46–47, 48, 62–64, 83, 130, 132
natural resources, 143, 160, 165, 169, 172
Neale, Ron, 75, 76
neoclassical economics, 49, 82, 110, 124, 132, 143
new cultural history. *see* cultural history
New Left scholars, 106, 109
New Public Management, 11, 115–116
new social history. *see* social history
New South Wales University of Technology, 71

Newcastle University College, 71
Nicholas, Stephen, 57, 76, 119, 121, 128, 147, 148
business studies, 149–150
Convict Workers: Reinterpreting Australia's Past, 104–105
No Paradise for Workers, 107–108
Noel Butlin lecture, 157, 158
North, Douglass C., 122
Northcott, Clarence, 33
Australian Social Development, 36

O'Hanlon, Seamus, 153
oral history interviews, 19, 199–200
orthodox school, 46, 52–62, 64–66, 80–81, 99, 138, 169
Oxford University, 29, 41, 128
reputation, 76
Oxley, Deborah, 5, 6, 135, *171*, 185
Australian Research Council fellowships, 119
career, 77, 128
Convict Workers: Reinterpreting Australia's Past, 104
women in economic history research, 135–136
OzClio, 175–176

Pagan, Adrian, 86
Panza, Laura, 176
pastoralism. *see* wool industry
Patmore, Greg, 174
Perkins, John, 76
Pincus, Jonathan, 83, 123, 128, 140, *171*
at ANU Research School of Social Sciences (RSSS), 58
editorship of *Australian Economic History Review*, 101n132, 120
Government and Capitalism: Public and Private Choice in Twentieth Century Australia, 110–111
studies at Stanford University, 77, 82

supervision of postgraduate students, 84
political economy, 23, 39, 105–107, 110, 131
pollution, 153–155
Pomfret, Richard, 141
Pope, David, 58, 80, 81, 84–85
Portus, Garnet Vere ('Jerry'), 29–30, 33, 35, 36
postwar reconstruction, 42–43
  see also Commonwealth Department of Postwar Reconstruction
professional enclosure, 178–179, 182
property rights, 143
public enterprises, 36, 37
Pursell, Garry G., 54

race, 107, 125, 177
  see also Indigenous Australians
railways, 48, 149
rankings, 116, 180–183, 184
real estate market, 48
Recovery from the Depression, 86, 110
Rees, Yves, 174
Reid, A.J.S. ('Tony'), 158
resource extraction, 109, 143, 154, 169, 172
  mining history, 155–156
  resource curse theory, 143
  see also environmental history; natural resources
Rhodes scholarships, 41
Richards, Eric, 77
Richardson, Sue, 83
Rimmer, Gordon, 74, 75, 76, 101n132
Rivista di Storia Economica (journal), 40
Roberts, Stephen Henry, 31, 41
  History of Australian Land Settlement, 31, 35–36, 38
  The Squatting Age, 31, 36
  war service, 42

Robertson, Dennis, 88
Rockefeller scholarships, 41
role of the State in the economy. *see* government
Routledge Handbook of Global Economic History, 166
Rowse, Tim, 109
Royal Statistical Society, 21, 41
RSPacS. *see* ANU Research School of Pacific Studies (RSPacS)
RSSS. *see* ANU Research School of Social Sciences (RSSS)
rural development, 97

Saito, Osama, 158
Salsbury, Stephen, 75, 127
Sammartino, Andre, 149, 151
Schedvin, C.B. ('Boris'), 6, 66, 90, 94, 100–101, 128, 148
  Australia and the Great Depression, 91, 110
Seltzer, Andy, 119, 127–128, 149, *171*
seminars, 60–61
Serle, Geoffrey, 87
settler capitalism, 107–108, 160–161
Shanahan, Martin, 77, 121, 141, 142, 143, 157, 160
Shann, E.O.G., 3, 35, 47
  An Economic History of Australia, 26
  background, 26–27
  career, 32
  research approach, 28, 36, 62
Shaw, A.G.L., 29, 31, 35
Sheldon, Peter, 152
Shergold, Peter, 76, 128
  Convict Workers: Reinterpreting Australia's Past, 104–105
Sheridan, Tom, 58
Shermer, Elizabeth, 165
Shlomowitz, Ralph, 80, 102, 105
Siminski, Peter, 144
Simkin, Colin G.F., 51

INDEX

Sinclair, W.A. ('Gus'), 48, 54–55, 62–63, 75, 80, 95, *96*
slavery, 81, 104–105
Snooks, Graeme, 80, 158
  at ANU Research School of Social Sciences (RSSS), 80
  Coghlan Chair, 131
  editorship of *Australian Economic History Review*, 101n132, 120
  household sector research, 131–133
  influence of Butlin, 58, 59
  Portrait of the Family within the Total Economy, 131
  research approach, 109
social history, 99, 106, 107, 125
social indicators in economic analysis, 83
social sciences, 17, 28, 38–39, 106, 118, 121, 153
socialism, 37, 138
sociology, 33
Spenceley, Geoffrey, 139
squatters, 26, 35–36, 107
  The Squatting Age, 31, 36
  see also land settlement
state socialism, 37, 138
Statham, Pamela, 130, 140
Sugihara, Kaoru, 158
Sutcliffe, James, 23
Swan, Trevor, 55, 58, 64, 74
Sydenham, Diane, 128

Tang, John, 176
taxation, 85
tertiary education. *see* higher education
The Australian Economy in the Long Run, 86
Thomas, Brinley, 65
Thomas, Mark, 82
Thornton, Tim, 122, 142
trade
  exports, 23, 51, 65, 92, 95, 168
  protectionism, 34, 107, 143

tariffs, 26, 34, 35, 143
trade cycle, 61
trade union movement, 32, 34
Tsokhas, Kosmas, 81
Tuck, Jacqueline, 123
Tucker, Graham S.L., 75
Turner's frontier thesis, 65

UNE. *see* University of New England (UNE)
unemployment, 84, 107
universities. *see* higher education
university departmental structure
  closure of departments, 114, 139–145, 148–150, 178
  departmental divisions, 73–74
  duplication, 53–54
  expansion, 69, 73
  impact on collaboration, 61, 93–94, 111
  impact on funding, 123–124
  impact on research, 6, 70, 188
  as silos, 78–79
University of Adelaide, 27, 30, 31, 80, 140, 141
University of Chicago, 41
University of Melbourne, 29, 30, 31, 41, 136
  Cambridge Economic History of Australia workshop, 171
  economic history department, 87, 93, 114, 148, 194–196
  economics department, 142
  Melbourne Business School, 148
  Melbourne University Labor Club, 27
  visit by Kenneth Boulding, 100
University of New England (UNE), 65, 73, 75, 103
  economic history department, 114, 197–198
  economics department, 139
University of New South Wales (UNSW), 71, 75, 103, 104–105, 136

213

economic history department, 114, 198–199
economics department, 139
University of Queensland, 140
University of South Australia, 143
University of Sydney, 29, 60, 75
   Business and Labour History group, 174
   economic history department, 114, 140, 197
University of Tasmania, 30
University of Technology (New South Wales), 71
University of Western Australia, 26, 29, 140
University of Wollongong, 142, 144, 184n81
university rankings, 116, 180–183, 184
UNSW. *see* University of New South Wales (UNSW)
urban history, 153
urbanisation, 47, 99, 137

Valentine, Tom, 86
Vamplew, Wray, 76–77, 80, 103, 128
van der Eng, Pierre, 127, 154
Vanden Driesen, Ian H., 140
Ville, Simon, 118, 119, 127, 137, 142, 144, *171*
   The Big End of Town, 151
   business history, 147
   The Development of Modern Business, 148

Wakefield's theory of systematic colonisation, 35–36, 39
Waterman, A.M.C., 58
WEA. *see* Workers' Educational Association (WEA)
WEHC. *see* World Economic History Congress (WEHC)
wellbeing, 144, 164
Wells, Andrew, 77, 80, 106, 108, 109

Wheelwright, E.K. ('Ted'), 106, 107–108
   Essays in the Political Economy of Australian Capitalism, 107
   No Paradise for Workers, 107–108
Whitwell, Greg, 77, 97–98, 121, 158
   The Treasury Line, 98
Williamson, Jeffrey, 176
Wilson, John K., 141, 143, 160
Wilson, Roland, 34–35, 41, 83
   Capital Imports, 31, 39
Withers, Glenn, 77, 85, 128, 140, 152, *171*
Wollongong University College, 71
women scholars, 133–136
see also feminist economic history
women's history, 95
Wood, Gordon Leslie, 30, 34–35, 39
wool industry, 26, 35–36, 50–51, 55, 65, 119
   The Simple Fleece, 56
Wool Seminar, 56–57
Workers' Educational Association (WEA), 10, 26, 30, 32–34, 41, 187
World Economic History Congress (WEHC), 2, 156
World War II, 42–43
   postwar reconstruction, 70–71

Yuzawa, Takeshi, 158

www.ingramcontent.com/pod-product-compliance
Lightning Source LLC
Chambersburg PA
CBHW042043240426
43667CB00048B/2966